Praise for

Father Joe

"Extraordinary, luminescent, profound . . . belongs in the first tier of spiritual memoirs ever written. . . . I beg you to read this book."

—Andrew Sullivan, *The New York Times Book Review*

"Smart, funny and ultimately inspiring . . . This book is a standout."

—*People* (four stars)

"Hendra's book is so funny at times that you wonder if you'll get through it for laughing. At other times, it truly brings a lump to the throat and a tear to the eye. It is splendidly crafted and a welcome reminder that what true religion is about is learning how to love."

—*The Philadelphia Inquirer*

"*Father Joe* is a many-layered memoir of a god-driven Englishman, Tony Hendra. When I read passages to my wife and my voice began to give way she said, 'Keep going, keep going.' I really didn't need much urging. I could easily have read the whole book in one sitting, but it's too rich, too powerful, overwhelming. You might see some of yourself in Tony Hendra. If you see anything of yourself in Father Joe, you are blessed. Like me, you might cherish this book so much you'll keep it on the shelf beside Saint Augustine, Saint Teresa of Avila, and Thomas Merton, and when you dip into it, you might hear Gregorian chant from the monks of Quarr."

—Frank McCourt

"*Father Joe* may be the best, most important nonfiction book I have ever read. This true story is filled with wild escapades, ribald humor, moving religious experiences and profound thoughts on the meaning of life."

—Fort Worth *Star-Telegram*

"A fine spiritual memoir, and one of the best primers on grace, on holiness and on friendship you may ever read . . . It is beautifully written, well paced and funny to boot. . . . The author not only describes a model of contemporary priesthood that is both inspiring and realistic, but also . . . offers the best description in contemporary writing of the goal of the chastity and celibacy in religious life: love." —*National Catholic Reporter*

"Hendra, with all his personal and professional exploits, no doubt added a vicarious dimension to Father Joe's life. But it was the constant grace that Father Joe bestowed on Hendra that was the true gift for Hendra and for the reader of his inspiring memoir."

—Associated Press

"Tony Hendra's superb *Father Joe* reminded me that the reason we are invariably thunderstruck by goodness is because we have so little experience with it. . . . It's the best book to be found on the best-seller lists . . . but it's more than that. In the person of Father Joe, Hendra shows us a man with the feel of something eternal, something called kindness, perfectly embodied in a book that just might become a classic." —*The Palm Beach Post*

"[Hendra] might just be the most interesting—and unlikely—mystic you've never heard of. . . . [Readers will] find themselves happily caught in the complex web of humor and spiritual vulnerability Hendra deftly weaves. . . . A confessional that rings true."

—*Chicago Sun-Times*

"A surprisingly serious book from a very funny man. . . . Readers would do well to listen to the story of this lovely, spiritually refreshing book, surprisingly funny, deeply engaging."

—New Orleans *Times-Picayune*

"A poignant and humble memoir of a hilarious and sinful life."

—*Vanity Fair*

"A worldly-wise and heavenly book . . . beautiful and lyrical, incisive and tender, funny and bittersweet. *Father Joe* is the kind of work you'll return to again and again for the sheer joy of good writing."

—Portland *Oregonian*

"Part memoir, part biography, part historic wisdom–meets–twentieth century . . . Full of timeless advice and thought-provoking anecdotes, this book will redefine your notion of 'saint.'"

—*Deseret Morning News*

"In the hundreds of books spewing from the presses each week, a few real gems come forth. One of the best of the year is *Father Joe: The Man Who Saved My Soul*. . . . Few people have influenced a life the way Father Joe influenced Hendra's. It is a beautiful story."

—*The Sunday Oklahoman*

"This is a book that should appeal to any thinking or feeling person, without respect to religious persuasion. . . . A book of depth that makes Mitch Albom's *Tuesdays with Morrie* seem like *Cotton Candy for the Soul* by comparison. . . . Announces [Hendra] as a top-shelf writer to be taken seriously."

—*The Buffalo News*

"This is a beautifully written book, with nearly every page providing a fresh, effective metaphor, or a keen insight into such subjects as Catholicism, monasticism, humor, England, America and family life. Best of all is Hendra's cumulative portrait of Father Joe. If you read this book, and he doesn't stammer his way into your heart, call a cardiologist."

—*The Charlotte Observer*

"Hendra recounts his life with crackling prose, punctuated in many passages by dry English wit. But this is a serious effort that often moves readers to tears, especially in the final chapters when a dying Father Joe helps Hendra find his true calling—not as a monk or satirist but as a husband and father."

—*The Columbus Dispatch*

"With his moving and unexpected new memoir, Hendra shares his spiritual mentor with the world, making it possible for Joe's memory to serve as a beacon of hope for any lost soul."

—*The Onion*

"Surprises and inspires . . . heartfelt and candid . . . You don't have to be Catholic to find spiritual sustenance in this story."

—*Boston Herald*

"I opened the book and couldn't put it down. I was fascinated by Tony's spiritual journey, his probing insights into his own soul and his growing disillusionment with his celebrity status. . . . One can only wish that we, like Tony, could know such a man of pure and simple goodness." —*The Roanoke Times*

"The soul-scraping honesty of [Hendra's] meditation on faith and friendship is a testament to the monk's continuing influence."

—*The New Yorker*

"Hendra is a gifted writer, and this is a wonderfully composed, touching, humorous, and surprisingly intellectual volume. . . . *Father Joe* remains a ray of hope in a foundering genre." —*Commonweal*

"I picked up *Father Joe* intending to read just a couple of pages before bed—and found that I couldn't put it down until I'd finished it. The nature of a wise man, and the true nature of what wisdom feels like in action, are beautifully captured in Tony Hendra's portrait of Father Joe, who is one of the few convincing saints in recent writing. The book's last episode, when Hendra brings his son to meet Father Joe, brought unexpected tears to my weary eyes."

—Adam Gopnik

"Tony Hendra has accomplished one hell of a lot in his life, and doubtless has many achievements ahead of him, but this memoir of his spiritual journey, and the monk who guided it, will almost certainly be his masterpiece." —CHRISTOPHER BUCKLEY

"I just read *Father Joe* in one gulp and I'm in a state. I've convened everybody in my house. It's been years since I've been grabbed like this. The book is funny, unexpected, incredibly smart. I've always thought Tony was a good writer, but this is writing like almost nobody is doing—jazzy and funny and sharp. Not a note out of place—not a word he doesn't get. I pretty much think that almost everybody writing nonfiction today is a kind of writing-model simulator, but Tony's book reads like it came out of the golden age of nonfiction." —MICHAEL WOLFF

OTHER WORKS WRITTEN, EDITED, OR PRODUCED BY TONY HENDRA

WRITTEN WORKS

National Lampoon's 199th Birthday Book

Not the New York Times (with George Plimpton and Chris Cerf)

The '80s—A Look Back (with Chris Cerf and Peter Elbling)

Off The Wall Street Journal

The Sayings of Ayatollah Khomeini

"Meet Mr. Bomb!"

Not The Bible (with Sean Kelly)

Going Too Far

The '90s—A Look Back

Born to Run Things: An Unauthorized Autobiography of George Bush

Brad '61 (with Roy Lichtenstein)

The Book of Bad Virtues

The Gigawit Dictionary of the E-nglish Language

Brotherhood

BROADWAY SHOWS

Smith—A Musical (with Dean Fuller)

Lemmings (with Sean Kelly)

ALBUMS

Radio Dinner (with Michael O'Donoghue)

Lemmings

FILMS

The Missing Link

The Big Bang

The Great White Hype (with Ron Shelton)

TELEVISION

Disco Beaver from Outer Space

Spitting Image (with Roger Law and Peter Fluck)

Grape Expectations

Father Joe

TONY HENDRA

FATHER JOE

THE MAN WHO SAVED MY SOUL

RANDOM HOUSE TRADE PAPERBACKS

NEW YORK

Father Joe is a work of nonfiction. Some names and identifying details have been changed.

2005 Random House Trade Paperback Edition

Published in the United States by Random House Trade Paperbacks, an imprint of The Random House Publishing Group, a division of Random House, Inc., New York.

RANDOM HOUSE TRADE PAPERBACKS and colophon are trademarks of Random House, Inc.

Originally published in hardcover in the United States by Random House, an imprint of The Random House Publishing Group, a division of Random House, Inc., in 2004.

Photograph of Dom Joseph Warrilow, Order of Saint Benedict, on title page courtesy of Quarr Abbey.

LIBRARY OF CONGRESS CATALOGING-IN-PUBLICATION DATA

Hendra, Tony.
Father Joe : the man who saved my soul / Tony Hendra.
p. cm.
ISBN 0-8129-7234-1
1. Hendra, Tony. 2. Catholics—England—Biography.
3. Catholics—United States—Biography. 4. Warrilow, Joseph.
5. Benedictines—England—Biography. I. Title.

BX4705.H468A3 2004
282'.092'242—dc22
[B] 2003065541

Printed in the United States of America

Random House website address: www.atrandom.com

9 8 7 6 5 4

This book is for

Judy, Carla, Katherine,

Jessica, Nicholas, Sebastian,

Lucy, Christopher, Timothy,

Julia, and Charlotte.

ACKNOWLEDGMENTS

It would have been impossible to write about Father Joe without the inspiration of The Moth and the encouragement of its Creative Director, Joey Xanders; without the hard work, dedication, and boundless confidence of Dan Menaker, Jonathon Lazear, and Webster Younce. Most of all my thanks go to the Abbots and Community of Quarr Abbey, past and present, especially Abbot Cuthbert Johnson, Dom Matthew Tylor, Dom Robert Gough, Brother John Bennet, and Brother Francis Verry. The encouragement, spiritual and otherwise, of Father Joe McNerney. The help of Father Tom Faucher and Arthur Wells.

Finally, I owe a debt of gratitude the size of the federal deficit to George Kalogerakis for his perspicacity, patience, and good friendship.

PAX

Father Joe

PROLOGUE

There he stands on the muddy clay of the little promontory, hands under scapular for warmth in the chill, his wide rubbery mouth beaming serenely at the gray turmoil of the English Channel. Hooked over vast ears, framing a fleshy groundhog nose and battered granny glasses, is his black monk's cowl, ancient and rudimentary shield against the blustery rain. Farther down: irredeemably flat feet in black socks and big floppy sandals, these emerging from scruffy black robes whipped by the squalls and revealing—if you're lucky—glimpses of white English knees so knobbly they could win prizes.

Dom Joseph Warrilow is his formal monastic name, but everyone calls him Father Joe. I have seen him in this pose and place countless times down the years, in the flesh or in my mind's eye. Never once have I been able to stop a smile from coming to my lips. He's as close to a cartoon monk as you could imagine. And he is a saint.

That poor, weary, once-powerful word—bowed and enfeebled by abuse—is not used lightly. "Saint" does not mean merely dedication, or selflessness, or generosity, though it subsumes all those. Nor does it mean the apogee of religious devotion, though it can subsume that too—sometimes. There are many pious people who believe themselves to be saints who are not, and many people who believe themselves to be impious who are.

A saint is a person who practices the keystone human virtue of humility. Humility in the face of wealth and plenty, humility in the face of hatred and violence, humility in the face of strength, humility in the face of your own genius or lack of it, humility in the face of another's humility, humility in the face of love and beauty, humility in the face of pain and death. Saints are driven to humbling themselves before all the splendor and horror of the world because they perceive there to be something divine in it, something pulsing and alive beneath the hard dead surface of material things, something inconceivably greater and purer than they.

This man is one of those rare, rare creatures. Gentleness and goodness come off him like aftershave. For all his irrepressible curiosity and concern, for all his love of talking and listening and then talking some more, a great stillness surrounds him in which he will fold you without your knowing it, numbing the pain of your most jagged obsessions, soothing away the mad priorities of your world with the balm of his peace.

For more than forty years, since I was not much more than a boy, this lumpy gargoyle of a man has been my still center, the rock of my soul, as steady and firm as the huge oak on the curve of the hill where the monastery stands, the hill that runs down to the sea. I have lost and found him more than once, gone far, far astray from the haven of his presence, but never ceased, however dimly and distantly, to love and revere him and hunger for his company. His was the wisdom I craved—though it was never what I expected; his judgment alone I feared—though never once did he pass judgment on me.

All my conscious life he was my strongest ally, the cherished gatekeeper of my lost Eden, a lighthouse of faith blinking away through the oceanic fogs of success and money and celebrity and possessions, my intrepid guide in the tangled rain forest of human love, my silken lifeline to the divine, my Father Joe.

Years ago the promontory of clay where he stands was much farther out, but the waves' erosion is relentless. He's gazing at the gulls swooping and diving for their lunch. He turns to me and smiles that fond crooked smile:

Tony dear, I was just thinking of you. How are your beautiful children?

More beautiful than ever. Happily as they grow older they bear less and less resemblance to their father.

And you, dear?

Still alone, Father Joe.

You are not alone, dear. We are never alone.

I remember. And every time you said that, I felt God's presence. But I felt it in you, *through* you. *Now I am a void.*

He smiles again, the old "no" smile—a "no" which has always meant "yes." Taking it as an invitation, I move a little closer. Hoping. Just this once . . .

But he melts away, still smiling, into the eternal rain.

The bare ruined trees drip their drizzle, chill my aging body. The tide snaps and tugs at the reluctant clay.

How to make my dear, good friend live again? Roll back the rock from the tomb, take him by the hand, and lead him out into the light. See him laugh and teach and heal once more . . .

Part One

CHAPTER ONE

How I met Father Joe:

I was fourteen and having an affair with a married woman.

At least she called it an affair; she also said we were lovers, and on several occasions, doomed lovers. An average teen, I was quite content with these exalted terms; in practice, however, I only got to second base with her. (I didn't yet know it was second base, as I was growing up in England.)

It was only rather later too, when I saw *The Graduate,* that I realized my Mrs. Robinson may have been somewhat older than she admitted to—which was twenty-two. To my unpracticed eye she could certainly pass for that; I was still young enough that any woman with breasts and a waist and her own teeth was roughly the same age as any other—which is to say a grown-up—and the mysterious repository of unimaginable pleasures deserving . . .

. . . hideous, very specific torments. The fly in the ointment of this relationship was that we were both Catholics. At least in theory

(theory to me, practice to her), there was a terrible bill being racked up somewhere, calibrating the relative sinfulness of everything we did, every gesture made, every word exchanged, let alone every kiss. Should death strike, should lightning fork from one of the huge trees outside into our concupiscent bodies, should one of the experimental jets being developed over the hill at DeHavilland's disintegrate and plummet to earth (as they often threatened to do when trying to break the sound barrier), turning her trailer into a fireball, down, down we would plunge, into the bowels of Hell, unshriven, unforgiven, damned for all eternity to indescribable suffering.

A lot of what little conversation we had—much more the norm were interminable, agonized, what she called "existential" silences—concerned whether we should even be having a conversation, should even be together for that matter, doomed lovers in the throes of a hopeless and illicit liaison, wrestling with the irresistible temptation of being in the same neighborhood, town, county, country, planet, dimension. We were so bad for one another, she said, such a monumental occasion of sin for each other, it was playing with fire; oh, if only we'd never met and plunged ourselves into this cauldron of raging emotions from which there was no escape!

These sentiments were very new to me. My instinctive response was that they were pretty goofy, but what did I know? I dimly recognized that I was going through some kind of passage out of childhood and would from now on be required to learn, without being taught, how grown-ups acted and spoke. Best not to rock the boat, by suppressing a classroom splutter. I had a good thing going. Mrs. Bootle was no slouch in the looks department. Perhaps this was the way women always spoke *in extremis.* Books were my only guide and so far it all seemed pretty true to form—like being in *The Thorn Birds* if it had been written by Christina Rossetti.

But it had been a long time since the first hesitant kiss, and we'd done lots of kissing since. I was getting restless, anxious to find out what would be the next cauldron of raging emotions from which there was no escape.

Now on a bleak Saturday morning in the damp, dank early spring of green, green Hertfordshire, England, The World, The Solar System, The Universe, in the year of our Lord 1956, I was about to find out.

She stood at the kitchen end of the trailer, where the sink was, surrounded by dirty dishes, her back to the picture window through which a waterlogged plot ran down to the river, swollen and sullen in the rain, the depressed little green caps of her higgledy-piggledy vegetable garden poking through the mud. "Should we?" she said in an agonized half-sob. "I think we should," I replied, having no idea what she was talking about. "But . . . but" (she never used just one "but"—always at least two) "it will be the end, the point of no return, all will be lost." "Well, then," said the voice of proto-adult reason, "perhaps we shouldn't." "No! no! yes! yes!, how can we help ourselves, I'm swept away, I tell you, let's cast all caution to the winds! Turn round."

I did as I was bid, averting my head and closing my eyes, mad excitement welling up through my body from my heels to my eyelids. This must be it, whatever it was. From behind me came surreptitious noises: rustling clothes, eyelets popping, zippers unzipping, hot little pants of effort.

"Turn round," she whispered hoarsely. I did. "Open your eyes." I did. Her eyes were now closed, her head inclined to one side, long hair draped over her white, slight, naked shoulders, framed by the rain-drenched window, the Madonna of the drizzle. My eyes ratcheted nervously down to her breasts. They were quite small, of slightly different sizes, and rather flat. Well, actually very flat. Making the nipples seem somewhat larger than I would have expected. The baby—to all appearances a sweet little scrap—must have been a voracious feeder.

These were my first live breasts. The only ones I'd seen to date had been in nudist magazines. Were they all like this? I'd just read *The Four Quartets* for the first time: the image of Tiresias popped into my head and wouldn't budge.

Then she kissed me. Her lips and face were hotter than usual, like my little brother's when he had a temperature. She came closer. I could feel the warmth of her skin through my shirt and then what must have been those nipples. I put my hand inside her rolled-down dress between her hip and her belly. "No! no!" she whispered, covering my hand with hers. But she pushed it down infinitesimally. As I followed her pressure, she resisted, pulling it up even more infinitesimally. "You mustn't!" she sobbed. "Think of the sin, the mortal sin, the eternal flames!" Then the downward pressure again. A textbook case of no-but-yes—though I was too young to grasp such psychosexual antics. I followed her hand down for a few millimeters. It resisted. Up we went. But not so far—we were definitely making headway. Down . . . up, down, up, down . . . My whole hand was inside her dress now, inching inexorably earthward. Her skin was silky and her flesh deliciously soft. And it kept getting softer. Where were we? Way down there, surely? Waves of—some unknown emotion—shuddered through me. I was dizzy with excitement, Tiresias having definitely taken a powder . . .

Ben and Lily Bootle had first appeared at the local Catholic church a year earlier. She was petite and slender, he was big and rangy, a head or more taller than his mate. Though she was very pregnant she wore a clingy, full-length shift-like dress, emphasizing her milky breasts and bulging belly. Open leather sandals advertised tiny, shapely feet. Her outfit had a distinct bohemian flair in a Sunday congregation made up for the most part of dowdy English widows and hungover Irish laborers with the occasional large unruly family and cigarette-ashen wife.

Ben looked as though he'd just emerged from a night of electroshock. His thick wiry hair stood up in uncombed clumps and spikes, his clothes were always rumpled with at least one element undone, and he wore battered tortoiseshell-rimmed glasses of impressive thickness.

They seemed to have no friends and kept very much to themselves; no one even knew where they lived, least of all our ancient and embottled parish priest, Father B. Leary (the "B."—for Bartholomew—leading us altar boys to call him Father Bleary).

In due course a baby Bootle appeared, which Lily carried in a rather self-consciously peasanty manner on her hip. Its gender was unclear, since it wore no conventional baby garments, being wrapped regardless of season in what my mother acidly called "swaddling clothes." But still no one had found out a whole lot about them, except that Ben was some kind of scientist doing hush-hush work on jets or rockets or something. Since the church was the only place they made contact with us earthlings, it had also been noted that Ben was quite devout. As well as Sunday Mass he would appear at non-obligatory services like Rosary evenings to pray for the Godless Soviets.

Though our paths hadn't crossed, serving Mass was also one of my chores, which I loathed not only because of the tongue-twisting Latin responses but also because Father Bleary had last brushed his teeth to celebrate victory over the Kaiser and his breath would have stopped even the leper-hugging St. Francis dead in his tracks. One moment of the Mass in particular, the Lavabo, at which the server is required to ritually wash the priest's fingers, putting the anointed face inches from yours, was like being gassed in the trenches at Verdun.

My level of devotion was at a fairly obligatory level. I was the product of what the Church called a "mixed marriage"—one between a Catholic and a non-Catholic, which in my father's case meant nothing fun like a Muslim or a Satanist, but simply a desultory agnostic, a "nonbeliever in anything much, really." Ironically, he was a stained-glass artist, so he spent far more time inside churches and knew far more about Catholic iconography than his nominally Catholic brood.

My mother was what the priests called a "good" Catholic. She attended Mass every Sunday and holiday of obligation, went to confession once a month, shelled out handfuls of silver when required, but otherwise, as far as I could tell, didn't allow the precepts of the Gospels and their chief spokesman to interfere much with her daily round of gossip, bitching, kid-slapping, neighbor-bashing, petty vengeance, and other middle-class peccadilloes.

One aspect of my mother's behavior did seem to me to be well up the scale of venial sin, if not all the way to mortal: she shared with local non-Catholics a broad prejudice against the Irish laborers who were appearing in our village in considerable numbers, as they were in many other parts of England, to work in the ongoing reconstruction of postwar Britain, particularly the new motorways. All of whom were Catholic.

The vast majority of these workers were fleeing chronic unemployment in the new Republic and brought with them habits of poverty that didn't sit well with the upwardly mobile Protestant burghers of southeast England: the drinking and plangent midnight singing in the street—naturally—but also the taking a leak round any old corner, the possession of only one jacket and pair of trousers—worn to the construction site every morning, to the pub every night, to church on Sunday, and to sleep in anytime.

Mostly they were loathed just for being Irish. The depth of British odium for a people they robbed, murdered, enslaved, and starved for eight hundred years is hard to exaggerate; I often experienced it at second hand when gangs of local toughs would run me to cover as I walked home from school, screaming "dirty Catholic go home" and heaving stones at me. True, British anti-Catholic prejudice harked back to the seventeenth century and was institutionalized in many ways, but it's unlikely these troglodytes had the excesses of James II on their tiny minds; for them, "Catholic" and "Irish" were interchangeable slurs.

I hadn't made this connection yet; kids tend to take prejudice in their stride, a fixed peril you find a route around on your journey toward adulthood. For the moment its larger meaning was opaque and my dealings with it open to compromise if not outright collaboration.

Example: every November fifth in England, Guy Fawkes—a Catholic conspirator of the early seventeenth century who almost succeeded in blowing up the Houses of Parliament—is burned in effigy on thousands of bonfires across the land. While it's fine that Guy Fawkes be remembered for what he was—an odious anti-democratic terrorist—this custom has for centuries also expressed and refueled anti-Catholic prejudice. So every Sunday before Guy Fawkes Day, Catholic priests would condemn it and order Catholics not to participate. For me—a serial pyromaniac—the prospect of no bonfire was bad enough, but it also meant missing the truly glorious part of Guy Fawkes Day: fireworks.

In a mixed marriage this sort of thing could be sheer poison. The arrangement my father worked out was as follows: (a) fireworks, naturally—kids have to have fireworks; (b) smallish bonfire (though I'd always creep out in the night and pile it higher, and if possible stick tires in it); (c) absolutely no guy (as the effigy of Mr. Fawkes is known). When my mother objected that we were still symbolically burning a Catholic, Dad would reply yes, but every time we let off a firework we were symbolically blowing up the Houses of Parliament.

So then we'd celebrate the same prejudice that got rocks thrown at my head on the way home from school. And the same prejudice that had the good villagers muttering about lazy drunks and refusing to rent rooms to the Irish or serve them in their shops. I found this obnoxious in them and, to the degree that she agreed, in my mother. I'd like to pretend that I was smart enough at fourteen to have worked all this out in total consistency, but in fact I had simply picked up from somewhere an aversion to discriminating against people because they had next to nothing and did work no one else wanted to do.

Unbeknownst to me there was more at work than mere altruism; a deeper bond made me take the Irish side.

If challenged, Mum would have said she was just being protective in putting as much distance as possible between us kids and the boyos down the pub. (She certainly did in church, where she would sit as far away as she could from her boozy coreligionists, moving up a row or two if they got too close.) Something much juicier, however, was going on beneath these maternal protestations.

She always insisted that her maiden name—McGovern—was

Scottish, even though it began with "Mc" as all the finest Irish names do, not "Mac" like all the finest Scottish ones. She and the other four McGovern sisters had indeed been born in Glasgow, so she did have that on her side. But as one of her older sisters would say, less skittish than she about their true origins: if a cat has kittens in the oven, are they biscuits? Nonetheless Mum stuck to her guns; we were Scottish and proud of it, *och awa' the noo.* Of course the British weren't much fonder of the Scots than they were of the Irish, but on the spectrum of Anglo-Saxon anti-Celtic prejudice she evidently felt it was better to be ridiculed as Scottish than despised as Irish.

Once when I was about ten, Dad brought home a book of Scottish tartans—he was painstaking about the heraldic and chivalric symbols he used in his windows—and I got very excited over the rich old aristocratic patterns. Surely with our deep Scottish roots we must have a tartan? That in turn would mean we could wear a kilt, *och awa' the noo.* This line of questioning threw Mum for the biggest loop so far. "Um—that one," she said, pointing at the Campbell tartan. "But that's the Campbell tartan," I objected. "Well," she fired back, "the McGoverns are part of the Campbell clan."

Only later, when I moved to New York, where I met dozens of McGoverns, every one as Irish as a pint of stout, did all become clear; I realized that the closest my maternal ancestors had ever come to the Highlands and a Campbell kilt was the wilds of County Leitrim.

If I'd known at the time how Irish I was, I mightn't have been so pleased about it. I wasn't a whole lot keener about being a Catholic. This had less to do with being on the receiving end of prejudice than with the growing gap between what I heard in church and learned in school. Not that my mother hadn't tried to prevent the gap from growing. The mixed-marriage contract the Church required the infidel half of the couple to sign said that all resulting offspring had to be brought up in the Faith. If humanly possible, this meant being sent to a Catholic school.

Between the ages of five and eight, therefore, I had gone to the nuns, in this case Dominicans, followers of the intrepid Spanish preacher Domingo de Guzman, aka St. Dominic, scourge of the

Cathars and inventor of the very first version of the Inquisition. The good sisters were known by baffling names like Sister Mary Joseph, Sister Mary Frederick, and Sister Mary Martin. While they never actually condemned us first-graders to an auto-da-fé, they certainly devised some Inquisition-level torments to instill the One True Faith in us; and, to be fair, they were effective. (*Why did God make you? God made me to know him love him and serve him in this world and to be happy with him forever in the next.*) There are several concepts and assumptions in this catechesis which might be a little beyond a six-year-old, but half a century later I can still recite it in my sleep.

The next stop after the good sisters was the good brothers.

These hard men ran a joint called, benignly enough, St. Columba's, quartered in a sprawling old Victorian mansion. I've blanked on the name of their order; I'd like to think it included some phrase like St. Aloysius The Impaler, but it was probably more along the lines of the Holy Brothers of the Little Flower. They were, to a man, Irish; in all my years in and out of the Church I've never come across a gang so utterly unholy. They dressed in lay clothes and wore lay haircuts, and as far as anyone could tell, they performed no religious observances whatsoever. Nothing distinguished them from what they appeared to be—members of a sleeper cell of the IRA or participants in some particularly vicious form of organized crime.

They beat us with their belts, they beat us with their metal rulers—the thin side, not the flat. They set dogs on boys who strayed into their quarters, they had beer on their breath at morning assembly. They encouraged the older boys—especially if they had Irish names—to beat the crap out of the smaller ones *ad majoram Dei gloriam.* This toughening-up process would turn us seven- and eight-year-old boys into good soldiers of Christ. Religion was invoked only as a prelude to violence; the fires of Hell awaited any infraction or indiscipline, especially the mortal sin of being anywhere near a Holy Brother with a morning head. Threatening the fear of damnation had limited force—as far as I could tell, I was already in Hell.

Disputes between boys were settled on the spot by boxing bouts—not with padded sparring gloves either, but ten-ounce ring gloves. The first time this happened to me, I tearfully objected that I didn't know how to box and couldn't I run a race or something, whereupon Brother Colm, who happened to be headmaster, snarled, "You'll settle it with the gloves—as Christ intended." I scrolled mentally through the Gospels for occasions where Jesus had gone a couple of rounds with the Pharisees or Sadducees. Nothing. Then the other boy hit me in the face and knocked me out.

After I came home for the umpteenth time with a bloody nose or my arse covered in welts or a smashed hand bandaged in a handkerchief—there being no school nurse at St. Columba's, the soldiers of Christ performed their own first aid—my parents decided that the mixed-marriage contract notwithstanding, my Catholic education was at an end.

My first Protestant stop was a small Church of England prep school with pretensions to be rather classier than was merited by its location—a nouveau-riche dormitory town north of London. I didn't like it much, and perhaps as payback to some greater educational authority in the sky, I became possessed by a demon of petty crime, a juvenile delinquent playing right into the stereotype of the perfidious Irish Catholic.

Excluded from morning prayers each day and C of E religious instruction several times a week, I spent the time allocated for spiritual reflection rifling through the pockets of my classmates' coats and jackets in the cloakroom. I could garner vast sums this way—sometimes as much as ten or fifteen shillings a day, a huge sum for a preteen in the mid-fifties. The proceeds were then spent at the local Gaumont cinema.

My visits were so regular that Mum became convinced that it really did take three and a half hours to get home on the bus, not the official hour or so. I caught—at least four or five times each—the Ealing comedies, Olivier's *Henry V,* Billy Wilder's *Sunset Boulevard,* and a long succession of early Technicolor Hollywood goodies, best of all the garish biblical epics that aging 1930s moguls were pumping out to nip TV in the bud (and in some cases to subliminally bolster the scriptural claims of the new state of Israel). My all-time favorite was *Samson and Delilah,* with ravishing Yvonne de Carlo as the hair-clipping houri and bulging Victor Mature as Samson. It riveted me that Samson's breasts were almost as big as Delilah's. One of my earliest sexual crises had been rage and bafflement that I would never be able to have a baby, and I found Mr. Mature's bosoms strangely comforting.

I became adept at theft, staggering my raids and leaving the heavier copper and bronze coins in the victims' pockets so they wouldn't discover their loss till they were out of school, where it could be blamed on their own carelessness. I'm sure the authorities were leaning over backward to be Christlike and tolerant, hesitant to conclude that the school's only Catholic was ripping off his Protestant classmates.

Eventually the well-meaning dolts put a patrol on the cloakroom, but by then the demon had parted as abruptly as it came, leaving me with no further taste for felony. I'd scored high in the eleven-plus exams and won a place at the best school in the county; then, to everyone's surprise, including my own, I won several events at the end-of-term athletics meet and was declared my year's champion. A top student and a track star could hardly be a thief. So the good Prots not only provided me with a small fortune in stolen goods and a solid grounding in Hollywood movies, they sent me on my way with a silver cup.

Robbery, violence, Hollywood—all classic enemies of Catholic piety. By the time I arrived at St. Albans School at the age of eleven, I was already drifting away from Holy Mother Church. St. Albans was nominally C of E; it was also the oldest surviving school in England, having been founded by the Benedictine monks of St. Albans Abbey in A.D. 948. This meant, for what it was worth, that it had been Catholic far longer than it had been Church of England, from 948 to the Dissolution being roughly six hundred years while the Protestants had had it only since then, a paltry four hundred. Up until the Second World War it had been a minor public school, but by the time I got there, the socialist leveling that was transforming British education had swept most of this religious and classist history away. St. Albans was a government-funded feeder school for the coming meritocracy, and academic excellence was its overwhelming concern.

The level was scary. Where up to this point I'd had little trouble making it to the top rank of any class, here I was just one of the anonymous striving middle. The aim became simply to keep your head down and your marks up. The syllabus included Latin and Greek, but there was no doubt about the long-term utilitarian emphasis—math and science, with English (and French) literature a distant third.

Our classes were seated in alphabetical order, and right in front of me for my first three years was an inarticulate homunculus named Stephen Hawking. The great utility of Hawking to his classmates was that he could do math and physics homework at the speed of light—a concept, by the way, only he seemed able to grasp. He usually had the homework finished by the end of lunch hour, and the thuggier element in his class—including me—found it easy to persuade him to share it. Our math and physics marks were terrific, until the inevitable day of a test, which Hawking would finish in minutes and sit snuffling and grinning and doodling for the remainder of the hour, while the rest of us sweated through the now-incomprehensible scientific runes.

The custom of using Hawking as a source for spiffy homework marks persisted until sometime in the third year when he began moving at warp speed. Now he would take a fairly simple problem of, say, calculus as the pretext for a far-ranging dissertation expressing itself in pages and pages of equations and formulae that no doubt stopped just short of the event horizon. The cloddier types duly copied all this out, figuring it would lead to massive bonus marks. It didn't, and soon Hawking disappeared from all math classes to pursue his destiny alone.

The fine print in the Church's mixed-marriage contract demanded that where offspring were forced to attend a non-Catholic school, religious instruction should counteract the heathen lies with which their little ears were filled. In practice my syllabus was so arduous that I had no time for religious instruction even if it had been available in a small country village. So there was no counterweight to my favored subjects, history and organic chemistry, leading my education in an increasingly secular direction.

History textbooks hadn't caught up with postwar historical thought or research; they tended to be Anglocentric, casually anti-Catholic, and often virulently antipapal. This was very much the case in my favorite period—the Middle Ages. One of the more egregious examples of skewed papal history concerned a local lad, Nicholas Breakspear, who in the mid–twelfth century rose from being Abbot of St. Albans to become Adrian IV, the only Englishman ever to attain the papacy. Breakspear, it was emphasized, was that very rare bird: a good Pope.

A teenager eagerly and uncritically lapping up all such great stuff, I had no frame of reference to judge it by. As the Curial bureaucrats who wrote the mixed-marriage contract no doubt foresaw, I much preferred the new analysis to the old, maternal, pro-Church one.

My fascination with chemistry added fuel to the heretical pyre. The clear message of chemistry—especially of lab experiments, which I'd never done before—was that everything in the phenomenological world had an explanation, and that if it couldn't yet be explained, further research would soon do the job. It didn't take a genius to figure out that the standard proof of God's existence ("someone must have made it all") began to get a little rocky in the lab. There was the evidence in the microscope slide: amoebas reproduced all by themselves without a flash of lightning or a big finger pointing at them, just as they had long ago in kicking off the chain of evolution that led to Hawking.

For me there was another factor too, in some ways more all-encompassing and from a strict doctrinal point of view more insidious. I had fallen in love with the Hertfordshire countryside.

Hertfordshire contains many of the signature images of the great landscape artist John Constable: slow, meandering streams winding through lush meadows intersected with vast stands of elm; gentle hills and soft bosomy fields trimmed with neatly laid hedges of hawthorn and hazel; animals of all kinds, wild and domestic, in huge profusion; rich clay and loam, its vegetation moist and bulbous, bursting with primal juice. You could hardly break a stalk in the meadows without some thick or milky essence bleeding from the plant.

I don't mean I passed my youth in a Wordsworthian trance. I had goals. The most important was the killing of small waterfowl and the roasting of them over an open fire. Hunting in turn required the construction of weapons—first spears with, for one brief and frustrating period, hand-chipped flint tips, but later and more practically, bows and arrows.

In the wonder years that I spent wandering the countryside with my lethal weapons, I never managed to kill a single living thing, let alone roast it—though I did once find an arrow sticking in the rump of our neighboring farmer's Guernsey. (She didn't seem to mind; he was livid.)

I was fixated on a tubby little waterfowl called a moorhen—ducks were iffy since they might belong to someone—but when moorhens broke cover they ran in crazy evasive patterns and you couldn't get a bead on them. But failure didn't matter. My self-image as an intrepid hunter alone in the wilderness, surviving on my wits, implacably tracking my prey, was reward enough.

I built a succession of secret huts from interwoven reeds and boughs and grass. I got quite good at siting these in natural blinds and clumps of vegetation to minimize construction. (Which made them even more secret.) Nothing better than to sit in the mouth of a secret reed hut after a hard morning's hunt, a campfire sizzling in the drizzle, toasting a slice of bread or a sausage and puffing on a dried, rolled-up dock leaf. Tomorrow, always assuming I could figure out how to pluck it and gut it, a fat moorhen would be spitted over this very fire and my entire life would be fulfilled.

Nobody knew where I was, nobody could find me. I was one with my allies, the trees and leaves and folds in the earth, the banks and hedges and stands of wild grass. On fine days the sunlight became a coconspirator, filtering through the filigree of leaves and vegetation to make a second, even more secure dimension of dappled camouflage—and me even more invisible.

This was when I first came across Marvell's

Annihilating all that's made
To a green thought in a green shade.

No doubt I was creating an alternate or fantasy life (food, shelter, security) in rejection of the one my parents provided. But nothing so tediously psychological ever occurred to me. I was happy without knowing it, at peace long before I knew how crucial and elusive peace is.

One summer a terrible epidemic called myxomatosis ran through the entire wild rabbit population, and there were little corpses of my former prey everywhere, their eyeballs forced halfway out of their skulls by the jellylike tumors the disease causes, making their eyes, still staring wildly in death, look like tumors themselves. There were trophies everywhere, meat for the taking, but I could only think *what a horrible way to die*—for my friends and coconspirators to die—and that in some implacable way my callousness had caused their agony.

Why was all this a doctrinal threat? Because my woods and meadows seemed a much better church than the Church. The irresistible force of life—the tiny eggs appearing in the nest, the buds on the dead wood of winter—evidenced a much more immediate presence of something divine than the presence that was supposed to exist in the tabernacle on the altar.

There beneath a flickering red lamp that was always lit to indicate he was home (the Savior is . . . IN) was Christ himself, really present in the Holy Eucharist, a chalice full of consecrated wafers. We were taught this was a *sacramental* presence, the outward sign of inward grace. The standard exegesis was that while the outward accidents of the bread did not change at the moment of consecration, its essence—that which made it bread and bread alone—had been transformed into the essence of Jesus Christ, that which made him and him alone the son of God. A neat analysis and, if true, a mind-boggling miracle. The trouble was I felt nothing gazing up at Christ's little brass hut. No presence at all; just the exotic odor of last Sunday's incense and that dusty mushroomy smell of decay all churches have, whatever their age.

Whereas under my canopy of sun-dappled leaves I certainly felt the presence of something, and something I was quite prepared to say was divine, powerful, benign, even loving, and if beyond my ken, not that far beyond. It could be God or a god, or more likely a goddess, the spirit of sun-dappled leaves. The lazy River Lea, polluted though it was, was still a miracle, a whole liquid universe of life.

One early summer evening, down along the River Lea, following my best moorhen route, I came upon something I'd never noticed before, concealed by thick curtains of willow fronds and giant reeds: a decrepit trailer with saggy old power lines running into the trees, painted a morose green. In the yard outside, a couple, one with a baby on her hip, were tending a newly turned garden. I'd come upon the secret lair of Mr. and Mrs. Mystery—Ben and Lily Bootle.

Contrary to my standard reaction on sighting other humans—to become a green thought in a green shade—I decided I'd initiate a meeting. I don't know why—perhaps I thought that these oddballs skulking in the rushes were kindred spirits. The first few minutes were awkward: three woodland creatures toting the customary baggage of English social inhibitions, nosing around each other, testing out the possibilities of contact. It was like an early draft of *The Wind in the Willows,* before Grahame decided to focus on rodents. Evidently they felt some level of comfort; after the usual stammered apologies and overlapping courtesies, we all ended up in the trailer.

Inside was chaos incarnate. At one end there was a sleeping area entirely filled with an unmade double bed and a baby's cot draped with diapers, possibly clean. At the other end was a narrow kitchen piled with dishes and used food. In between was an unkempt living area stuffed with books, littered with discarded clothing, and dominated by a handsome old upright piano, a Bechstein.

Ben was an odd bird. He wore Coke-bottle glasses askew his large pointy nose, which had a little ball of flesh on the end as if to protect you from the point. He always seemed to be looking over your head, or through you to some far horizon. Together with his stuttery upper-crust accent, this gave him an arrogant air, mitigated somewhat by a wildly disorganized exterior.

Lily was timid and retiring; she had little to offer in the way of information or opinion that wasn't simply echoing the lord and master. Ben stuttered that a cup of tea might be nice, and she hurried busily back into the kitchen area but then did nothing, and the tea never materialized.

The rather stilted conversation turned to where I went to school. "St. Albans," I said. Ben looked shocked. (Naturally, so did Lily.) "But that's a Protestant school," stammered he. I explained about the local lack of acceptable Catholic secondary education. He became quite agitated, his glasses glinting with concern at the peril in the distance. "Is anyone giving you religious instruction?" I said no. "But that's terrible!" He was now blinking fast and twitching. I was only fourteen and on uncertain ground. I agreed it was terrible, but it was a fantastic school and . . . "That's irrelevant!" snapped Ben. Lily agreed mutely in the background. "It's a question of your immortal soul!" A bit much only five minutes into our first meeting—these were words I'd only ever heard in an Irish brogue.

Ben was now staring intensely at someone far, far away over my left shoulder. "I have an idea," he said; "I'll give you instruction." I didn't know what to say. I looked at Lily to see if there was any other opinion in the room before the chairman banged the gavel. She smiled at me in a saintly way as if to say: tonight a soul has been saved. "That's that, then," said Ben, standing up abruptly. "I'll speak to your parents tomorrow."

My mother was agreeable; Ben had a toff's accent and a Cambridge degree, and his proposal assuaged her guilt at my being in a heathen school. My dad took his normal hands-off attitude toward the whole subject. And so it began.

There was a reason for Ben's uncompromising doctrinal stance.

He was a recent convert with the recent convert's bright-eyed enthusiasm for all things Catholic. After meeting Lily and a speedy courtship he'd proposed; she being a practicing Catholic, the marriage would have to be the good old mongrel kind. According to the fine print, Ben, just like my father, had been required to take a test-drive through the Big Doctrines. Unlike my father, he had been blown away by the logical beauty of it all.

His conversion was no born-again rush of emotion. Ben would claim with a glint of weird humor in his glasses that he had no emotions (Lily nodding with rather more warmth than usual). Ben took pride in being "cold," "detached," "objective," "logical." This was not altogether a pose: he had a first in mathematics from Cambridge at a time when the university had an unparalleled reputation for physicists and mathematicians (Bertrand Russell, Fred Hoyle, et al.). The parish scuttlebutt that he worked on something hush-hush like nuclear research wasn't totally inaccurate. He had taken a high-level defense job when he came down from Cambridge, which probably got him out of his two years' national service. He didn't talk about it much except to say he didn't like the work and was hoping to become a teacher.

His oddest self-description was that he was intrinsically "Teutonic." The gleam in his glasses would get even weirder on this tack. He had a Teutonic temperament, his lack of emotion was Teutonic, his coldness and logic were Teutonic, Teutonic discipline was his model. In fifties Britain with the flowers still fresh on the war graves and bombed-out cities still waiting to be rebuilt, all thanks to a certain gang of Teutons, this was cheeky stuff. It might indeed have begun as some undergraduate *épater-les-bourgeois* pose.

However it had started, wherever it came from, the Teutonic thing suffused his self-image. And it was at the core of his relationship with his wife—the only thing that brought Lily to life. She, according to Ben's analysis, was the diametric opposite of his Teutonic temperament, being French by birth (though raised in England) and therefore consumed at all times by uncontrollable emotions. She was happy to embrace this stereotype: it gave them something they could agree upon, a template on which their marriage could function. A Teutonic temperament and a French temperament living in uneasy harmony across an emotional Maginot Line, cold blood versus hot, logic versus impulse, head versus heart, mind versus matter, stoic versus swept-away, Alsace-Lorraine versus the Saarland . . . it was rich, it explained everything, it even got a laugh once in a while. "That's so Teutonic, dear," she would murmur when he mowed the reeds outside in straight rows. (Except how else would he do it?) Meanwhile she'd agree that getting depressed about housework and thus not doing it was typically French and overemotional. (Except that French wives are house-proud to the point of psychosis.)

As my visits grew more regular, I joined in the fun—an easy way to ingratiate myself. There was an awkward moment when I first crashed the party, as if they weren't sure whether they wanted someone else in the game. (I tried to defuse some tense domestic moment with a crack about the Franco-Prussian War.) But once I was in, I was part of the family—it was the exact opposite of three's a crowd. A third person gave new energy and validity to the template.

Throughout that summer and the autumn I spent more and more time in and around the decrepit green trailer. There was something appealing about its invisibility—that neither my parents nor my siblings, nor the only village subgroup I belonged to, the Catholic parishioners, knew where I was. The trailer was the latest version of my secret hut—a new green shade for new green thoughts.

There was plenty to think about. Ben was a ferocious docent. I'd just turned fourteen but he taught at his level and what he could grasp, not at mine and what I could. On the positive-indoctrination side (our team) I got mostly his beloved Aquinas (the proofs of the existence of God and exegesis of the mysteries, e.g., the Trinity, the Eucharist), with some Cardinal Newman for ballast. On the negative-reinforcement and much more rigorous side (their team) was a shooting war on error: the reasons why every Western philosopher from the Reformation on had got it all wrong. He blew up the errorists from Bishop Berkeley to Bertrand Russell. Much of the error was over my head, but what did stick I found rather more interesting than Ben's refutations.

My carapace of faith in Catholicism was flimsier than I'd realized. Philosophy—not taught in my school or most English schools—was new and engrossing. So whenever I found something inconsistent in Ben's argument against the enemy, I balked and argued the point as best I could.

Lily was fascinated with these exchanges (which I never got the best of). She'd sit at the table after dinner or out on the trailer steps on a summery evening and nod and smile at my points. I was naïve enough to think this was because she actually agreed with them, instead of my being the surrogate for something she didn't have the nerve to do—talk back to Ben. One evening I got hopelessly entangled in some contentious point having to do with faith and reason and didn't the distinction between them have to be taken on faith? I hadn't the foggiest idea where I was going with my argument and Ben was demolishing it anyway. I became quite tongue-tied and pissed off. "Let me finish! Leave me alone! You're wrong! Wait, wait! . . ."

Ben came out of the objective, detached, Teutonic trance in which he taught and actually looked me straight in the eye. "No need to be so prickly," he said.

Lily laughed—for the first time I could remember. "That's it!" she cried at me. "You're a hedgehog! When things get too much, you roll up in a prickly ball and hide from the world! From now on," she said, "I'm going to call you Hedgehog."

She gave me a dazzling smile. Another first. Ben just looked bemused at this flood of Gallic feeling.

So now I was Hedgehog. Our Hedgehog, my Hedgehog, silly old Hedgehog, Hedgie, Hoggie. A typical teen with the self-confidence of your average mollusk, I was delighted that I had enough identity to warrant a nickname.

There was a lot of work to do in the trailer and garden that autumn, and I volunteered to help out in my spare time. Because Ben was now looking for teaching work, he was often away for whole evenings, and for the first time I was with Lily alone. She was jollier than when Ben was around and treated me as an equal, which I appreciated since she was, after all, a grown-up, a member of the parental class, my tribal superior.

One sunny autumn evening I was clearing some rotten lumber from the reeds when I began to feel I was being watched. It made me self-conscious and it puzzled me—I'd never seen another soul down there. I kept going, ignoring whoever it was. It got too much. I had to look round. No one. Then I noticed Lily staring at me through the picture window of the trailer. She had her hands crossed at the wrists over her breasts. It looked bonkers to me—as if she were posing as the effigy of a medieval saint.

I waved. She came out of her trance and waved back. I returned to my chore. Minutes later the same sensation. Now Lily stood just a few yards away. The setting sun behind her shone through her brown hair. She was wearing a long white dress in her customary slinky style, hugging her hips and belly. She was looking at me wide-eyed as if I were a stranger and might be dangerous.

"Hedgehog—do you feel what I feel?"

"What do you feel?"

"As though something was drawing us together. Some terrible temptation. Do you feel that?"

"Um, no, well, not really."

Mostly I was feeling very nervous.

"I feel as though there's a devil pushing me toward you into your arms."

And she did come toward me just as if someone were pushing her—till she was right up to me. Her eyes were still wide. Her lips were trembling and her chin puckering. "Oh God, Mrs. Bootle, please don't cry."

She took my hands and put them on her hips.

"Hold me!"

Now I was really nervous. I pulled her to me in an awkward clinch, as if she were an aunt at Christmas. Then she kissed me. It happened so fast I didn't have time to close my eyes—but I could see hers were shut. Her mouth was soft but rather dry. She could have used some ChapStick.

She opened her eyes. "You demon."

I had no idea how to take this. "Demon" was a schoolboy adjective meaning supercool. But she didn't mean that. There was a long beat of silence. It began to dawn on me what had just happened—my first kiss!—and how pleasant it could be if repeated. With perhaps a bit more planning. I lunged toward her. She shook her head violently and stumbled back as if I were trying to bite her.

"You must go."

"I haven't finished doing the wood."

"Finish it tomorrow."

She turned, strode into the trailer, and slammed the door.

I walked home through the chill fall mists on the meadows, floundering in confusion. Somewhere on confusion's outskirts was wild excitement that I'd finally embarked on my love life. But I couldn't be sure. For one thing, she'd seemed pretty angry at the end there. Had I done something wrong? Should I have kissed her back harder? Should I have tried harder for the second kiss? Should I not have tried at all? Did she hate me now?

What I didn't feel was guilt or remorse, connection of any kind between what had happened and my religion, despite the fact that it must come under the general heading of adultery, an exceptionally juicy mortal sin.

But—most curious and confusing—I wasn't aroused. I hadn't been aroused when she kissed me either. And yet physically Mrs. Bootle was streets ahead of the schoolgirls who traveled to various educational establishments on my bus, several of whom had been the objects of my perpetual love.

Unlike these bulky English Roses, she was small and slender with that antique, seductive French carriage that comes from being taught from the age of six to walk with a book balanced on your head: straight back and shoulders, flat tummy tapering to coy groin, butt pushed out behind. A stance which sets up the heart-melting glance over the shoulder, the delicious French art of using the back as a sexual characteristic.

Her face was pretty and petite also; she could have made gamine if it hadn't been for a rather prominent nose. This was true of many of the women I subsequently fell for and all the ones I loved, a feature I never noticed when I fell in love with them but which later, in moments of anger or alienation, would begin to appear grotesquely large.

My own nose, I hasten to add, is nothing to write home about.

The more I thought about the undeniable cuteness of Mrs. Bootle, the more this aspect began to dominate all others. And since she had not sparked the usual bestial acts in me, there must be something better and purer about this love, if love it was, and what else can it be when you're fourteen and a pretty, grown-up woman kisses you?

The next morning, churning with a high-octane mixture of wild excitement and utter terror that I might have got it all hopelessly wrong, I showed up to finish doing the wood. Ben wasn't there, but she was, standing on the steps of the trailer waiting for me, holding the baby for protection. She was quite the opposite of the day before, a hostess almost, chatty and outgoing and apologetic.

"Hedgehog, I'm so sorry about what happened yesterday. I—we shouldn't have done that. But . . . but . . . there we are. I do hope you'll forgive me and that God will too. I know you want to get started on the wood, but why not come in for a moment?" She took my hand with her free one, entwined her fingers in mine, gave me a bright smile, and pulled me inside.

We sat at the table across which so many fine points of morality had been pounded—obviously none too effectively—into my immortal soul. In Ben's absence she adopted the instructional mode.

"Hedgehog, these impulses sometimes come over us, and we mustn't give in to them. I believe even discussing what happened could bring on the impulse again, which is why social contact between us may itself be sinful."

I nodded dutifully, desperately disappointed.

"Being together like this is an occasion of sin, and we will have to avoid being together alone in the future—until these impulses pass. You do understand, don't you, Hedgie? Now I expect you want to get started on the wood."

Then she got up and just stood there. Her eyes turned all wide and tragic and she shook her head operatically.

"Oh, my love." She rushed round the table and cradled my head in her arms. "I can't help myself and I don't care."

I stood up. This time I was ready. I kissed her, eyes closed, grinding away on her lips as I'd seen Victor Mature and Burt Lancaster and Stewart Grainger and Errol Flynn do so effectively.

She flopped her face on my chest, sobbing. "I love you I love you I love you. I want ordinary corrupt human love! Go before I do something rash, something unforgivable!"

I did go, in a glorious glow of love. I was in love, she was my lover, I was her lover—possibly a Great Lover. I had handled a love scene. Love was great and I was in it.

And that was as good as it got. With variations, the same scene repeated for months. We really had little to talk about except being in love and how tragic it was and how we shouldn't even be together alone talking about it, which would set one of us off again—at first her but then, as I got into the rhythm of the thing, me too, since I always wanted to get to the kissing part as quickly as possible. Which would be the end, for she would be aflame, or out of her mind with desire, or something equally Verdi-esque, and so I would have to leave and trudge off, fulfilled once more, bursting with obscure feelings of warmth and pride and excitement at how grown-up I was—up the lane in the wintry moonlight. The wood never did get done.

That odd phrase occurred again more than once: "ordinary corrupt human love." Pressed, she admitted that it wasn't original—it came from one of her favorite books, *The End of the Affair* by Graham Greene.

I'd heard vaguely about Greene from my mother, who disapproved of him. He wasn't a good advertisement for Catholicism, she said. But then he was a convert and didn't know any better. Ben also disapproved of Greene—violently—so Lily's reading had to be sub-rosa. She lent me her copy of the novel and I devoured it. Most of Greene's tortured introspection was over my head, but I was transfixed by its sexuality. The descriptions of Sarah's orgasm, "that strange sad angry cry of abandonment," and in particular for some reason "her secret hair," turned me on like mad. Oddly, I made no connection between the deeply sexual Sarah and my actual flesh-and-blood lover. But I had little trouble grasping the intensity of feeling, the forbidden fruit of infidelity, and certainly Lily's longed-for parallel. I too longed to be like Bendrix, to have such full-blooded and complex and grown-up emotions as hate and jealousy and despair.

Lily, though, was an unhappy and lonely woman, and sometimes that winter she'd be so low that even she wouldn't have the energy for such convoluted dramaturgy. Usually at such moments new information about her marriage would emerge.

It turned out that not only was Ben Teutonic in the garden, at the piano, at table, and in everyday life, he was also a Teuton in bed. He made love, she said, like a machine, the same way he played Bach, as if he were a human metronome.

Ben, of course, had a rationale for his Teutonic approach to intercourse. (He always called sex "intercourse" in our instruction sessions, which continued as before.) His rationale came directly from Rome, inspired by that old sexpert Pope Pius XII. Taking pleasure in intercourse, even properly-married-and-Curially-approved-birth-control-free intercourse, was, while not a sin, a weakness. The supererogatory path, the more saintly option, was to *avoid* pleasure. Therefore, since intercourse was for the sole purpose of procreation anyway, Ben avoided all pleasure during the act of love, speeding Lily along the path to salvation by making sure she experienced none either. To make doubly sure, Ben insisted that they pray before intercourse to ask God's help in killing pleasure and creating life when they finally got down to business.

Lily's intimacies took things to another level. They were not playacting. They were real, unnerving. They were intended to induce pity, and to the degree that I understood the emotions involved, I tried to be sympathetic. But they also turned me on, in a way nothing had so far in the relationship. Whenever she talked of this I felt a delicious rush of confused, definitely illicit, definitely impure emotion.

Guilt arrived with the knowledge that there was more to this than a pure and innocent game called love—these were dangerous and fascinating undercurrents. The absence of pleasure she bemoaned was a pretty clear message about her needs and the depth of her frustration. My fear of Hell began to appear now that I knew what I was playing with, but so did my excitement. Maybe I could do better than this guy. Maybe I could make her happy. When I thought about what that might entail, shadowy though it was, it was intoxicating, and I wanted it to happen soon.

Which is how we came to be standing in her tiny kitchen on a cold spring morning with my hand under her smaller one, far down beneath her dress now, beyond the tightness of the waist, where nothing was left as an impediment, smoothing over her hot skin, at the top of her groin surely, I felt her sweat, oh God we were there, she was guiding me into the unknown, the unimaginable . . . her secret hair!

"No!" she yelped suddenly, tugging my hand out of her dress. She twisted away from me, melodramatically sobbing "Go, go, oh, what have I done, why did I ever meet you? You demon, you devil, *get thee behind me, Satan!"*

Then Ben's face was at the trailer door, followed by his body, his very big body, filling the doorway. He took in his wife as she turned, gasping at his sudden appearance, holding the undone top of her dress up around herself; and then over toward me, scanning through the Coke-bottle glasses for whoever else was there in the shadows of the kitchen. He was a very big guy indeed. I'd never noticed before that when he came into the living area his head grazed the ceiling. I had no idea what would happen next. There was incomprehension in his mouth, and his glasses had some new and different glint. But what? Rage? Jealousy? Murder?

CHAPTER TWO

Where Father Joe lived:

Our train trundled out of Waterloo Station en route to Portsmouth on the south coast of England. Ahead of us lay a two-hour train ride and a half-hour ferryboat journey to the Isle of Wight, a midsized island a mile or so from the mainland. There a short bus ride would take us to our destination: a place called Quarr Abbey.

Ben resumed his lecture on the recent ecclesiastical history of France:

"By the end of the century, the anticlericalism of the French government had become chronic, and in 1901 the Law of Association was passed, giving all French monks the effective choice of either betraying their vows or fleeing the country."

He'd kept this up—or something like it—for the two-hour bus and train ride to London. "Keep it light, bright, and polite" was evidently how Teutons—at least the civilized British branch—dealt with the rather awkward situation of being confined in public transportation with a boy who's given you, if not horns, two sizable lumps on the cranium. I found this odd, but then I'd found Ben's reaction to catching Lily and me in semi–*flagrante delicto* odd. Lacking any experience of a husband's normal response to finding his wife with her top off in the presence of another male, I knew enough to realize that it wasn't "hello, you two." Yes, there had been a certain strained quality to the greeting. But still.

However, I had not been interested in making this a learning experience. Sliding as smoothly as I could between the Bechstein and Ben's looming bulk, I'd remarked that I'd better be getting along, to which Ben had replied with the first hint of menace that yes, perhaps I should.

For the remainder of the weekend I was scared silly. I had no one to turn to, no means of finding out if there were consequences for what I'd done. It was Saturday and hence time for the weekly sacrament of penance, but I was not about to confess to the rusty grille that I'd been caught by Mr. Bootle with my hand down Mrs. Bootle's dress. I suspected the seal of the confessional might get a little leaky in the parental direction. Not going to Confession meant I had to feign sickness the next morning and miss Sunday Mass so that I wouldn't have to go to Communion with a mortal sin staining my immortal soul. On the other hand, missing Mass without a valid excuse was also a mortal sin. I couldn't explain to Mum that I'd skipped going to Communion because I was an adulterer, just like Scobie in *The Heart of the Matter.* Lily had often compared our predicament concerning the sacraments of Confession and Communion to Scobie's. I hadn't seen it.

Now I got it. I was piling up eternal liabilities like a drunk in a casino. Perhaps the priests were right. It was appalling how far I'd fallen from the insouciance of a mere twenty-four hours ago; once you started down the road of concupiscence the sins began swarming like bees.

There was also the possible criminality of the thing. Every day Dad's *News Chronicle* dripped with people being jailed for crimes of passion, which in almost every case seemed to mean having it off with other people's mates. What if I was a bona fide delinquent, nicking first people's bus money and now their wives? Could Ben have me arrested?

Late on Sunday afternoon I got a summons from the trailer. The Bootles had no phone, so the message came as a note conveyed by a kid from a nearby farm—formal enough to raise my parents' eyebrows. Would I like to come down for supper? On the whole, not really. But given my usual alacrity in accepting any invitation from them (despite Lily's rock-bottom cooking), declining would definitely have set Mum's antennae twitching.

A very long trudge down the lane that evening. Last time I'd made the trip—months ago, it seemed—I'd been a great lover striding toward his mistress with a delicious intimation of new and unimaginable favors. Now I'd regressed to the guilty what-have-I-done-then? defiance of a hapless teen.

"Hello, Hedgehog," said Ben heartily from the trailer door, gazing as usual at the faraway person on the horizon. I had never wanted less to be called by my nickname. "Do come in."

The trailer was unnaturally tidy. Lily was nowhere to be seen. She was resting, said Ben, she'd been putting the house in order. Ominous. Was I hungry? Not in the least, but it was a good way to delay whatever was coming.

"Starving," I said.

"We'll eat afterward," snapped Ben. "Please sit down."

We sat facing each other across the rickety table of catechesis. My stomach was churning. I had no clue what was going on. Were we teacher and pupil, or males locking horns? Ben didn't seem to be experiencing any emotion at all. If anything, he was going into his customary detached, glaring docent trance.

"We will say the Rosary for guidance," he intoned. He knelt beside the table and produced his large wooden nun-issue rosary. I hesitated. "Don't you have your rosary?" he snapped, as though it were an essential piece of equipment in resolving adulterous imbroglios. I shook my head dumbly and knelt too.

I'd always hated the Rosary, which involves endless repetition of the Hail Mary, or Ave Maria. The Ave splits into two halves, the first intoned by the priest or leader and the second by the faithful (in this case me). The first or Hail part is positive and cheerful, complimenting the Virgin on her quasi-divine attributes and her achievement in giving birth to Jesus without a husband; the second or Holy part, as always in Catholic ritual with the bits the faithful have to say, is about being sinners and needing major help, "now and at the hour of our death."

We said the Sorrowful Mysteries—five "decades" of the Rosary, or fifty Aves. Fifty times I was required to repeat that I was a sinner and needed serious divine intervention now and on my deathbed. There may have been some malicious method in what seemed more and more like borderline madness, but I doubt it. While nothing whatsoever in the way of guidance occurred to me during the interminable prayers, for Ben it apparently did the trick. He accelerated into the final "glory be" with an upbeat air and resumed his seat.

"We're confronted with an unfortunate situation," said Ben to the guy on the horizon. "You and I must resolve it." What did that mean? Fight a duel?

"We will have to bring the matter to a priest," he continued. I began to panic. Presenting Father Bleary with our unfortunate situation would not only do no good, it would lead inevitably to parental retribution.

"But not just any priest," Ben continued. There was a monastery he knew of, in the South of England, where dwelt a monk whom he and Lily had consulted on some prior marital matter. We—meaning he and I—would travel there as soon as possible. It happened to be the school Easter holidays, so we could leave in the next day or two. He would make the arrangements. He was willing to tell my parents the white lie that it was part of my instruction.

"This monk," pronounced Ben, looking at me directly for the first time, his cold, gray, alien eyes made colder and grayer and more alien by the permanently skewed lenses, "will know how to handle the matter." *The heart of the matter,* I thought. Ben's tamped-down hostility struck a chill into my gut. The matter was *me.*

* * *

Monks were a mystery. They probably were to most English Catholics, except for the small, tightly knit Catholic aristocracy whose sons attended schools run by Benedictine monks. The top two of these—Downside and Ampleforth—were considered the Catholic equivalent of Eton and Harrow. One of Ampleforth's sales tags was that it was "what Eton once was [i.e., before the Reformation]: a school for the sons of Catholic gentlemen."

Even if one was privileged enough to know the Benedictines who ran these places, teaching orders weren't monks in the strict sense, because they weren't contemplative.

Contemplatives, who spend their lives in a cloister, in minimal contact with the outside world, better fit the immemorial image of monks. Raised on Anglocentric history, I, like my schoolmates and doubtless most of my other fellow citizens, imagined monks as hooded, faceless creatures, gliding through history along dark cloisters, bent on intrigue and treachery, the Romish occupation forces of a country yearning to be free and Protestant.

The behind-closed-doors aspect of monastic life, its inherent secrecy, not to mention the vast wealth amassed by monasteries down the centuries, had bred a long tradition of monstrous tales about what went on "in there." Monks were rumored to be drunks, gluttons, lechers, catamites, or worse. A decorating cliché of English halls and bathrooms was the nineteenth-century satirical print of (usually fat) monks doing things they shouldn't. *The Monk* by Matthew Lewis was one of the first horror novels in Romantic literature. Nuns had a cheery or naïve image; they'd even starred in their own hit movies. But not monks. Most people assumed contemplative monks to be a thing of the past, a very endangered species—and good riddance.

This monk and this monastery were contemplative.

What was Ben thinking? How could a monk help us? A man who must spend a fair amount of his life and energy putting stuff like adultery and dresses and what lay under them forcibly out of his mind? To make things still more puzzling, the monastery was of

French provenance, having been founded by French monks early in the century. Since the unfortunate situation had arisen in large part, according to Ben, from Lily's fiery, impetuous Gallic temperament, why were we off to see a monk who, chances were, also had a fiery, impetuous Gallic temperament? Shouldn't we be heading for Germany?

If I'd been a year or two older I might have resisted this trip. But I wasn't much more than a boy, and a country boy at that, and in my constricted world Ben held all the cards. He was "the injured party"; he had been and still was a powerful intellectual influence on me. And he had a killer ace up his cuff: if I refused his guidance he could simply tell my parents what I had done. God only knew what the fallout of that would be—physical or otherwise. More shadowy and therefore more scary: what was my moral responsibility here? Just how bad was this sin?

A half century later it's easy to make light of fifties Catholicism's minute calibration of sin. But good and evil and where I stood on its spectrum did concern me, as it concerned many others.

The cultural zeitgeist made moral agonizing natural. From its grave, German militarism cast a long shadow over all that was done and written and felt in Europe, however optimistic it might appear to be. The ungraspable suffering caused by one small group of determined men, along with a happily passive population acquiescing in their claims to be acting for good and against evil, was fresh in the memory, sixty million wrenching absences in the lives of the living, the photos unfaded, inescapable.

But a few years earlier—indeed, it was the first news story of which I was really conscious—another small group of determined men, in Washington, had begun to talk blithely of murdering in a few hours as many civilians as had fallen in the entire Second World War, and another happily apathetic population seemed to be just dandy with the idea (many of them because they believed Christ would—or did—agree). The new militarism cast an even more terrifying shadow across the future than the militarism behind us—insisting yet again that one side was good and the other evil—an absurdity on a simple historical level, given the fathomless sacrifices of the Russian people, the means by which the Wehrmacht had been checked and broken.

Yet while their heroes were still warm in their graves, the Russians had betrayed their memory, behaving toward their neighbors with brutality indistinguishable from the Nazis', racing to catch up in the development of the most cowardly weapons in the history of warfare, claiming that good, if not God, was on their side and only evil on the other.

My two authority figures, Dad and Ben, could hardly have had more divergent views on the menace of communism. For my dad, socialism had been the hope of his life, the force that had lifted him from his working-class background into fulfillment as an artist and which in the hands of the Labour Party would lift me and my sisters and brother still further. He knew Stalin was a monster, but communism was still socialism and should not be judged by those who'd betrayed it.

As a boy growing up after World War I, surrounded by the ghastly evidence of what bestial militarism coupled with cutting-edge technology (politely known as modern warfare) did to those unlucky enough to survive it, my dad had become a pacifist. When Nazism boiled over, the socialist stared down the pacifist, but he joined the Royal Air Force in a dull despair that stayed with him all his life. Like most working-class people, he mistrusted the heroics of the arrogant, self-aggrandizing Churchill but accepted his leadership as a necessary evil. If the future of socialism could be assured by defeating the century's true enemy, fascism, such accommodations had to be made. The only joy my father took in victory was bittersweet: he and his partner painted the "Battle of Britain" window in Westminster Abbey, the nation's memorial to his fallen RAF colleagues.

Ben saw communism through an exclusively religious filter as the intellectual, spiritual, and political enemy. Not only did it deny the existence of God, it held that spirituality was just another tool of capital by which labor could be kept fearful, docile, and exploitable. It was uncompromisingly materialist, denying the divinity of man and the universe, promising that a material paradise in which all humans would receive the greatest possible good was achievable. For Ben communism was the mirror image of Catholicism. Once the leap of non-faith—the absolute nonexistence of God—had been made, all else flowed from that posit with Thomist precision. Communism was the One True Faith of the material world, the Un-holy Universal Church. He had a grudging admiration for its theoretical completeness, its dialectical purity.

His complete embrace of Catholic doctrine also meant that he saw the struggle between good and evil as absolute, astride this world and the next. Given the Cold War standoff, victory for the moment was just a lovely dream, a new dawn tinting the horizon. In the interim, prayer was the weapon of choice. And since prayer was efficacious in direct proportion to one's standing with God, personal self-improvement was demanded of you. The better you became, the more pressure there would be on the Devil and his communist dupes. Thus the external struggle between good and evil became internalized, and where you stood upon its spectrum, of crucial importance.

Against such an all-or-nothing backdrop, it was hard to argue that sin was a private affair. Sin helped the enemy, sin let Christ and Mary's side down. Ben's relentless insistence that sin led not just to Hell in the afterlife but to the hell of communism in this life had its effect, if not on my intellect, certainly on my id. Neither my parents, nor the nuns, nor the brothers, nor regular attendance at the sacraments, nor a fine liberal education had done a thing to sharpen my moral self, but Ben put good and evil front and center on my inner stage by a time-honored Catholic technique: fear. Or as we fearless moderns prefer to call it: guilt. I was unpersuaded by Ben's doctrinal rigor, but under his tutelage I developed impressive reserves of Catholic guilt, billions of barrels of it, a lifetime supply.

The refineries were working at full capacity as we got off the train to board a rusty ferry in Portsmouth Harbour, bound for the Isle of Wight. (The Isle of Wight was once Queen Victoria's southernmost redoubt, a royal favor which had guaranteed, despite its pastoral charm, that it was gripped by suffocating fustiness. It couldn't have been more grimly English, a little haven for cozy retirement cottages with names like "Little Haven.")

Embarking for its misty shores a mile or so away, I felt very far from home, descending like Dante into a doleful bark upon a dismal Lethe with my personal Charon, Ben.

Foremost on my mind: what will they do to me, this monk and this monastery? Having only the Holy Brothers to go on when it came to male religious models, I was worried that the punishment ahead might be major. And physical. Didn't they brick people up behind walls and stuff—or make you spend the night in spook-ridden crypts with your arms stretched out like Christ on the cross?

Ben was of no use here. I could hardly ask the injured party what my punishment might be for injuring said party. In any case he was keeping up his light, bright history patter. We had moved on to the Benedictine order, founded in A.D. 534 by St. Benedict, an aristocratic young Roman who, growing sick of the corruption of post-Roman Rome, had disappeared into the hills of Umbria to be a hermit but ended up establishing the first pan-European monastic order.

There had been monasteries before this, communities of men or women—in Ireland, men *and* women—living apart from the normal world, the better to contemplate its shortcomings and improve their chances of salvation. These monasteries were mostly found in the Eastern Church—Greece, Asia Minor, the Middle East—small groups living in the harshest and most ascetic of conditions and the most inaccessible of places. A parallel tradition of hermitage had grown up in North Africa, even more devoted to self-mortification and self-denial, of which the most celebrated exponents were the Desert Fathers.

There was, in the social and spiritual chaos of post-Roman Italy, great interest in withdrawing from the world, but the abnegation and asceticism of the Desert Fathers didn't appeal to the post-Romans.

St. Benedict took a very different tack. A charismatic man and a brilliant organizer, his two masterstrokes were, first, to insist that the monastic path to salvation was communal and, second, to put it in writing. Benedict's Rule—actually a collection of Rules—governed every aspect of communal life, from the most spiritual to the most mundane.

The Rule plays down self-denial: "since the monks of our day cannot be convinced [not to drink wine] let us agree to drink moderately and not to the point of excess. . . ." For self-mortification Benedict substituted prayer and coherent organization. His monks were required to take vows of stability, conversion of life (including poverty and chastity)—and, most significantly, obedience. Instead of exhibitionist displays of self-flagellation and sunken-face fasting, Benedict insisted on work. The monk's day was divided between work and prayer, "work" meaning anything from high art to academic research to making wine to cooking dinner or mucking out the cows.

But work in the Benedictine tradition, enjoyable or not, exalted or humble, is in no conflict with the spiritual. Indeed, it too is prayer, a principle best expressed in the classic Benedictine dictum *Laborare est orare*—"To work is to pray." There is no separation between work in the sense of secular, non-spiritual toil and the spiritual in the sense of uplifting relief from its tedium. Benedictines were the first people in history to claim that work is sacred.

Ben's history lesson got us across the choppy gray Solent—the channel separating the Isle of Wight from the mainland—its irritable squalls slashing rain past the greasy cabin windows. But even he lapsed into silence as our journey neared its end. The green double-decker bus crawled up narrow streets lined with tea shops and pharmacies, the tea shops full of pensioners, the pharmacies full of prosthetics and corn plasters and walking devices by means of which the pensioners could make it to the tea shops.

The bus reached the outskirts of town and the retirement-cottage belt, endless cul-de-sacs of squat gray stone dwellings whose tidiness alone made you feel suicidal. Every cottage had a cute name filched from the common fount of sentiment: Fair Harbour, Dunroamin', Mon Nid, or, in a more imperial vein, Kilimanjaro, Bangalore, Botany Bay. Several were called "The Laburnums" and almost all sported those flowers, just coming into bloom, their sopping fronds of pus-colored buds drooping over trim fences and neat walls.

Then we were in open country, speeding through lush fields and dense woods. Almost immediately, off to my right, sprouting out of massive oaks and dark evergreens, I saw an odd round brick spire shaped like something between a gnome's cap and a warhead. The bus wheezed to a halt by a long driveway leading in its direction. The far end of the driveway was dark and overgrown, a wet green mystery.

Absolutely nothing suggested what to expect up there. Could be a county jail. Could be a modern version of the Inquisition for underage adulterers. With that spire it could even be an overseas branch of the Kremlin.

Suddenly I felt an overwhelming need to resist, to run away, to return to my parents and what I knew, to call this demented man's bluff. I wasn't obligated to do what he said. I didn't really know him at all. He could go utterly bonkers on me, aided and abetted by whoever was up that driveway. If I went up there, something cataclysmic, life-changing, perhaps life-ending, could happen.

But I was a nicely brought up British kid. And nicely brought up British kids don't make scenes in public.

So up the driveway I went, to Quarr Abbey.

CHAPTER THREE

The first impression was of utter silence, stillness so palpable that you had to stand for a moment to see if anything would disturb it. It only increased my apprehension: in my experience nothing got this quiet unless it preceded a major explosion of trouble. But the silence persisted.

The entrance area appeared spacious and welcoming, except that when you examined it, you saw it was enclosed on all sides, save for the driveway and two massive iron gates marked PRIVATE. Two sides of this enclosure were formed by the brick walls of an extensive vegetable garden. On the third side, facing us, was a high multistory building with many triangular vaulted windows and one vast wooden door in the shape of a truncated Gothic arch, the kind of door that once thwarted the axes and battering rams of besiegers. The fourth side was a handsome, compact church whose entrance was an even bigger truncated arch.

The architecture wasn't English, but neither was it French. Nor was it very old. Built of pink and yellow brick, the buildings had many crenellations and blunt triangular turrets; at second glance, in fact, triangles were everywhere—like the spire which I could now see was atop a bell tower. In context it looked less like a warhead than a streamlined minaret. The two-color patterning of the brick and the triangular theme gave the structures a Moorish feel, at once elegant, exotic, and mildly forbidding. Other than the church, though, they didn't look like something that could go by the name of "Abbey." The three-story building facing us looked more like a girls' boarding school or one of those new enlightened postwar reformatories where nobody got flogged.

Without announcing us at Reception, checking our luggage, calling the bellhop, or whatever you did in places like this, Ben ducked inside the church, pulling me with him.

Later I absorbed the fine proportions and stark simplicity of the interior, its un-Catholic lack of adornment, free of soppy-eyed lumps of plaster in the shape of the Virgin and saints, of the garish mismatched side altars and hideous gobbets of congealed wax hanging like polyps from the candle racks.

None of that struck me at the time, because of the music.

To say I'd never heard Gregorian chant before wasn't strictly true. Snatches of it survived in Catholic liturgy, but the atonal croakings that passed over our good pastor's gingivitic gums had never conveyed an iota of its beauty.

It seemed far away, but deep inside my head. It soared, but softly and serenely, quite unlike the robust choral music—Mozart's Requiem, Beethoven's Ninth—that Dad loved to play on our miraculous new twelve-inch LPs. It hung in the air, it caressed the rays of light striking through the long nave windows, the pauses between the phrases as limpid and evocative as the melodies themselves.

If "melodies" was the right word. The music's tonality struck my teenage ear as foreign, exotic, Eastern, and ancient, incredibly ancient in fact, pre-Christian. It didn't seem Catholic or medieval or even holy. Its associations were much farther back: Mediterranean, but from a distant and more pristine sea, an age of more local mysteries, with gods of wine and goats and olive groves, before the advent of a remote and impersonal deity.

I don't mean it sounded pagan—a churchy word that suggests hedonism. The chant was the exact opposite of hedonistic. It would never induce the delicious surges of despair or longing or nobility of purpose that Beethoven and Brahms and Schumann could. It was a music of the spirit, seeking peace, not emotional release, expressing the hunger of the soul rather than the heart. A way of sequencing notes so ancient it might be music's mother lode, its Fertile Crescent. It wouldn't have grated, I felt, on the ears of ancient Greeks or Egyptians or Mesopotamians or Sumerians—or even on the august auditory equipment of the Buddha or Lao-tzu.

Before me on a slightly higher level and about a hundred feet away were two long rows of curved, carved choir stalls facing each other across the nave. In these stood some sixty men of all ages, thirty or so on each side. They were dressed in black from head to toe; hanging from the back of every robe was that telltale hood.

It was Holy Week, so there was a special gravity to the hymns and antiphons. They were intercut with longer sections of simpler, repetitive incantation, sung alternately by each side of the choir. Ben whispered details of what was going on, but I took in very little as I sat there awestruck, washed by waves of sound, alone on the shore of a new ocean of experience.

The service ended—Vespers, I learned later, combined with None, the Office of the ninth hour or afternoon. The monks left their stalls and paired off, genuflecting together toward the altar, then turning toward us to walk out of the church. They walked in silence, heads and eyes cast down, their arms crossed under the front flap of their robes, completely ignoring their public (several widowy-looking women and us), the younger ones in step, the older ones shuffling or limping. Some of the most ancient put up their hoods as they came toward us, apparently for no more sinister reason than that it was freezing in the church.

I scanned the faces anxiously, looking for the hard-faced (but please, sweet mother of God, fair and merciful) disciplinarian who was going to know how to handle the matter. I saw no one who fit the bill. Many of the faces looked Continental—the English called Europe "the Continent" in those days, meaning the lesser tribes beyond the English Channel—but among the Gallic olive-tan and gaunt gray Anglo-Saxon mugs there was no likely candidate. If anything, they all looked exceptionally mild-mannered.

We were shown to our rooms by a decrepit old monk who hauled himself in agony up the stairs of the guesthouse, giving me ample time to sign a query to Ben as to whether this was the one. He wasn't. The guesthouse turned out to be the high three-story building I'd taken for a girls' school or a reformatory. The rooms were plain and simple; mine was on the third floor with tiny windows facing inward to the cloister. No escape down the drainpipe, then.

His exertions left the old monk uncommunicative. As he staggered back down the stairs, Ben hurried after him and said something in a low voice. No, replied the good monk loudly, the Guestmaster was not available; he was also the Sub-Prior—whatever that was—and was very busy until dinnertime. But he would try to greet the guests before dinner.

"And yes," he added, glaring over at me with pale watery eyes, "Father Warrilow is aware that you have a Special Problem."

My stomach clenched. So it wasn't just Ben. I had done something objectively obnoxious, a breach not just of Catholic morals but of standards and laws as yet unknown. Doubtless the whole monastery knew what the blond-haired kid with the squint had done to a helpless woman. The fearsome Father Warrilow was even now devising some punishment or torment worthy of my sin. Would he have a study, like the headmaster of my school? Or a ghastly, fuggy living room like that of Father Bleary, where I'd go when I'd committed a sin beyond parental reach? No—it was more likely some dark, intimidating space beyond the guesthouse wall, a room with a secret door behind a tapestry and steps leading down into cryptlike gloom lit by one tall candle. Behind it, unseen, would be Father Warrilow's grim, relentless basso, demanding an explanation for my crimes and satisfaction for an infuriated deity.

Why hadn't I turned back at the bottom of the driveway?

Ben nodded with relief that the authorities had been informed. He headed down to the second floor and the guest room.

St. Benedict's Rule stipulates that all guests who arrive at the monastery are to be accommodated, whatever their rank or condition, on the rationale that they represent Christ and to respect Christ's words: "I was hungry and you took me in." Within reason (you have to make a reservation and you can't stay for months), the Rule still holds fifteen hundred years later. Not surprisingly, therefore, the guesthouses of most monasteries often contain some serious weirdos.

There are guests with straightforward goals: most commonly priests on retreat or young men thinking about joining the community, less often people like us looking for some specific spiritual relief. But there are always two or three shabby, gray-faced organisms of indeterminate age who might best be described as monk groupies.

These men, if men they be (and only men are allowed to stay in the guesthouses), are the male equivalent of Church Ladies. They rise to attend the earliest Offices (before dawn for much of the year); they know all the responses and chants and when to kneel and stand and bow the head and utter saintly ejaculations. You will often hear them behind you, tunelessly groaning the gorgeous cadences of the chant.

But it is backstage that they really come into their own.

Monk groupies are also Cathoholics, with an insatiable thirst for pious gossip and intrigue. On matters of faith and doctrine they're reticent; they'll know where so-and-so in the diocese stands on an issue or whether such-and-such an episcopal policy is likely to get this or that luminary's blessing. They rarely have opinions of their own.

On the other hand, they always have detailed knowledge of late-breaking news in the monastery itself: every minor disaster in the kitchens or on the farm, the disagreement between the Abbot and the Cellarer over whether the Sunday cider should be bought from the off-license or made on the premises from the apples in the orchard (which go to waste every year, you know), every political eddy in the chapter house (the chamber in the monastery where a chapter of the Rule is read each day and monks discuss their community's internal affairs); and, with the greatest relish, who is recently dead, near death, or not looking as if he'll make it through the winter. Many of these Gollum-like creatures have tried the monastic life at some point and didn't make it, and so have a burning, shame-driven interest in new postulants (those who present themselves to enter the monastery).

There were a couple of them in the guest room, a book-lined, newspaper-strewn room hung with holy paintings, smelling of cigarettes and stale cookies, as untidy and overflowing with worldly detritus as the cell-like rooms were stark and plain. Ben listened delightedly to all the gossip. Nothing could have interested me less. I was by now in a glassy-eyed catatonia of apprehension.

But they were interested in me. The appearance of a teenager in the guest room meant only one thing—I was a potential postulant. Young too. Intriguing. They plied me with oblique questions, trying to find out whom I knew, making veiled hints about the terrors awaiting me in the cloister. All this increased my apprehension, which in turn incited them to further obscure utterances, which in turn brought me closer to complete collapse. Ben volunteered that I had come to see Father Warrilow. Ah, purred one of them with a nasty, knowing smile: I would find that Father Joseph—all monk groupies refer to the idols by their first names—was a very *different* kind of monk.

Time for dinner. We trooped downstairs, my knees knocking as I prepared to confront Father Josef Varilau, Butcher of Quarr. But it was only the old monk again. The Benedictine Gruppenführer had been further delayed—perhaps to give a recalcitrant postulant a lie detector test.

Dinner went by in a blur. The refectory was a huge, austere, handsomely beamed room. Monks lined the walls on heavy benches, eating in silence, as inscrutable as they had been when they left the church. The guests sat at a long table in the center of the room with their backs to the monks, so that while every monk could see the guests, the rules of decorum forbade you to inspect them. I could feel my soon-to-be inquisitor's piercing eyes on my back, staring at me from the anonymity of the benches along the walls, sizing me up, pondering how the matter might be handled.

One monk was at a lectern reading aloud from an improving book, *The Lives of the Saints.* As far as I recall, though my mental condition could have affected my grasp of the story line, the saint by whose life we were being improved was a martyr from the early Church. She'd had all her limbs and other appendages removed by her tormentors—the Romans, probably—but had somehow managed to keep calling on the name of her Savior despite being reduced to little more than a blood-soaked cube of meat with a head. In the end they cut off her head too, but the head kept joyfully professing its (or her) faith in the reward hereafter. Not an appetizing story at the best of times, but I had no appetite anyway.

Then there was another office—Compline—the last of the day, with more of that wondrous chant, beautiful beyond description, in the darkened church. But even this comfort ran cold. Definitive word had been passed by way of the testy old monk: Father Joseph Warrilow would see me after Compline. Without fail. I was to wait for him in my cell.

So here we were, Ben and I, in my little room with the tiny windows. Outside it was dark and cold and raining. No escape now. Why Ben was there—as ally or accuser—I wasn't sure. I didn't have the nerve to ask him to leave. At the end of the day—literally—this was his call. My moral sense told me he had every right to be there. My moral sense, largely shaped by Ben.

All of a sudden there was the sound of sandals squishing along the corridor and the swish of long skirts. The door opened. And there stood one of the oddest human beings I'd ever laid eyes on.

CHAPTER FOUR

The sandals first. They were huge and stuck out from floppy, flapping black skirts at an angle of sixty degrees. They contained the flattest pair of feet imaginable. Thick black socks could not conceal their chronic knobbliness.

Knobbly too: the big pink hands like rock lobsters sticking out from frayed black cuffs, the scrawny neck rising from its frayed black collar, the award-winning Adam's apple.

A fleshy triangular nose sported granny glasses that must have predated the Great War. The crowning glory: gigantic ears, wings of gristle, at right angles to the rather pointy close-shaven skull. The long rubbery lips were stretched in the goofiest of grins.

Father Joseph Warrilow was as close to a cartoon as you could get without being in two dimensions.

"Ben—my dear!" He came toward Ben, arms outstretched for the big hug, but Ben, no devotee of physical contact, converted it into a handshake. Holding on tight, the good monk hustled him toward the door.

"Out we go," he grinned at an open-mouthed Ben, who began to protest as the door closed on him. "Tony and I want to be alone."

He turned to me and gave me the hug instead. Then a smacky kiss on the cheek, as if we'd known each other for years.

"What terrible weather you brought with you, my dear." He gathered his skirts around his knees and plopped into the only armchair. "But it's always remarkably wet in Holy Week. Then on Easter Sunday, out comes the sun!"

He had a hurried, eager, very English manner of speech, his *r*s always threatening to become *v*s.

I went to kneel beside the chair as I had with Father Bleary when he heard my confession in his lair. "No no no no," said Father Joseph Warrilow seventeen times. "Sit down next to me." He reached over for a little wooden stool at the table and pulled it to him, patting the seat.

I sat down. Without looking at me he took my hand in his—big, surprisingly soft—and held it on the arm of the chair. His long mobile lips pursed and unpursed several times; he blinked rapidly until finally his eyes closed. Evidently it was his way of concentrating his energies. His hand relaxed slightly over mine and I began to feel its warmth. The intimacy took me aback, but I was drawn in by something stronger. There was a stillness in the room, the same stillness I'd noticed earlier when we'd arrived, this time without any apprehension. A calm suffused me, a physical sensation running through my body like a hot drink on a cold night. For the first time in a week, all my fears melted away.

"Now, dear," he said, eyes still closed, "tell me everything."

So I did. I told him how Lily and I had met, how it had started, where it had started, the things she said to me, the things I said to her, the kissing, the existential silences, our deception of Ben, the dinginess of the trailer, Gallic versus Teutonic, the religious indoctrination, the parallels with Graham Greene, everything I could think of.

His lips continued to work, pursing and unpursing; occasionally there was a flurry of blinking, but his eyes stayed closed as he listened without comment or prompt, concentrating on every aspect of what I had to say, as if he were meditating as I spoke, murmuring "yes yes yes" from time to time, his whole knobbly, lopsided body focused on my story. When I came to the parts that had made me privately laugh or had seemed absurd, he smiled and nodded but didn't laugh. The only time he frowned was when I threw in a self-castigating "mea culpa," as if this was an irrelevant intrusion into the narrative.

Inevitably we came to the part I dreaded, the breaking point, the unhappy ending, my adulterous eyes on the breasts of another man's wife, my adulterous hands under her dress, my adulterous fingers inching their way into another man's wife's vagina. To my complete surprise, this didn't seem to merit a different response from anything else I'd said. His lips went on working, his eyes, as always, closed. They didn't purse and unpurse at any greater tempo or blink any more rapidly. None of it seemed to warrant any of the shock or horror I had anticipated.

And so my tale was done.

A beat of silence, his busy face at rest. "Poor Lily," he murmured.

It drifted across my mind, as he sat there saying nothing further, that this had been a cue; he'd gotten me to open up, now *wham*—punishment! The door swinging open, younger, tougher monks pulling me to my feet . . . Even as the fatuous thought passed into the limbo of fatuous thoughts, I knew I'd just met a man from whom would come none of the usual responses I'd learned to expect from priests. Some unknown fuel drove his engine. Gentleness bubbled out from the funny figure in the scruffy black robes like clear water from solid rock. It was flowing into me through his dry warm hand. I felt on the brink of learning an entirely new set of possible responses to the world.

He hadn't questioned a thing I'd said; he hadn't asked me to repeat or clarify, or was I sure that so-and-so had happened or that I hadn't left something important out? He seemed to assume that I was telling the truth—which I'd tried to the limit of my ability to do—or he knew by instinct that my account could be trusted. That alone was remarkable: no authority figure had ever failed to question me, directly or indirectly, about any account I'd ever given of anything. Adolescent life is governed by cross-examination.

When he finally spoke, his words were slow and stilted, his face beginning to work again, as if he were trying to puzzle out what was being said by someone speaking to him through a spiritual earpiece.

"You've done nothing truly wrong, Tony dear. God's love has brought you here before any real harm could be done. The only sin you've committed is the sin of . . . s-s-selfishness."

The soft, hesitant emphasis on the word made it quite clear he regarded this as a far more serious crime than the one that was officially on the charge sheet.

The verdict was gentle, final, the last word of, well, a father. A father unlike mine or anyone's I knew, unlike the men we were accustomed to call Father or even—according to all reports—the God we called Father. I'd confided something that had confused and tormented and terrified me to this father. And the matter had been handled.

"You won't see her for a while, will you dear? Not alone, anyway. It wouldn't be fair to her."

I nodded, swept by waves of relief, then by a new consternation, that I'd never once considered the pain of a hungry, trapped, unhappy woman. Yes, selfishness. Lily came into sharp focus; I saw her anguished, longing face, a real person with a real inner life whom I had treated as a mere extension of my nerve endings, a prop for my young posturings on the stage of adulthood. For the first time, I felt toward her something like love, or at least the gentleness I owed her. How had he done that?

He murmured the words of absolution and made a tiny cross on my forehead with a big long thumb.

"No penance. I think you've already done a good deal of penance, haven't you?" He shot me a little grin, sidelong and conspiratorial. And how did he know that?

He got up awkwardly and a fuss of departure began, words tumbling out of him in his funny rushing prattle. I didn't want him to go. I'd never felt so safe and secure with anyone in my life. I wanted to tell him everything that had ever happened in my few years. There were a million things I wanted to ask him. No, two million. He'd been with me only five or ten minutes, for Heaven's sake. (I realized later that it had been nearly three quarters of an hour.)

"Can't you stay a bit, Father?"

He chortled. "I'd love to, my dear; I'm a night owl—if they'd let me, I'd talk all night. But these old bones must be up at the crack of dawn for Vigils. Now don't you try and come like these others, silly things—it's much too early for sensible people. We'll see each other again and talk and talk. God bless you, my dear."

Again the hug, again the swirl of skirts, again the super-sandals squeaking away down the linoleum.

Then silence. And peace.

CHAPTER FIVE

The next day was Good Friday, the holiest day in the Catholic calendar, the commemoration of Christ's death, a day of fasting, penitence, and prayer. I woke very late in the morning—I must have been out for thirteen or fourteen hours. There was no one in the guesthouse, the church, the porter's lodge. I assumed everyone was in super-holy mode and retired to my room to read. Ben appeared for lunch, but he avoided my eye and hurried away afterward. The same happened at the afternoon service and at the evening meal. I put it down to piety rather than pique, all the other guests, especially the monk groupies, being in a state of advanced solemnity.

I was too in some fashion. I always enjoyed Holy Week. The Passion and Crucifixion are great stories, full of action, arrest, good guys, bad guys, conflicted guys (Pilate, Peter), double crosses (Judas, the Jerusalem mob), and R-rated violence (flogging, torture, the carrying of the cross), and ending with a spectacular death scene—all the more gripping because the good guy dies—the whole miseen-scène made more authentic by brilliant narrative touches like Veronica offering Jesus the cloth to wipe his face, the soldiers dicing for his robe under the cross, and the bad thief crucified beside Jesus who tells the Savior of the Universe to get lost (which I always thought took real guts—far more than the obsequious good thief who had nothing to lose).

One was supposed to be sad and penitent on Good Friday, but I always felt cheerful and turned on, as if I were actually part of a biblical epic complete with Israelites in flowing robes and Romans in brass skirts and people shouting lines at each other in temples and tents.

What I was focused on this Good Friday was: when would I next get to see Father Joseph Warrilow? At the services I went to, I couldn't spot him in the serried ranks of monks, and I worried that this might be because I had taken away a mistaken image of him the night before and now couldn't recognize him.

After minimal human contact all day, I finally tracked down the old monk just before bedtime: could he ask my new friend when I might see him again? Snappishly he replied that Father Joseph had many duties and other guests to worry about and music to rehearse for Easter Sunday—apparently he was also the organist for the community, which is why I hadn't seen him in church: he was out of sight in the organ loft. But he would convey my message to Father Joseph if humanly possible (which I took to mean "provided same was not up a substantial number of steps").

The next day was Holy Saturday, as uneventful a day as Good Friday is packed with action, since Jesus is now dead. (According to Catholic tradition, he kept busy nonetheless, descending into Hell for the Harrowing of it: the release of good men and women who had had the misfortune to live before he made salvation available.) Still, nothing happens in the church, which is empty, stripped of its usual furnishings, its decorations concealed by funereal purple cloth.

It was the middle of the morning and I was bored. Ben was once again nowhere to be found. I didn't feel like meditating on the meaning of Easter, and the books in the guest room were either painfully academic or nauseatingly pious. I was used to physical activity, walking or cycling or exploring the countryside, and there was nowhere to be active except the enclosure in front of the monastery, which was fine for the other guests—whose idea of aerobic exercise was pulling a cigarette from its box—but left me restless and tetchy.

I'd been told we were only a few hundred yards from the sea, but I didn't know how to get to it. It was a wild, windy day, the kind I loved; I peered through the tiny panes of my window at the racing clouds and cavorting trees and felt very left out. I wasn't sure about this place. Music, definitely okay. Father Joseph Warrilow, more than okay. Otherwise monastic life seemed like a gentlemanly version of jail.

All of a sudden, that squeak of sandal on lino, that swoosh of skirts, and there he was in the doorway, ears as big as before, feet as flat—I hadn't exaggerated my image of him at all. He was funny-looking enough to make you smile whenever he made an entrance. Before I could stop myself I was laughing.

"Dear Tony, sorry to be late. I do so love the organ, it's hard to tear myself away. How about a walk? It's wild and windy today, my favorite weather!"

He thrust his arm through mine and off we went down the stairs, out into the enclosure, and through one of the huge gates marked PRIVATE.

Tranquil and rustic though Quarr appeared from the entrance area, there was no way to guess at the full beauty of its surroundings. The gate marked PRIVATE was the door into a secret Eden.

A broad earthen path ran beside the church and past a tiny cemetery containing rows of plain stone crosses, then through massive oaks to curve round a great sweep of newly ploughed fields, brown and soft against the wild blue and gray sky, disappearing into a grove of horse chestnuts and dense woods of more oak, beyond which heaved the turbulent, white-capped Solent. Off to the right in a lush sea-level meadow were scattered the ruins of an early twelfth-century Cistercian monastery. Where white-robed monks had once tended their ancestors, a flock of sheep chomped on grass rooted in their shepherds' remains.

It took my breath away: the curve of the great path, the contrasts of raw earth against rushing cumulus, of tumbled old stone against tall young grass, of leaf-speckled oaks against the sea. A very different landscape than my placid, green-shaded Hertfordshire; this was impeccable and classic, every element of natural beauty in exact harmony, a foretaste of perfection, an *amuse-bouche* of Paradise. It had the dignity of a mighty painting, but I felt in it and of it. I knew this place. I had read about it in a poem or dreamed it once.

I stopped and he did too, our arms still linked, his eyes doing their signature blink, his rodent nose twitching with pleasure in the swirling air.

"Oh yes, dear, yes yes yes. Whenever I come round this corner, I'm sure I'm seeing it for the very first time!"

We walked down the wide path to the grove of horse chestnuts. They were in bloom, their conical flowers scattered like massive Christmas candles in the boughs. As most English schoolboys did, I played conkers—a conker being the large, smooth, mahogany-colored nut of this tree. You'd make a hole in the middle of your conker, then suspend it from a piece of knotted string about a foot long. Conkers was played by two boys: you took turns holding up your conker by the string while the other guy took a shot at smashing it using his conker like a miniature mace and chain. If he shattered your conker with his conker, he won the bout; if not, you got a shot at his. The skill of the game came in selecting the right conker (large nuts were not always desirable, since they split easily) and in wielding your nut so that it came down with maximum force on the other guy's nut. The ultimate aim was to own a conker that had racked up an impressive number of kills; a fiver had murdered five other nuts, a tenner ten, and so on. You were supposed to use only the current year's conkers in their natural state, but unscrupulous players would toughen theirs by cooking them in a low oven or soaking them in vinegar or—lowest of the low—using last year's nuts.

I was a bit old for the game itself, but no English male worth his salt could pass under a chestnut tree without assessing its conker potential. These trees looked very promising, young and robust. "There'll be some terrific conkers under here in a few months," I said.

"There will indeed," he replied; "they give wonderful conkers." He searched the ground as we walked. "There's one!" He picked up a medium-sized nut from under some leaves.

It must have lain in a dry place, for instead of being soft and rotten it was wizened and hard as a rock.

"A beauty!" He tapped it with a practiced knuckle. "At least a tenner or twelver."

"But, Father, it's from last year! You can't use that."

The venerable monk shot me a rubbery naughty-boy grin. "Who says I can't?" He pocketed the conker.

The path came to a little promontory. The sea heaved and tugged at the soggy shoreline below, the wind whipping spume off the chop farther out. Across the Solent, you could see the smudge of Portsmouth, which had been a major naval facility in World War II and in every war for centuries back.

We stood arm in arm, still, gazing at the far-off mainland. It seemed much farther than two miles away and getting farther by the minute.

He blinked and closed his eyes meditatively.

"A world away."

"I'm not sure I want to go back, Father Warrilow."

The eyes blinked, the lips pursed. "Oh, but you must, dear."

Suddenly gusts of wind ripped round us, whipping his robes up around his thighs. He yanked his arm from mine, trying clumsily to hold down his skirts. Marilyn Monroe would do much the same over a subway grate in New York City later that year, but she couldn't come close to him in the knobbly-English-knees department.

Finally he got his wayward garb under control, spluttering "oh my goodness, oh my goodness . . ."

"Well!" he laughed. "Now that you've seen my knees, you can hardly call me Father Warrilow."

"What should I call you, then?"

"Everyone calls me Joe."

A bit radical, I thought. This monk did nothing that other priests did; he talked to me like an equal, not a sinner, and so far had made no mention of that ultimate sanction used by all Catholic adults, Hell. But still. He was a priest.

"How about Father Joe?"

"Father Joe it is!" He retucked his arm through mine and back we went through the wind-whipped woods.

I don't remember everything we talked about that wild spring morning, but it was life-changing in ways I could never have conceived when I'd stood two days earlier churning with fear at the end of the driveway. There was plenty to discover as we ambled down muddy paths, through meadows of fat cattle, around fields of winter crops, beneath more mighty oaks, circumnavigating Quarr Abbey's extensive farm, all two hundred acres of it, for an hour or more.

Father Joe had been a monk for thirty years, having become one at seventeen—which made him several years older than my father. But I wouldn't have pegged him as my father's senior. It wasn't his appearance; he could have been thirty or sixty. It was more that he was in tune with or appropriating my rhythms, he followed my sequence of thoughts. He didn't have to explain his terms to me nor I mine to him.

He really did appear to perceive things as a young man might, to be seeing, hearing, thinking things for the first time. The incessant workings of his face marshaled his responses, but what in another could have been a means of controlling the dialogue seemed in him quite unconscious. He gave one the feeling that his experience of any stimulus—a bird on the bough, a chance meeting, an idea he must have heard a hundred times—had never been quite the same before nor would be again. This one time—and hence the person he was talking to—was utterly unique.

He hailed from Essex, with the usual Irish antecedents that make

English people Catholic; but he couldn't have looked more English. And therefore to me Protestant. When later I began to study *Piers Plowman,* I instinctively projected his bony, asymmetrical face onto that English archetype—and early harbinger of the Reformation.

But he had a very un-English lack of inhibition and an even more un-English love of the French. He'd spent the first part of his career at another French-founded Benedictine monastery called Farnborough, but in some internal monastic politics had been transferred to Quarr. He'd flourished in these French microclimates.

"Such an expressive language, don't you think, dear? It comes off the tongue like honey. Or vinegar, depending on what you're saying. You must do French at school—I expect you speak it very well?"

My French was appalling—I hated its regimented grammar and impossible obsession with genders—but I was fully prepared to give it a second chance on his say-so.

"And the cooks here—ah, Tony dear!—we've been fasting all week, but just you wait till tomorrow! And of course"—his granny glasses in my face, eyes shining with undisguised epicurean lust—"there'll be wine!"

"If you love French things, you must have a Gallic temperament. Like Lily."

"I don't think Lily has a Gallic temperament, dear. I don't think she thinks so either. I think she has a very Catholic temperament."

Startling. For me, absent glaring evidence to the contrary, adult self-description was always to be taken ex cathedra.

"What about Ben, then? Do you think he has a Teutonic temperament?"

"Good heavens, no! Ben's as British as steak-and-kidney pie. It's just his way of controlling his feelings, you see. And Lily's feelings too, of course."

He'd had a Good Talk with Ben the night before and would have one with Lily within the week. That would mean—best of all—he would get to meet her little baby.

I was dimly aware that there were other mea culpas than my own in this triangle; indeed, I would have been delighted to have this confirmed. But I was also learning that I would never know for sure. Father Joe had nothing bad to say to others about those who consulted him, however much he might have found fault with them in private. Which only augmented your trust. Anyone who blames the other party to your face blames you to theirs.

Being a monk, he spoke of God. But rarely unless linked with the word "love." And while he spoke of God as "he," it wasn't a "he" I recognized at all, that far-off, knee-weakening authority, Headmaster of the Universe, invoked to enforce discipline or morality or compliance with doctrine.

Father Joe didn't appear to need the clerical metal ruler of do-it-or-I'll-tell-your-father. The "he" of his God was gentle, generous, endlessly creative, musical, artistic, an engineer and architect of genius, a "he" who felt his joy and your joy deeply, who could be hurt just as deeply but would never give up on you, who showered you with gifts and opportunities whether you acknowledged them or not, who set you tasks but didn't abandon you if you failed them. Often, in fact, "he" fit much better into my fifties-shaped notion of "she." Father Joe spoke of this person fondly and gratefully, with respect but more than a hint of intimacy. Familiarity for him had bred no contempt. Fear wasn't even on the board. His God might have untold trillions of other concerns, but definitely had time to be Father Joe's best friend.

And there was something else, which I realized later as I went over and over every detail and impression of that walk: unlike the pious, he didn't speak of Christ very much. But then, neither did Christ.

Soon we were strolling through an orchard, and the considerable extent of the monastery was apparent above the trees. We passed its working areas: wood shop, metal shop, leather shop, garages, repair facilities, barns and granaries, dairy, bakery, kitchens; places to produce sustenance of all kinds, places which in the outside world are redolent of obligation and tedium and exploitation and discontent, but here were embraced as prayer, another and very different form of sustenance.

We came to the other great gate marked PRIVATE. Father Joe hauled it open and held my hand for a long moment in his big warm one. He would not see me again, he said. The demands of the Easter liturgy were great and we were leaving the next day, Easter Sunday, after lunch. He hugged me tight and again gave me the smacky kiss on the cheek, which I now knew was a time-honored Benedictine custom, the kiss of peace.

The exit door to Eden closed on the black flapping figure.

CHAPTER SIX

"*Lavabo inter innocentes manus meas . . .*" Father Bleary turned toward me, his baggy face speckled with dried blood from a hurried shave in an ill-lit bathroom, what little hair he had the color of wet rat fur, his meaty old Celtic mitts shaking from the whisky which had briefly kept death and failure and despair at bay the night before.

He could hardly hold the tips of his thumbs and index fingers together over the chalice as I poured water on them from a little glass flask. As always, his head slumped a bit over the task. Then he lifted it to continue reading. Here it came—the Breath of Death:

". . . et circumdabo altare tuum, Domine."

It was always that *-dabo* and *Domine* that did it, the d syllables releasing fetid waves of long-dead dinners fermenting in his gums.

I welcomed it, with a joyful prayer of thanks; I gratefully inhaled the horrible stink, offering my selfless nostrils up to God for the unfortunate souls languishing in Purgatory, my saintly sacrifice knocking several centuries of torment off the meter for some long-dead sinner.

The Lavabo (literally "I will wash") was the beginning of Act Two of the Mass, the good part, where the action kicked in, the big magic began to happen. The ancient Latin words never failed to scare up a cloud of butterflies in my now-fifteen-year-old belly. I accepted without question that the wobbly heap of scrofulous humanity in the threadbare robes was a vital link in a mighty chain that stretched from our dingy little sanctuary back down twenty centuries of courage, wickedness, conflict, sanctity, high art, arrogance, generosity, savagery, creativity, suffering, ecstasy, humility, hypocrisy, scholarship, and self-sacrifice to another dingy little public place where another young man gave his friends a farewell supper knowing that in three days his Roman masters would crucify him. And through the power invested in the wobbly heap, not only was that farewell supper commemorated here almost twenty centuries later, but the young man himself, Jesus of Nazareth, Messiah, Savior of Mankind, Son of the Father, Second Person of the Trinity, would in a few minutes enter the wafer that lay between those cracked and dirty fingernails—the living, throbbing presence of God.

I believed it all now. It all made perfect sense. Ben's crystalline theological theorems had fit nicely together, like the hexagonal representations of molecules in my chemistry diagrams, clustering around the central molecule of belief in the existence of God. From this and the concomitant existence of evil, lines connected to all the other molecules of faith: the necessity of redemption, the Incarnation, the Crucifixion and Resurrection, the Apostolic Succession, the Church's labyrinthine and gargantuan tax system for salvation, the Eternal Revenue Service.

But I never believed Ben's diagram. It was all on paper, abstract, removed from the continuum of time and space in which one talked, walked, studied, admired the scenery, ate, drank, pissed, shat, and, most important, sinned. It was true only in some parallel dimension, the dimension of religion. It had never been real.

Not until Easter Sunday, the morning after my walk with Father Joe.

Like the rest of Holy Week, Easter is also a terrific story. It starts as tragedy: the hero broken and bloody, against all expectation dead, his followers' joyful hope in him entombed with his corpse, the rock rolled into place, sealing their despair.

But the curtain doesn't fall there. The next morning at dawn they discover the rock has been rolled back. The tomb is empty, the body's gone! A missing corpse? Great stuff. A whisper of comedy. Now a touch of farce as Mary Magdalen and the guys chase frantically around looking for help, or the corpse, when suddenly, out of nowhere, up it pops—alive!

Of course it's Jesus, who's done the impossible and beaten death.

And they're so amazed they think he's the gardener! It's a payoff way beyond the Hollywood ending: all the flooding emotion and uplift of a tragedy followed by all the bubbling joy and optimism of a comedy.

Is that possible? Not just to live happily ever after but to die—and still live happily ever after? It's the most audacious claim of Christianity, the one element that marks the brand indelibly, that trumps the claims of all other major faiths. And of course I'd never really believed it either; the Resurrection was in that same parallel dimension, an amazing trick performed by the character Jesus in a gripping story—like those Disney characters, Pinocchio or Snow White—who would die or be murdered and utter despair would grip the Enchanted Kingdom until suddenly, by some agency—*bingo!*—their thyroidal eyes come slowly open, their pallid faces break into a smile, the strings swell, the massed voices soar, and death has no dominion.

I'd never considered any of my religion's great stories to be actually, factually true. As true as the eggs in the nest in spring, the sticky green lumps pushing from the dead branches, things I could see and stroke and know their actuality, the outward signs of inner grace. Nor had I ever met a man or woman true in that sense, as natural and simple as the eggs and buds, beneath whose untidy exterior pulsed that same evidence of the divine. But now I had.

As I sat in the abbey church that Easter Sunday, the morning after our first walk, the sun flooding through the chancel windows—he'd been right about that too—the triumphant *alleluia* of Easter bursting from every phrase of the chant, the music pure and odd and unique, its tonalities never going quite where occidental ears would expect, another sacrament in fact, alive with divine promise, it suddenly struck me for the first time in my life that the Easter story was not just a story. It had actually happened in this dimension, the one I existed in, the here-and-now—or the there-and-then.

This morning had been celebrated a mere 1,923 times—1956 minus 33 for Christ's age. It wasn't an enormous number of times when you thought about it, approximately the number of pounds Dad earned in a good year; a graspable, tangible figure from which you could count backward—pausing to get your bearings over historical blips like the French Revolution or the discovery of America or the fall of Rome—until there you were, back at zero, and it was actually happening, early one morning in a city called Jerusalem which was still there at the other end of the Mediterranean. Just 1,923 of these mornings ago—a woman and two men rushing wildly around the burial ground looking for their friend's body and bumping into . . . the gardener.

Which brought Christ into focus too. He wasn't just the hero of a great yarn or the *quod erat demonstrandum* of a neat syllogistic proof (and probably not the doe-eyed soap star of the soppy statues either), but a man alive, perhaps as odd as Father Joe, untidy and uneven, exuding gentleness and peace, with sandals larger than you'd expect, or funny-looking, with a big nose or ears, someone you would mistake for the gardener, an actual, factual guy, walking, talking, eating, drinking, shitting, pissing, just like us, in the everyday miracle of an ordinary human body.

And what if this singular man in some unprecedented, unrepeatable way was in touch with the divine, was divine as claimed—which, with the evidence of Father Joe before me, did not seem quite so outrageous a claim as before? What if the story of the Resurrection was actually, factually true, not just an extra crowd-pleasing narrative twist but a once-in-the-planet's-lifetime occurrence designed to demonstrate that there was hope after death and that the resurrectee was everything he said he was? Then the world and the universe would be totally different places. True good might even be attainable in life as well as the self-evident evil.

If one part was true, why not all of it? The lines of force on Ben's diagram which had connected to all the other Big Doctrines flashed from unconvincing black and white to living color. In the monastery church the stately Latin sonorities of the Mass were reaching their climax in one of those Big Doctrines, the Transubstantiation; soon the fragile flour-and-water wafer would become the flesh of Christ, confining within its fraction of an ounce the infinite dimensions of something beyond universes and event horizons, behind and above all existence.

What had been baffling claptrap all my life suddenly became more than a proposition—it became true and real. I felt a welling, overflowing excitement in the perception that God existed and therefore so did I.

As I took the host a few minutes later, all the conflicting and confusing thoughts and feelings I normally experienced, the usual objections and reservations and logical, sensible, commonsense hesitancies were swept aside, fused into a whole of certainty. It was all perfectly natural, it all made perfect sense—this was bread just as Christ had used bread, this was a meal just as the Last Supper had been; how else would you take your God into yourself but through your mouth, consuming him in this ordinary, mundane way? The ordinary *was* the divine, where common sense met mystery, where logic kissed the cheek of the inexplicable, the immeasurable, immemorial spirit throbbing like veins beneath the hard gray asphalt of quotidian life.

What had always bothered and often panicked me—the wafer sticking to the roof of my mouth and having to be poked and peeled away sacrilegiously with the tip of my tongue—was welcome now, intended, a way to savor its nature before its material vehicle dissolved. The host practically burned my mouth with the presence of what it contained; I felt as if a shaft of light had pierced the top of my cranium and lit me up from the inside out.

As Mass ended I ran from the church, unable to contain myself any longer, shoving aside the startled Cathoholics. I banged through the huge gate marked PRIVATE and ran past the massive oaks down the great path, through the sweeping blossom-dappled chestnuts, to the white-capped, sunlit sea. I danced as I ran, yelled whatever came into my head—bits of songs, schoolboy whoops, Latin tags—I flung myself around in mad pirouettes, I tried to run up the trunks of trees. I began to scramble down the muddy promontory overlooking the Solent and gave it up, jumping the last fifteen feet or so and crashing in a heap on the pebbles, feeling nothing. I tore along the beach as if I were doing a victory lap, a happy champion, happier than I could ever remember being. Truth existed and so did I. I was real, me, a Me, not an idea or a possibility or someone else's incomplete theorem or a mutinous bundle of neurons.

The lunch was excellent—Father Joe proving to be right yet again—and there was wine, the first red wine I'd ever tasted, which I was allowed to pour myself, as much as I liked. I felt no regret as Ben and I walked away from Quarr Abbey, down the driveway, back toward the world. Whose voice or what part of me, I wondered, had warned me not to go up that driveway? Did the voice know how cataclysmic was the change that awaited me up there? That I would find at Quarr not just a sanctuary, an Eden, but most precious of all, a home? There was no need for regret—I would be back, and right speedily.

Everything had changed too between Ben and me as we followed the interminable bus-ferry-train-subway-train-bus rigmarole back across the South of England. He was subdued and reticent, far from his usual declamatory self. I got the feeling the visit had been not at all as he intended or expected. Once in a while I caught him actually looking at me instead of his pal on the horizon, as if he were trying to puzzle out why I was so bright and cheerful when I ought to be dour and penitential.

Even his iron Teutonic carapace could hardly have failed to detect that something had happened to me; I felt like a spiritual version of Road Runner, zooming past Wile E. Bootle as he assembled a complex gadget in the road to slow me down or sabotage me. I said how great Father Joseph was, how saintly. "Saintly" wasn't quite the word I wanted, but I couldn't think of a better one. "He's wonderful," agreed Ben, "but intellectually slight." I didn't really hear this till later; it was so far off my meter it didn't register. In any case I'd borrowed a book by the great Benedictine historian Dom David Knowles from the guest room and was completely engrossed in it. Ben made approving noises at this studious choice, but I didn't much care what he thought. I was tearing through it, soaking it up like a sponge. I think Ben knew he'd lost his pupil.

When we parted outside my house, he asked whether I'd be down for my usual Tuesday-evening instruction, and I said, "No, Father Joseph thinks Lily and I shouldn't see each other for a while." An odd, confused expression crossed his face; this was something his calculus ought to have predicted but hadn't. "Well, I'll get rid of her for the evening," he said with a stab at manly jocularity. I saw Lily's small pale face in the gloaming as she pushed the baby's pram toward the village on some trumped-up errand, knowing full well why she'd been sent away. "I don't think so," I said, and the last page of that volume turned and it was over.

The glow of Quarr did not fade.

I'd always been a creature of crazes; I was aware of this and often depressed by it, not that that stopped them from coming. I'd measured the effective life of my crazes: they averaged three weeks.

I'd been an astronomer, archeologist, research chemist, brewer and vintner, race-car mechanic, minimalist poet (twice), numismatist, lepidopterist, reporter, concert pianist, angler, munitions expert, operatic tenor, Olympic track and field star, lumberjack, and spelunker.

These were more than mere hobbies; they were all-consuming full-blown passions. When a craze bit me, I'd devour data for days, write away for free information, and project myself furiously into the role, babbling newfound expertise as I conducted crucial field tests. Since these always involved equipment or raw materials and I had no funds, elaborate improvisation would have to take place. As astronomer I found a pair of binoculars in the attic and hacksawed them apart for the lenses, which I glued into an old drainpipe. I never did get a very clear view of Saturn, but Fred Hoyle and I had some furious debates, all of which I won.

As brewer I fermented every plant in the garden, from nettles to lichen, making my sister quite sick when she mistook a toadstool stout for cold tea. Munitions expert meant nicking nitrates from the farmer down the lane and sugar from the larder (and leaving a gaping hole in the back of the garage). Spelunker in the flat clay of Hertfordshire meant actually digging my own caverns (with disastrous results for the same farmer's tractor when it rolled over one of them). The three-week life of my enthusiasms had a lot to do with the limits of my ingenuity or getting sidetracked for days trying to come up with a working version of an indispensable piece of equipment. No lepidopterist can function without a butterfly net—his mum's old bra just will not do.

A little voice sneered that Quarr too was a craze and would fade within the regulation period, but I desperately didn't want it to, and as the weeks rolled by, I grew more confident that this time was different. Like all my other teen dreams, the new identity was like a tailor's fitting as I turned this way and that to see how it looked in the mirror of self-consciousness. But unlike the others, it was more than an inwardly directed choice that for the moment felt right. There was an outwardly directed component this time—a new way of looking at the world around me that also felt right and made sense, indeed, transformed it.

The sheer force of my experience at Quarr, this new grasp of the realness of things, lit up unexpected areas of my life—areas I'd preferred to ignore or endure up till then. History, once my most and then my least favorite subject, resumed center stage. It had become a tedium to study, a forgettable rat's nest of dates and places and people, every one of them stone-cold dead and of no relevance to me here and now. Just as Latin was a dead language, history was a dead subject. I asked Mum once why we had to belong to such an incredibly old religion—weren't there any new ones? (She didn't agree or disagree, but she did give me a lurid pamphlet the Jehovah's Witnesses had left behind.)

Now, driven by the need to dig farther and—just as urgently—to experience the actuality of everything I could, history became my new frontier, the past became my future, a vast terra incognita, every discovery of which was another chunk of virgin territory I could claim, bringing with it the glow of ownership, the anticipatory thrill of further exploration. Wars and treaties and royals still bored me silly, but how real people lived and thought, what they had done with their hands and minds, obsessed me and—when I got a flash of what it might have been—cheered me in some obscure but wonderful way. History was a way to live extra lives, to cheat the limits of flesh and blood, to roll the rock back from the tomb and free the resurrected dead.

Of none was this truer than of the Benedictines, my new heroes, my men in black. And there was plenty to know—it was a tradition so deep you never heard the stone hit bottom. Almost anywhere in England—or Europe, for that matter—you ran up against the Benedictine legacy, whether it was simply a place name or something embedded deeper in the culture, like the bottle of Nuits-Saint-Georges my father treated himself to at Christmas or the university colleges I was being urged to start thinking about. Right under my nose was the most obvious example of all—my own school, a Benedictine monastery from its foundation in 793 until the dissolution of the monasteries in 1539.

So far St. Albans School had been for me, well, a school—an unexceptional late-nineteenth-century complex of assembly hall, corridors, labs, classrooms, etc., whose dominant features were a big central bulletin board—where you found out your end-of-term marks and whether you were on a school team—and various nooks and crannies where cigarettes could be frantically sucked on. The library was housed in a medieval gateway; it was built, in the old style, of flint, but so were many official buildings in that part of England. Nearby was a large Protestant church—of little interest to me, since Catholics were excluded from it during prayers and services. The outlines of ancient stone structures were scattered about the lawns; their chief utility was as picnic tables when we ate lunch outside.

Now all this became a living place, a treasure site, a lava pit of intoxicating emotions I'd never experienced before. That flint gateway had been the entrance to a vast enclosure of monastic lands, granaries, dairies, bakeries, storehouses, stables, byres, pigsties, fishponds, forges, workplaces; that Protestant pile had been a Benedictine abbey where a thousand years before, on any afternoon, I could have heard exactly the same soaring chant of Vespers I'd heard on my first afternoon at Quarr.

The foundation of St. Albans Abbey came on the upswing of a mighty sea change in the era fatuously dubbed—during the dark age of Queen Victoria—"the Dark Ages." A time when men and women of good sense must have been in a tumult of excited hope as a great reforming king reached his life's goal: a unified Europe. An entity transcending tribal, national, and dynastic ambitions, stretching from the North Sea to the Pyrenees, from Italy to the Atlantic, one and at peace, centuries before the brutal idiocies of patriotism tore it into bloodier and bloodier shreds. The first Holy Roman Emperor, Charlemagne, a ruler known not as most rulers are, for his skill at mass murder, but for his restraint and deep respect for learning, notably that of the man he called "Master," leader of a great intellectual revival at the imperial court in Aachen, the English Benedictine, Alcuin of York.

I acquired a duffel coat that autumn, one of those shapeless felt things with a large hood and wide sleeves to accommodate thick existentialist sweaters. I took to gliding round the abbey precincts and the abbey itself after school with the hood up and my hands tucked together in the sleeves in a rough approximation of monastic garb, conjuring up the occasion when Alcuin himself came all the way from Aachen to see how the work was going, with me as his guide, or being some good brother on exactly this day of this month and this time of the evening in, say, 1156, padding round the cloister, dreaming of a nice fish dinner from the fishpond at the bottom of the hill . . .

One early winter afternoon when the abbey was empty of visitors, I stood in the choir and sang a few phrases of Gregorian chant I'd picked up. The plangent notes rose into the cold darkness of the chancel arches and echoed along the old stones of the nave, separate from me and yet still my voice, stirring the ghosts of a millennium.

Unfortunately, my duffel coat was fawn-colored, so rather than looking monastic, I probably struck anyone who bothered to notice as a seriously strange kid who stood in strange places for strangely extended periods. But inside my hood I was a man in black, centuries gone, lost on a sea of time.

For the new identity, the non-craze, the one that had stuck, was *monk.* More than a year it had been now—long enough for twenty crazes to have been born and died. And this one had survived.

I was a Teenage Monk.

My school pals were deciding whether their musical allegiance should be to Chuck Berry or Dave Brubeck; my musical hero was a sixth-century Pope named Gregory the Great. To them, Peter, Paul, and Mary meant folk. To me, it meant the top two Apostles and the mother of Christ. Other guys were groping girls in cars; I, who had had a torrid affair with a married woman, had renounced the world and its fleshpots. They were eyeing the emerging schism between Mod and Rocker and wondering which way to jump in the crucial matter of hair; I couldn't wait to shave a bald spot in mine.

Since my first Easter at Quarr, almost a year before by now, there had been many contacts with Father Joe, other visits, a flow of letters. All broadened and deepened my sense of certainty, of a world which hung together intellectually and spiritually.

I got to know every emotional way station of the long trip down to the Isle of Wight, the fidgety excitement at setting out, the monastic detachment as I jostled with London's millions in the Underground, the anticipatory cross-fade from the city's hideous southern rim to the suburban greenery of Surrey and the soft downs of Sussex, the feeling of leaving the world behind entirely as I set out across the Solent on the ferry, the renewed excitement as we neared the shore and there was the abbey's gnome-hat minaret sticking out of the oaks.

And always that squeak of sandal on linoleum, the swish of robes outside in the corridor, the knock, the funny bony face poking round the door, the catalyst and exemplar and still center of my transformation . . .

There was Father Joe sitting in a field in July, sweating rivers in his robes but transported, granny glasses intent on a cornflower, his knobbly digit caressing its petals.

"Everything we need to know is here, Tony dear. God's love for us, that he surrounds us with such beauty; God's love for his creation, his beautiful cornflower. Beauty that existed for eons just for God, long before we came along. Beauty for its own sake, *in idipsum.* Order and harmony: look at the blue of those petals, dear, exactly the blue of the summer sky."

He held it up to the sky, and he was right.

"How could such beauty exist without God? There would be nothing, surely?"

And I thought: everything I need to know is here indeed—the delighted eyes squinting through ancient lenses, the giant, twitching nose with its unclipped hairs, the elastic lips stretched in ecstasy at the little round of sky in his fingers. This was what I had to become, this clear, this simple, this present and alive.

There was Father Joe the mischievous, admitting that he could get irked by the Psalms:

"We have to say all hundred and fifty of them every week, you see. Of course they're wonderful and they shape our lives, but that old psalmist, golly, he can be a grump: 'O Lord, I'm so depressed this morning, nobody loves me and besides, I have boils. Hear my voice from the depths O Lord and *pl-e-ease* do something about these boils. (*Chanting*) A-a-a-a-men.' "

Or that he'd sneaked an extra helping of pudding from the kitchen after supper—a fairly large Rule-of-St.-Benedict no-no—or overlooked a prank played by a novice because he thought it was funny. All these transgressions accompanied by: "d-d-don't tell the Abbot!"

There was Father Joe expounding the meaning of *contemptus mundi*—literally "contempt for the world"—a phrase I was much enamored of, with that great, uncompromising absolute.

"But does *contemptus* mean 'contempt,' dear? Of course not. That would imply arrogance, superiority, pride. So much that we call worldly is actually just flawed or being seen through a cracked lens. Imperfect or imperfectly understood. Who are we to judge as contemptible a thing or person whose existence God sustains? Everything, however imperfect, has its purpose.

"No, Tony dear, *contemptus mundi* means '*detachment* from the world,' seeing the world sub specie aeternitatis. Enduring or celebrating it, but never forgetting—even when it seems perfect and forever—that as the Bible says: 'all this shall pass like grass before the wind.' "

There was Father Joe's retort in answer to some enthusiastic piety of mine about the sanctity of the community and its high purpose:

"Good gracious, dear—we're not silly old monks, mumbling prayers all day long. We've got a job to do!"

And my laughing but being a bit startled too. Until I realized how like him this was, how unpious, how down-to-earth, encapsulating his immensely generous view of the ordinary. Every word he spoke was drawn from a deep well of generosity. He had built it up, fed it to the brim over decades of contemplating people; and whatever their defects or defenses or eccentricities, however unappetizing they might be personally or morally, loving them without reserve. His gentle power sprang from a straightforward assessment of the world and his job in it. That job was love.

There was morning Mass in the crypt of the abbey, the dawn's orange-golden glimmer edging through the slit windows. The crypt of my first day's nightmares was in reality a place of sacral mystery, a catacomb, Merlin's Cave become Christian, a cavern measureless to man. In the gold-tinged gloom were other priests at other altars, each lit by his two candles, whispering his Mass. I knelt behind Father Joe as he said his, quite resplendent in a white and red chasuble (the only time he actually looked like a member of the Catholic clergy), but transfigured, his eyes closed for almost the entire time, every Latin word—even those that changed each day—known by heart, relished through his smiling lips, pursing and unpursing as if he were savoring sips of wine.

By my second or third visit I was beginning to get to know other monks as well. My initial impression of uniformity, even anonymity, was quite incorrect. They came from all over the map, a suave and worldly chain-smoking ex-banker from Vienna (reputed by the Cathoholics to be a Jewish convert), an ageless irrepressible midget from Malta with skin the color of conkers, visiting Italians, a German or two, Frenchmen galore, a huge, tall, paunchy monk with a very pukka accent who looked like an ex–Cabinet minister in a witness protection program and was always dashing off to London on mysterious missions involving Jesuits and cardinals . . .

The second Easter—my anniversary—I spent my entire two-week school vacation at Quarr, and Father Joe began to let me hover on the fringes of actual monastic life. Nothing was more central to it, he believed, than the lay brothers.

Lay brothers were an anachronism even in the 1950s. Defined as those for whom long church Offices were not appropriate, whose talents lay in more practical directions, they did not take priestly orders. (Hence they were "Brothers," not "Fathers.") Most of the surviving lay brothers were French and by now very old, having entered the order as teens in the late nineteenth century and come over with the community when religious orders were expelled from France in the early twentieth. Every monk capable of it performed manual labor, but the majority, who were priests, divided their time between manual work and other, more intellectual pursuits—they were scholars, musicologists, skilled craftsmen, etc.—while the brothers worked mostly at menial tasks. Father Joe, who had been Master of the Lay Brothers, especially loved the old men, believing them to be saints—though he made relentless fun of their peasanty Norman and Breton accents—and when I begged him to give me some *laborare* I could *orare* to, put me in the charge of Frère Louis, the woodsman.

Frère Louis was seventy-five or eighty-five (he said he couldn't remember, and certainly no one else could). He was no more than five feet tall, entirely bald, his head the shape and color of a huge hazelnut, his hands the size of skillets, only harder. He was possibly the sweetest human being I've ever met: he had no teeth left and a seraphic half-smile parted his lips at all times. It wasn't the smile of an innocent or a fool of God; the serenity in his sharp old eyes had a sadness to it, as if it had been earned through a journey of suffering from which he had finally emerged at peace.

It was spring; the great oak woods were full of bluebells and the sky was bright, the light dazzling because the gray-green leaf clusters were still forming. Frère Louis gave me a heavy, curved old French hatchet and smilingly, in patient mime, showed me how to cut unwanted saplings with one diagonal blow as near to the ground as possible. He cut through one as if it were a nettle and handed me the tool. I tried a sapling of roughly the same diameter and barely nicked the bark.

Frère Louis had turned away, either because one lesson was sufficient or because he was too charitable to observe my pathetic woodsmanship. Bent almost double, the tiny nut-brown monk moved steadily between the oaks, amputating with one blow saplings twice the size of the one he'd demonstrated on. When the hatchet went clean through the trunk it made a dull but distinct clang. I started on smaller wood, not much more than twigs, and slowly got the hang of it, working my way up to saplings of a worthy size. The two of us—a difference of sixty or seventy years between us—worked without a word through the stately woods for the next two hours, the steady clang of his hatchet and the occasional clang of mine our only communication. At noon the abbey bells rang and he straightened up and bowed his head. I realized he was saying the Angelus, that most ancient of agricultural customs, said in the fields at noon on every farm in every Catholic country for more than a thousand years. I bowed my head and followed suit, happy, at peace, almost a monk.

Almost. And almost sixteen. I was no longer just a visitor. I was a supplicant. I wanted in. Father Joe became oddly hard of hearing on the subject.

"I'll be sixteen in July, you know."

It was the last day of my stay. We were strolling through the woods.

"Father Joe?"

"I was just admiring your handiwork, dear. What a wonderful job you've done!"

"Frère Louis cut ten to every one of mine. And mine were all tiddly."

"I'm sure you're being modest, dear. Now every time I walk in the woods I shall have this to remind me of you."

"What if I just stayed?"

"For once you can see the bluebells."

"Father Joe, I believe you're avoiding the subject."

"Am I, dear? Well, I shall have to pay more attention."

"You were only sixteen when you started thinking about entering Farnborough. You told me so yourself. So why not me?"

"I wasn't as clever as you, dear. I was a dunce. I still am. Everyone says so."

"In July I'll have done my O Levels and I can leave school."

O (for Ordinary) Levels were obligatory nationwide exams taken at age sixteen in a variety of subjects. I was on firm ground here. Boys often entered seminaries after their O Levels.

"Yes, but then there are A Levels [Advanced Levels, taken at eighteen], and of course university . . ."

"I don't want to take A Levels, Father Joe! And why would I risk my immortal soul at university? And that's three years from now! If I entered this year I could've taken my Final Vows by then and be a full member of the community."

Father Joe stopped and plucked a bluebell. He was unusually reticent. Before the bluebell became his only focus—a distinct danger—concessions were needed.

"Of course, if the community felt I should go to university, I would submit to anything required of me. After all, I would have taken a vow of obedience. But surely that would be best *after* I've taken my vows."

He said nothing, but neither did he go into raptures about the bluebell. We walked on. Away on the hill, the abbey bells rang for Vespers. He turned to me and took my hands.

"Dear Tony, your enthusiasm is infectious and precious. I don't think it's likely that the Prior will allow you to enter now, but I will mention your wishes to him, and when you come next, the three of us can discuss it."

"Father Joe! Thank you, thank you! God bless you!"

I hugged him tight. He hugged me back and we hurried up to Vespers.

For me this was tantamount to welcoming me with open arms. I went home on a cloud. I would get through my O Levels. Then I had the two long months of summer holidays to convince everyone—my parents, Father Joe, the Prior, the Abbot, the Pope if necessary—that St. Alban's School and all its works were a meaningless bauble compared to my monastic vocation, my future as a saint.

This had been the best year of my life, a year of clarity, of certainty, a year shot through with light. The light had refracted into every part of my world, transforming it, yet so solid was the structure of my belief, it seemed less a transformation than an inevitable outcome. Long dead were vague ambitions to become a scientist of some kind (mostly driven by the dream of a salary more reliable than my dad's). My consuming interests now were history, literature, philosophy, arts, and above all, theology. What had once been conflicts seemed mere intellectual exercises; what had once seemed like pleasures now seemed hollow and petty. What had once been duties were now pleasures.

Which is how I came to be serving Mass for our poor broken parish priest on a sunny June morning in 1957. The Mass was nearly over now and I was taking Communion, mouth stretched wide open, tongue extended as far as possible—thanks to those whisky hands, his aim with the host was not good.

O Levels were behind me, and they'd been a breeze. I had a few more weeks of school, then Quarr would be my only goal. I knew who I was and what I was going to be and that it was not a finite career path with a bell curve of promise-ambition-disappointment-pension. My path was a life free of grubbing after money and ridiculous, unfulfilling possessions, a life of pure thought and contemplation and self-betterment and divine rewards. I had a world-class tutor and I was ready to get started, to become a spiritual champion, bouncing on the balls of my spiritual feet, with energy and skill for anything.

That very same night, a late spring night, warm and balmy, a few weeks before my sixteenth birthday, the bottom fell out of my universe.

CHAPTER SEVEN

I slept in a room with my kid brother. He had the top bunk, I the bottom. He went to bed long before I did, but I didn't want any sibling knowing too much about my private affairs, in this case that it was my custom to recite the Office of Compline before I went to bed. Even for an eight-year-old kid—perhaps especially for an eight-year-old kid—this would've been irresistible ammunition. I performed my oblations silently by flashlight.

The best part of Compline is the final hymn to the Virgin, which changes throughout the year but in late May is a gem from the eleventh century called *Salve Regina* (*Hail O Queen*)—as it happened, Father Joe's favorite—which I knew by heart. I would have preferred to sing it aloud, but instead would kneel by my bed and sing it in my head, eyes shut tight, imagining myself in the darkened choir at Quarr, surrounded by the men of peace in whose company I so longed to live.

On this night, I put out the flashlight, knelt, and sang the song as usual; then I stayed kneeling for a few moments, imagining the young novice in the abbey church turning out the lights and my future brothers heading for their cells. Now the church was empty, pitch-black except for the far-off red light of the sanctuary.

Suddenly, though it was a warm night, there was a chill in the bedroom and in my heart, a surge of cold animal fear that some vast, irresistible force was circling me, stalking me, about to pounce. Instinctively I prayed for strength or protection when—just as suddenly—I was falling, in an elevator with its cables severed, accelerating down into the blackness of the shaft. I opened my eyes but I was still falling—faster now—plunging into a chasm with no bottom, its dark sides rushing by me, and I knew even as I fell that my faith was being torn from me by the slipstream of my descent, as if I'd been flung from the battlements of my certainty.

I squeezed my eyes shut, trying somehow to brake the descent, praying desperately *please God help me, slow me, grant me a miracle,* but there was no help or miracle and I was hurtling still farther into the depths, both down there and above, watching myself fall as one does in a nightmare, falling through myself, out of my own soul, which never existed anyway, incalculable distances below the solid rocks of faith and truth into fathomless cold dead space an infinity and eternity deep, where there was no God nor Christ nor faith nor hope nor certainty nor salvation and never would be ever again.

I had stopped falling. I opened my eyes again. I was in my small room. I could hear my little brother breathing.

It had been no nightmare. The terror, the agony of loss inside me, the utter desolation were real, cold, hard. I was sweating and trembling. My cheeks were wet.

I threw every ounce of mental effort into waking myself up, in case this was one of those nightmares-within-a-nightmare where you wake from waking. But no, I was awake and this was reality, the new reality of nothing—and worse, of having to continue to exist.

A terrifying word came into my mind, like an echo running round a dark valley: despair. *You have despaired. You are damned. For despair is the unforgivable sin.*

I begged the darkness to give me back my faith. But the darkness said nothing. There was no one there to give it back. To pray to nothing for faith in nothing was a closed circle. And I was trapped inside it, its prisoner for all time.

I was utterly alone. I had never felt such loneliness, to be existentially alone, alone in my existence; so nightmarish was the feeling that I wasn't even sure I did exist. Which threw me into an even greater panic.

Logic intervened: I had to exist to be able to ask the question *do I exist?* But this took me even farther down, reminding me that my existence stretched before me and beyond death into the afterlife, an eternity of inescapable existence circumscribed by God's nonexistence, incarcerated without parole in the prison of self.

Whoever or whatever had stolen my eternal freedom had also stolen my dreams of becoming a monk. They too had shattered in the fall. The shards were already drifting away into the trackless wastes of space, too distant to retrieve. And that loss was immediate and wrenching, as if I had seen a lover killed in front of me, vibrantly alive and present one second, dead and silent the next. Who was it that had committed this vicious, senseless act? Was it me? Was I guilty of my own destruction?

I don't know how long I knelt there, my brother's peaceful little body making a bulge in the bedspring above me as I swung between wild panic and utter mental paralysis; but suddenly there was sunlight in my eyes. It was morning. I had fallen asleep on my knees. My brother's bunk was empty and Mum was yelling up the stairs.

The pain and loss returned instantly, hit me like a hammer in the head. So did the realization that I had woken an hour late for school. The universe may have been without God or hope or faith, but it definitely contained a bulbous green bus belching smoke through the tranquil lanes of Hertfordshire and due to arrive in the village three quarters of a mile away in exactly twelve minutes. I washed, dressed, grabbed my things, and sprinted.

The cliché that mindless activity takes your mind off misery is a lie. I sat in the bus, surrounded by cigarette smoke and giggling pink girls in gray uniforms, lost in an internal battle to the death: on one side, me and my will holed up in my head; outside it, besieging forces of jeering, sneering, heavily armed doubts. Gone were the existential agonies of the night; now specific propositions were being fired at me like rockets. *God does not exist. Therefore Christ was not God. Christ was a fool who got himself killed for nothing. Christ was a phony, a two-bit snake-oil salesman.* There were endless Christ-rockets.

Throughout the half-hour bus trip the battle raged on as I forced the incoming doubts from my mind, grunting "no no no," shaking my head, clenching my fists. My seatmate, a buxom matron in a sensible coat, a feathery forties hat glued to the side of her perm, must have been aware of the quivering, muttering teen next to her, but when I took a quick breather from the battle to see where the bus was, she just stared politely ahead, a frozen smile on her lips. Not nice to notice the mentally ill, is it? Can't help themselves, poor things.

A sumptuous late-spring morning rolled past the bus window, the countryside a foaming ocean of white from the flowering hawthorns, the air swirling with intoxicated birds, sticky buds spreading into blossoms everywhere, stately white cloud-galleons sailing through blue skies.

There's no green to match the green that England turns in the spring, the nuclear explosion of its flora, the exquisite balance between the decorum of the countryside and the joyful chaos of rebirth. In springtime, England lets go its dank irony and murky ambiguity and rain-soaked rancor; the green and pleasant land bursts with uncomplicated energy. But I had only one thought as I rolled through all the new life—I could not afford to die. In this now hostile, lethally unpredictable world, my actual demise was just as possible as the recent demise of everything I believed in.

And death would mean damnation.

By the time I made it to school I was exhausted. You can't wage war against the massed armies of doubt and despair on two hours' sleep and an empty stomach. My class was in rollicking spirits; with the summer holidays in sight and the dread O Levels behind us, five long years of work had wound to its end. What remained of school was without much discipline and light on homework. Everyone was high as a kite, as I had been just twenty-four hours earlier. Now I oscillated between contempt for my pals' worldliness and shallowness and inanity, and envy that I couldn't participate, ever again, in their worldly, shallow inanities.

I couldn't dislodge the image of myself, a healthy athletic teen with no history of serious illness, suddenly keeling over and croaking. Lying there rasping my last shallow breaths, begging the concerned Protestant faces for a priest, who, even if he came in time, couldn't absolve me.

I remembered something I'd not paid much attention to when it happened a year before: a boy in my class had died suddenly while playing rugby. He had run the length of the field, scored a try, and collapsed dead. He'd had a rare lung condition but had never had the slightest symptom. Back then he had seemed more a curiosity than anything, that unfortunate member of almost every student body. Now his death confirmed for me the intense fragility of life.

That day there was a swimming match against another school. As vice-captain of the swimming team I couldn't avoid it, but I dreaded it. The pool seemed the perfect setting for some untoward fatality. The other school had a hopeless team: chubby, pear-shaped lads who looked as if they'd been chosen on the rationale that when they dived in at least they wouldn't sink. I was considered a shoo-in in my event, the hundred-yard breast stroke, but in the lead halfway down the second lap I suffered a particularly violent assault on the doctrine of the Real Presence, closed my eyes with the effort of repelling it, and slammed into the end of the pool. A boy twice my weight floundered to easy victory.

The bus ride home was even worse than the one in the morning. The assaults had abated somewhat, only to be replaced by a depression so profound and all-encompassing and inescapable it hurt. I trudged home from school through the blossoming hedgerows and past our little church. It had always been a warm place, reliable in its unassuming smallness, a fixed point in my daily world. Yesterday I had ducked in as I always did for a quick word with the Blessed Sacrament. But . . . now?

In my year of light, the Real Presence had been one of my most glorious discoveries—the most immediate point of contact with the divine. I not only believed in the doctrine; in front of the tabernacle I felt the immanence of a being I believed to be Jesus, as I felt that presence nowhere else. The presence was not of a person, exactly; it was somehow impersonal or supra-personal—beyond the confines of human personality—yet unmistakably there, filling the church. Sometimes when I became lost in prayer, the presence was so vivid and real that I almost had to run from the church before it overpowered me.

Today the little church looked ugly and rickety, a place where danger lurked. What new nightmare awaited me inside?

Nothing awaited me. Nothing hovered over the tabernacle like a dark cloud. Nothing sat on the altar like a pile of luggage, packed and ready to leave. Nothing glared at me triumphantly from the rafters, the pulpit, the pews, the Communion rail. The church was a void, gray and cold.

What was to become of me? Where could I turn? My parents would be no help. Father Bleary, right now pouring his first whisky of the evening in the rectory, even less. Ben and Lily were out. There was only one person who could help me, and he was far away—four or five hours' journey at least, and it was already six in the evening.

But it had to be done. My parents would be frantic, but what choice did I have? I turned back toward the bus stop. An express bus to St. Albans arrived. A good omen. In the early evening there were plenty of trains to London. I had just about enough cash. I was on my way to help.

But the journey was another nightmare. The hordes had developed a whole new generation of deadlier, more precisely targeted weapons. What if Father Joe was not what I'd always thought, the rock on which I'd built my church, but the cartoon he looked like, a holy clown in a black dress? How would Quarr seem when I got there? Home—or an asylum for other holy clowns?

Time slowed to a crawl; each leg of the trip—once so full of delicious, time-gobbling feelings—was interminable. My enemies seemed to have control of time itself, the ability to slow it down to nothing.

One moment stood out. I had to change at a Tube station in the West End which was packed with theatergoers, forcing me to the very edge of the platform. The train hurtled into the station. The center rail, with its pit beneath, seemed to quiver like a great silver serpent.

Not long before, Mum had told me that my dad's father had committed suicide. I'd been horrified, since it meant my grandpa was in Hell, but also fascinated that anyone could get to a point so distant from hope, a situation so without remedy that the only release would be to murder yourself.

But now I understood. I was surely in the same place my grandpa must have been—a prison cell with no door, a place from which no one could rescue me. Suicide was not an option—it would mean damnation—but since I was damned anyway for my despair, what was the difference? At least this wracking mental and physical misery would end . . .

A detail of my grandfather's suicide, on which my mother had dwelt with the vindictive relish of an unsympathetic daughter-in-law, was this: Grandma always maintained that Grandpa had killed himself by jumping in front of an Underground train, but in fact he'd hanged himself in the cellar. According to the finely calibrated values of the lower middle class by which my grandma lived, death by Underground was evidently a finer and nobler end than topping yourself.

For me in that moment, it made perfect sense. Jumping off a chair and hoping the rope would break your neck was fraught with the risk of living. Here all you had to do was fall forward and you were gone, smashed and ground beyond recognition, a zillion volts flooding through the remains just in case.

Do it. Fall forward. Embrace that silver snake! It'll all be over. Come on! Only a fraction of a second left! Decide!

But I didn't decide. Not to, that is. I simply hesitated long enough, then the train was past me, slowing, and the moment had been absorbed into the interpretable past. A whole new front into which the hordes rushed, to fill up with their willing dead. For hadn't I intended to commit the act, but been saved by circumstance? Intention being equal to the sin, I was now guilty not just of despair, the unforgivable sin, but of suicide, the unabsolvable sin.

I squeezed into the crowded carriage, hot and close, my skin clammy-cold from my brush with death and damnation. This was Hell nor was I out of it.

I'd never come to Quarr at night. It was past eleven, several hours after Compline. The driveway was pitch-black as I trudged up it, the mass of the monastery completely dark, unreadable to a heart yearning for comfort. The place was so still it could have been peopled only with ghosts; no movement anywhere except a speeding moon in the treetops behind scudding clouds. And there I was, the traveler, knocking on the moonlit door.

Nothing. I knocked again. Still nothing. I hesitated to ring the bell, having no idea where it sounded or to whom or how loudly, but I'd come halfway across the South of England and I'd lost my faith.

Almost immediately after I pressed the bell, a window opened above me. A testy voice said three times: "Who is it?" It was the old monk of my first visit, whom I'd never seen again. He peered down at me peering up. "Why, Tony," he said, surprising me no end, "it's you."

He disappeared. Bolts scraped and he reappeared, swinging back the big guesthouse door. "Come in, come in. Whatever's the matter, boy?"

I couldn't explain. There was just too much to say, too many words were needed.

"Please, may I stay the night?"

He squinted at me, puzzled but concerned, through his battered glasses, all testiness gone.

"Of course you may. I think Number 4 has been made up. If you don't mind, I—"

"May I see Father Joseph?"

He went to say no or to remind me of the hour, but nothing came out. He sighed a little at the unorthodoxy of it all. The stairs that had to be climbed.

"I'll see what I can do."

I hauled myself up the creaky guesthouse steps, down the drab corridor to Number 4, and sank on the bed. I was still twitching and gritting, but it was a reflex; there was a lull in the attacks. The hordes seemed less sure of themselves here. Time passed—too much time, I thought, if he was coming. I could not afford to sleep. I was shell-shocked, weary and wary. I had to stay awake.

A door opened far away. Slow steps mounted distant stairs. My heart sank. It was the old monk for sure. Father Joe was not coming. I would have to endure the night, then. Across the space between us I could feel the dark armies stirring. *Ah God, no, here they come . . .*

"Tony, dear, wake up."

And there was the long face, twitching and blinking as ever, glasses askew, for once not smiling, the collarless neck of an old-fashioned nightshirt trapped by his hastily donned robe. He squatted in front of me, holding my hands as I sat on the bed, waking.

"You're upset, dear. What is it?"

The tears exploded, all twenty-four hours' worth. I tried, gasping, sobbing, to explain that I had lost my faith, that I had despaired, I'd committed the unforgivable sin, and soon it was not grief that was making me incoherent but relief, overwhelming relief that he was not a cartoon or a holy clown in a black dress but a great rock, a calm harbor, a sheltering wing, my Father Joe.

He did nothing but listen. He made no attempt to calm me or cool the heat of this new development in the insane life of this insane child. He didn't try to explain why I was feeling these things, why what seemed so catastrophic was actually normal, common for my age, simply the result of the hormones raging through my plumbing. He didn't try to shock me out of my funk or manhandle me for my own good with tough love. He called down no higher powers to intercede on my behalf, nor did he invite me to join him in prayer. He didn't do anything that would have said: this is not as bad as you think.

He took my condition head on, as seriously as I took it. Tomorrow there might be other responses, the intellectual consequences of what I was saying to be dealt with. But not tonight. Tonight there was just a desperate boy on a cold and lonely cinder spinning through a meaningless universe, who'd come running across the Home Counties in a waking nightmare, convinced that it was all somehow his fault.

He did say one thing, after I'd cried myself out and sat there heaving and shuddering with fatigue and gratitude.

"There is no such thing as an unforgivable sin, Tony dear. God forgives anything and everything."

He made me take off my jacket and shoes and get into bed. He sat beside the bed and pulled the blankets up to my chin and put his warm hand on my brow. The gentle force that I remembered flowing into me at our very first meeting flowed into me now, filling cold and empty places. How long he sat there I have no idea—two minutes, two hours? Peace descended like snowflakes. My terror receded until it was far out to sea. The dark hordes were nowhere to be seen. Sweet oblivion came and I slept.

CHAPTER EIGHT

"No, dear, I'm afraid it was not the Dark Night of the Soul."

We were sitting on a log on our promontory by the sea. It was the middle of the next morning. Back at St. Albans, my classmates were heaving school supplies at each other behind M. Garnier's prim French back. A few days before, I'd started reading the poems of St. John of the Cross. It was a long shot, but I was hoping my great tribulation might have leapfrogged me into the major leagues, the youngest inductee ever into the Mystics' Hall of Fame.

"The Dark Night of the Soul comes only after years of discipline and meditation. It's the last stage, the final test, before the soul achieves perfect union with God."

"Have you experienced the Dark Night of the Soul?"

"So far, dear, I've not been that lucky."

I had woken, hours after the rest of the community, from a deep sleep, calm and relaxed but with a dull all-body pain, as if during the night I'd undergone major emergency surgery. At first I couldn't remember the reason, then gradually it came back: the crash, the aftermath, the miracle doctor who'd put me back together. I would live. Terribly disfigured, but I would live.

"You fell in love with God, you see, and now the romantic part is over. It happens to us all, I'm afraid."

"I'll never have that feeling of light and certainty again?"

"Someday you'll experience a much greater light and certainty than just feelings."

"Feelings are not good?"

"Feelings are a great gift, but they're treacherous if that's all we live for. They drive us back into our selves, you see. What *I* want. What *I* feel. What *I* need. A man and a woman pass beyond just feelings at some point, don't they? That's when they start to know true love. The love of another. The joy in another's existence. The wonderful ways that the other person is not like you, nor you like them. What you said about the p-p-prison of self you felt you were in—that was very exact. Love releases you from that p-p-prison, you see."

He'd arrived in Number 4, as I was washing my one pair of socks, with a cup of tea and a pile of toast. The night before, he'd sat with me for a while to make sure I was sound asleep, then called my parents before going back to bed. It had been midnight and they were a bit worried but not too much. They figured I was down at the Bootles'.

On our customary walk, he'd said he had a little quiz for me. He'd made me repeat all my inner battles, item by item, literally quizzing me, neatly dissecting the answers to refute my loss of faith. My agonizing over the unforgivable sin, for instance, showed I clearly still believed in God, otherwise why would I have cared about being unforgiven? Conversely it also meant I still believed in the forgiveness of sins. Worrying about my intentional sin of suicide meant I still believed in damnation and therefore the afterlife. And since I hadn't hurried off to some atheist for answers but to a Catholic monastery, I probably still believed a little in the Church's teachings. That was half the Apostles' Creed right there.

This was a new Father Joe, more authoritative, more analytical and definitive, a little more severe. A docent, even. But nothing like this had ever come out of Ben.

"Feelings trap us in the self, Tony dear. Doing a thing because you feel wonderful about it—even a work of charity—is in the end a selfish act. We perform the work not to feel wonderful but to know and love the other. It's the same with your romance. You may not feel your love, but God is still your loved one, your other."

"I can't get over the feeling there's no one there."

"God is there, dear. God is here now, with us."

For that moment anyway, it seemed undeniable.

I began to sense that there might be possibilities I could never have known while my world was overflowing with feelings of boundless possibility. Another level of belief, another kind of light, a profounder certainty.

"The other day Father Prior was telling me about a French writer, Jean-Paul Sartre. An existentialist. I'm sure a brain like you has come across him. One phrase of his particularly struck me: *'L'enfer c'est les autres.'* Do you think he meant that as a joke?"

"I don't think humor's a strong point with existentialists."

"I think it's p-p-poppycock. How can Hell be others? God is manifested in others. God is the Other. That's why the self must lose itself in love for the other. It's the self we must leave behind. Better to say Hell is the Self. *L'enfer c'est moi.*"

"L'enfer c'est les Sartres."

"*Oui oui oui.* Though *un p-p-peu* unfair to the rest of the Sartres!"

The seagulls swooped over the rolling breakers, eyeing their lunch. A momentary squall blew by, spewing rain on us. Neither of us moved; there was that little lull that comes after laughter. I was feeling nothing. But peace suffused me. So peace was not a feeling. Peace was less centered on self, less substantive. Like a force in physics, perhaps, a force that could only flow between you and another you, between two molecules called "Me"—as it seemed to flow now from Father Joe to me and, as far as I could tell, from me back to him.

"Define peace, Father Joe."

"Peace is love, dear, and love peace. Peace is the certainty that you are never alone."

I had not thought about my doubts, my problems, my anguish all day. It was not just Father Joe's logical demonstration that the damage I'd suffered was less than I thought. That was reassuring, but the desolation and loss were still throbbing like a fresh wound. Rather, it was his dramatic otherness that I trusted: I might have lost my faith but I could still believe that he was, to me and for the moment, God. God the Other. It didn't sound like God as I had ever conceived the term, but what else could it be? Love was a possibility, but that didn't fit any of my existing definitional templates either. Unless peace, love, and God were all in some way the same thing.

"God gave you a great gift that terrible night, Tony dear. He gave you a vision of Hell. Not that silly fire-and-brimstone stuff. True Hell. Being alone with your self for all eternity. Only your own self to hope in, only your own self to love. *In saecula saeculorum.* As you said, a p-p-prison with no door. I don't think that vision will ever come to you again. You must never forget it."

He was right, as usual. It never did. And I never did.

He made me go home the next day. I climbed the bus steps to the top deck to get a longer view of the gnome-cap minaret as it slipped away through the oaks and remembered what he had said in those far-off days when everything seemed clear and simple: on the next visit, we would discuss whether I could enter Quarr that summer. This had been that visit. It had never been mentioned.

Yet in a way it was academic. Once again I had come thinking I wanted one thing and left having discovered something quite different. Father Joe had been right: I had not been ready to enter the novitiate; I had been too innocent, too untried. My descent into Hell had forced me to consider the deeper nature of what I professed to believe, the life I wished to choose. For a year I'd basked in my faith as if it were no more my responsibility than a fine spell of weather. Now I had to fight for it, dig deeper foundations, prove how much it meant to me.

Thinking I'd been engulfed by darkness, I'd instead found enlightenment and strength of purpose. The way ahead would be a steeper, stonier path that led to grimmer, tougher places, the real world, hard issues, life as it was really lived. There would be more tests, more doubts. But doubts were normal, even to be embraced. By questioning where you stood, you moved forward.

I knew now beyond any doubt that this abbey was where I belonged, that in this community—not after all a choir of black-robed angels, but real men, others to whom and from whom flowed that quiet, mysterious peace I had experienced—I would spend the rest of my days.

CHAPTER NINE

Back home I was a stranger in the door. It was a Saturday evening and my father was out in the garden. Mum was beside herself with rage. At first I thought it was the running away, which I apologized for copiously, but as she raved on I saw that "the episode," as she called it, had brought home to her the hold Quarr had on me and that someday soon I was going to enter it and be lost to her.

"Isn't a Catholic mother supposed to be proud to give a son to the Church?"

"If you want to be a priest, that's one thing. But these—these—*pansies*—chanting and making pottery and honey and whatnot! That isn't Catholicism!"

"Of course it is. The Benedictines are the oldest order—"

"Escapism! That's what it is. Running away from reality!"

"No—discovering *true* reality, a life of prayer and—"

"Why can't you do Something Useful? After all the sacrifices we've made! Just you wait till your father gets here!"

On cue, my father entered. He took one look and knew what was going on. His face was grim.

"Robert, you must put your foot down once and for all about this monk rubbish."

Dad went over to the laundry cupboard and opened the door.

"In here, please, Anthony."

This couldn't be happening! The laundry cupboard—where the laundry dried—was actually a tiny boiler room. In times gone by, it was here he'd take me for punishment. For most infractions, a boxing of the cranial region; for capital crimes, a tanning with something made of leather.

I hadn't been in the laundry cupboard for years.

He shoved me in and closed the door behind us. I was much bigger than the last time, and I floundered in the laundry. I turned toward him just as he turned toward me and flung up an arm instinctively to ward off the blow. But there was no blow. In fact, he flinched as though I were going to hit him.

It was the first time I'd ever seen him flinch. I was a good inch taller than he was now, broad-shouldered and trim from track and swimming. He was out of shape, with thinning hair and a thickening waistline. In the long moment he took to recover himself, to pretend he hadn't acknowledged his weakness, he seemed literally to shrink as if I were looking at him through the wrong end of telescope, his head tiny, far away down there below.

The head said:

"I didn't bring you in here for the usual reason. It was to say something private I don't want your mother to hear. I don't mind what you do with your life. Do what you want, not what others want. I did. But don't hurt her. And you must finish your schooling. Is that clear?"

His head was the right size again. I nodded mine. From that moment on, we never had another fight.

Even before this I'd thought there was finally some chance of a relationship with my dad. A month earlier I'd announced that I wouldn't be going into Science Sixth Form after all but would be heading over to the arts side. Mum was deeply dismayed: perhaps she hoped I'd be the ticket to a degree of prosperity. I think she hated being married to an artist, living from stained-glass window to stained-glass window, with no fridge, no television, and a very-used car every year or so that broke down within weeks. Dad would buy these with at least forty thousand miles on them—a huge mileage in pre-motorway Britain—and though he'd been trained as an engineer in the RAF, he had no talent for car repair. Since he also refused to buy American, we became victims of superlative British workmanship. The Home Counties were littered with the corpses of our Morrises, Austins, and Vauxhalls.

Mum did have compensations, like getting to meet dignitaries at the unveiling of new windows. Usually these were fat churchmen or sozzled minor nobility. At the Westminster Abbey do, she actually got to shake the hand of the charming young Duke of Edinburgh, who, though sozzled, was not fat. But these occasions were infrequent—it takes several years to get a window from sketches to a hole in a church wall—and anyway, none of them translated into a fridge.

I suspected that Dad, officially in accord with her about my artsy-fartsy plans and coming lifelong penury, was secretly delighted. And that my monastic dreams, far from offending his agnostic sensibilities, tickled them. He wasn't a mere artist after all, but an artisan in an ancient craft. He set great stock in mixing his paint from the antique pigments his forerunners had used in the thirteenth and fourteenth centuries, which gave his glass intense, evocative colors; his windows had a certain authenticity from the traditional techniques of leading and aciding and firing he also insisted on. Forward-looking socialist he might be, for him "medieval" was not a dirty word.

Greater communication between us revealed how private and

saddened a man he was; our alienation hadn't been of his making, but of Hitler's. His reaction to the ghastly landscape created by the Cold War generals was not very different from mine; the Age of Faith may not have been perfect, but those benighted centuries had been a sight more civilized than this one. I don't mean we had an easy time of it; he was weak and had a foul temper and he cheated on my mother. But one thing remained rock-solid; I was deeply proud of what he had chosen to do with his life.

That summer I went to France for the first time, on a bicycle tour of Normandy and Brittany, with a school friend, Michael Church. Michael's last name was odd, because his dad was a C of E Vicar, the Reverend Church. He was a gentle, patient guy of a somewhat spiritual bent himself, who shared my new literary enthusiasms and would put up with my occasional religiosity.

He also shared my passion for churches, at least the great cathedrals of northern France; if he tired of having to stop in every other village to check out its nondescript place of worship, he was too polite to say so. I couldn't get enough of them. I'd never been in a Catholic country before, and this hard evidence of the Church's transnational reach and cultural depth gave me a reassuring sense of belonging—not something I often felt in England.

I told my parents the fib that we'd be in France for three weeks or more. Actually we were there about a fortnight, so I had almost a week to spend at Quarr.

There was no more playing at monk. I wanted to get as much training as I could in my chosen profession before actually entering the monastery. I stayed on the third floor of the guesthouse, which seemed to be the preferred spot for those interested in entering the monastery, and I regularly worked on the farm or on the grounds. I also started to get occasional instruction from the Prior, a formidable scholar and historian named Dom Aelred Sillem.

Other people found Dom Aelred a cold fish, but he filled a cerebral need I was feeling. His large and unforgiving intellect could grapple with formal questions of philosophy or theology which Father Joe tended to deflect. As I got to know him better, I found that he also had an intense mystical core, in sharp contrast to Father Joe's down-to-earth saintliness.

He came from a distinguished German family with origins in Hamburg and had entered the Benedictine order at the Abbey of Downside. Dom Aelred and several other monks, including the celebrated historian Dom David Knowles, grew unhappy with the worldliness of Downside (whose rich and prestigious public school had many secular liaisons) and began agitating for a new foundation which would live by a contemplative and far stricter interpretation of the Rule. They failed in this goal, and Dom Aelred came to Quarr.

He was a severe and ascetic man who believed in the virtues of order and discipline and could hardly have been more different from Father Joe. As the most prominent younger men in the community, its future leaders, they nonetheless complemented each other beautifully. Dom Aelred and Father Joe were the head and the heart of Quarr, a monastic Odd Couple, one living by logic and precedent, the other by emotion and intuition. The two were a real-life version of Ben and Lily's Franco-Prussian fantasy: a man with actual Teutonic roots and one who, if not French, had spent almost two thirds of his life speaking, thinking, and breathing French.

They represented the extremes of the Benedictine spectrum: at one end the ultraviolet of awe and order, at the other the infrared of love and community. Dom Aelred held that the fear of God led to the love of God. Father Joe never tired of telling me "we have to take the fear out of religion, dear." I never spent an hour with Dom Aelred that didn't leave me feeling I'd been through an intellectual car wash; it was with Father Joe that I felt safe. It was natural as air to call Dom Joseph Warrilow "Father Joe"; it would have been unthinkable to call Dom Aelred Sillem "Father Ael."

* * *

Dom Aelred sent me home that summer with a reading list for Mysticism 101—among others, Thomas à Kempis, Dame Julian of Norwich, the anonymous author of *The Cloud of Unknowing,* St. Teresa of Avila and her Franciscan mentor Bernardino de Laredo, who wrote a how-to of mystical advancement called *The Ascent of Mount Sion* which St. Teresa swore by. He also suggested that when I had time I should dip into the Desert Fathers, the dour, unyielding pillars of the early Church.

I found Thomas à Kempis pedestrian but Dame Julian beguiling. I was surprised by the Spaniards, who I expected to be intense and passionate like St. John of the Cross; instead I found them ferocious and absolute, their paths to salvation painstakingly laid out in dozens of steps and stages, with spiritual exercises to get you from one to the next and crammed with gloomy imagery minutely worked out (the great door of Grace might be opened with the doorknob of Constant Prayer on the hinges of Relentless Self-Denial). Or they would casually throw out daunting tidbits of information: *The Ascent of Mount Sion* estimated that the path to perfection—from a standing start to union with the Godhead—takes thirty years. If you make it—no guarantee that, at the end of Year Twenty-nine, within sight of the summit, you won't choke and slide back down to base camp.

In my sixteen-year-old hunger for learning and experience, I lapped it all up. In the back of my mind, though, was the hope that somewhere in all this strenuous and often inspiring piety would be one story or account or prayer or insight that would somehow spark a fiery and emotional renewal of my lost Eden, wipe out the ravages of my night in Hell.

Sensing there was probably something aberrant about this, I mentioned it to Father Joe.

"Well, dear, the whole point of the mystical path to God is that it's arduous. That's why it's often called the Way of the Cross. It takes years of dedication, hard work, and discipline, with few rewards. There are no shortcuts. Certainly not the *coup de foudre* you're looking for. We leave that to the holy rollers. The trouble with being a holy roller is, it's wonderful at the time, but what do you do the next day—and the day after that?"

Father Joe's favorite writers were those who inspired rather than systematized. Dame Julian he loved, and *The Cloud of Unknowing.* As for Thomas à Kempis, whose *Imitation of Christ,* written in the late 1400s, is one of the best known devotional texts of the Church:

"It's very sound. Solid stuff. But don't you think, dear, that Brother Thomas must have been a most uninteresting person to be with?"

This had been exactly my reaction, but I would never have dared express it to Dom Aelred.

"He'd have bored me silly."

"Of course, he did spend most of his life in Holland. That might have something to do with it."

Of the Spanish mystical contortionists:

"Dear me, no! I could never remember all those steps and exercises. Like learning to be a chartered accountant."

And of the august and adamantine Desert Fathers:

"Stay away from them! Silly old devils!"

Father Joe responded to the person, to the simplicity and limpidity of the writing, rather than to the degree of order which could be imposed on the volcanic and mysterious process of salvation. This may have been why he suggested the pithy, punchy, and passionate thirteenth-century German Meister Eckhart, a brilliant preacher considered by Protestant scholars to be an early precursor of the Reformation. Dom Aelred had specifically forbidden me to read him until much later, because he was "difficult."

I loved Meister Eckhart:

When God laughs at the soul and the soul laughs back at God,
the persons of the Trinity are begotten. When the Father

laughs at the Son and the Son laughs back at the Father, that laughter gives pleasure, that pleasure gives joy, that joy gives love, and that love is the Holy Spirit.

This was a Trinity I could live with.

One recommendation on which, surprisingly, both my mentors agreed was the Discalced Carmelite nun St. Teresa (Thérèse) of Lisieux, also called "the Little Flower." The Carmelites were the extremely strict order of enclosed nuns founded in 1562 by St. Teresa of Avila—whom Father Joe therefore called "the Big Flower."

Thérèse of Lisieux died in 1897 when she was only twenty-four after a harrowing round of physical and spiritual travails. Respectful though Catholic kids were taught to be about the saints—especially modern ones, with their relevant messages for our sinful young lives—the Little Flower was a figure of fun, because her following, while enormous, tended to be female, long in the tooth, and gag-me sentimental. Her statue was always the soppiest in the church, goody-goody eyes rolled up to Heaven, chipped plaster roses held to chaste bosom. I'd always dismissed her and her wildly popular autobiography, *Histoire d'une âme* (*The Story of a Soul*) as the worst kind of Victorian nun-slush.

There was a lot of three-hanky Victorian piety in *The Story of a Soul,* but to my surprise I also found a very tough-spirited young woman. I found her single-mindedness about entering Carmel inspiringly familiar. Even more familiar: the "curtain of darkness" she endured and the manifold doubts which constantly plagued her.

I was now in my first year of Sixth Form (the rough equivalent of American high school), a committed artist rather than scientist (as the Labour Party would probably have preferred). The armies of doubt which had attacked so suddenly and savagely a few months earlier had retreated but had not disarmed. The more I read and absorbed of my faith, of its defenders and expounders, the more there was to doubt. Every time they did attack, I would find they'd become more sophisticated, like bacilli that develop immunity to your body's defenses and return ten times more dangerous.

A useful distraction was English Lit, into which I plunged headfirst: not just the curricular Spenser and Milton and Dryden and nineteenth-century novels, but Pound and Graves and Eliot (and therefore the Metaphysicals), Orwell, and other twentieth-century novelists, like Forster and Conrad and Woolf and Waugh.

The only problem was how much I liked it. And liking it brought an instant reflex: that one day soon—if not tomorrow—I would have to try my hand at it. But—an enormous "but" for a proto-monk—the literature I was devouring, whether it was Shakespeare or Conrad or Pound or Orwell, dealt overwhelmingly with The World—and its evil and sin—and furthermore, seemed to get more powerful and memorable the more evil and sinful the subject matter. *Macbeth, The Heart of Darkness,* Donne's violent, searing love poems . . . the list was endless.

Obviously this was no problem for students and/or aspiring artists who were happy to live in the world and wallow in evil and sin, which gave them all kinds of juicy raw material to be artistic about. But:

"Here's my problem, Father Joe: if art describes the way things are in the world, not the way things should be—and the more memorably the better—isn't that, well, celebrating evil and sin? Doesn't someone like me, who's getting ready to leave the world and its imperfection behind, sin by enjoying it?"

"Good heavens, no, dear! At least I don't think so. Can you give me an example?"

"How about *Macbeth . . .*"

Tomorrow, and tomorrow, and tomorrow,
Creeps in this petty pace from day to day,
To the last syllable of recorded time;
And all our yesterdays have lighted fools
The way to dusty death. Out, out, brief candle!

Life's but a walking shadow, a poor player
That struts and frets his hour upon the stage
And then is heard no more: it is a tale
Told by an idiot, full of sound and fury,
Signifying nothing.

"That's said by a murderer who sees no salvation or meaning in life. So why do I, who know there *is* salvation and meaning in life, love it so much? Why would murder and despair inspire great poetry?"

"I know so little of art and literature, dear. But I'm sure the beauty of great art is intended by God. And nothing and no one in this world is so utterly evil as to be unredeemable. Imperfection is not irredeemably evil. Nor is it good, true. But making beauty out of imperfection seems to me very good."

"All right—can *you* give *me* an example?"

"Well, I don't see how an artist who depicts the horror of the Crucifixion and suffering of our Lord, and makes it terribly and wonderfully r-r-real to us, is sinning."

"What if he loves wallowing in all the blood and gore? What if he enjoys painting the nails being driven through Christ's hands?"

"I don't really know, dear, not being an artist, but I wonder, is the artist enjoying Christ's suffering, or is he enjoying rendering Christ's suffering so well? It must be very hard to separate one's feelings in the act of creation. And if creating beauty out of imperfection is good, it follows that the ability to create beauty is too."

"All right. How about this? According to my art teacher, the reason so many Madonnas—of the Renaissance painters, say, or the Dutch Masters—are so beautiful is that the model more often than not was the artist's mistress. Isn't it sacrilege to portray the Blessed Virgin Mother of God as someone you're committing adultery with?"

"I can't imagine why, dear. We have no way of knowing if Our Lady was physically beautiful, of course, but we do know that she was spiritually beautiful. That's hard to show in a painting, isn't it? Making her physically beautiful could be a symbolic way of showing her spiritual beauty."

"What if the artist doesn't believe in God, or the Virgin, or even the idea of spiritual beauty?"

"I wonder whether that matters. If the result is beautiful. God is still the picture, the poem, and the song."

"So is art somehow redemptive?"

"It might be dear, yes. What an interesting thought."

"The beauty created in the process of describing the world as it is, rather than the way it ought to be, compensates for the evil and sin which are being described?"

"That's a rather harsh way of defining art, don't you think, dear? Artists are creators. The beauty they create did not exist until they rendered it. In a way that's Godlike, isn't it? In that sense, art is an imitation of God."

"Wait—are you saying that God the creator sees artists as fellow creators?"

"I don't see why not, dear. Though it might be best not to repeat that to Father Prior."

"Or the Abbot?"

"N-n-never tell the Abbot."

"I still don't get it. If God has already redeemed the world, what's the point of art doing it as well? Does God need art? Does God like art? Does art like God? Where does God fit into the artist's version of the world? Is art a rebuke to God? An escape from God? A substitute for God? Why are so many artists atheists or agnostics?"

Father Joe said nothing for a moment. A little smile I'd never seen before played around his lips. It was mischievous and fond and—unusual for him—a bit private, as if he were contemplating something he couldn't share.

"Tony, dear Tony! I'm not nearly clever enough to answer these questions. But I think someday you will find the answers for yourself."

"Here's what really worries me. Could it be that the more saintly you become, the less you need art? And conversely that the less saintly you are, the better an artist you can be? That would mean to write a great novel I'll have to get to know some really wicked people. If I want to write a decent sonnet, I'll have to have sex with someone."

Again the mysterious smile.

"Why are you smiling like that, Father Joe? You look like the Mona Lisa."

"I just enjoy being with you, Tony dear."

I didn't find Catholic writers other than Greene much help in these concerns. Take Evelyn Waugh. I'd read *Vile Bodies* and *The Loved One,* which were cruel and hilarious; not much Christian charity going on there, and the less there was, the funnier. Ditto Alexander Pope: at his best when nastiest. Eliot I worshipped, but my favorite poems ("Prufrock," "The Waste Land") were devastating, compassion-free commentaries on desperate humanity—who presumably would not have been desperate if they'd found God, which a good Christian like Eliot must have known, so shouldn't he have led them in that direction instead of calling them straw men who end with a whimper? (On the other hand, I'd tried to read *Murder in the Cathedral*—a worthy stab at a wholly religious theme—and had fallen asleep.)

Conversely, as far as I could tell from my Quarr-mandated reading, it seemed that the holier the writer, the worse the writing. Prove-the-rules exceptions like St. Augustine or St. John of the Cross simply underlined the rarity of holy, unworldly writing worthy of the name "art." The Jesuit Gerard Manley Hopkins could be excepted; while I responded to his ecstatics, I sensed something else going on beneath his verbal fireworks that was not the ecstasy of the saved—this was another tortured soul, like Greene.

An even more puzzling thing: almost all the Catholic writers I'd read and loved so far were converts. Weird that Greene became a Catholic, then set out to disobey "our" rules (or wrote characters who did), wallowing in all kinds of highly artistic agonies. The convert thing went all the way back to Cardinal Newman and Hopkins—it even included the American poet (and fellow follower of St. Benedict) Thomas Merton. Why were converts setting the Catholic artistic agenda? Was it just my anti-Protestant prejudice, or could it be that Catholic angst wasn't acceptable in England unless it came in an ex-Protestant package?

Not that I had anything against converts. I was even trying to make a few. My first target was Michael Church. Mild-mannered and not at all argumentative, he looked like a pushover. I was rather surprised to find that High Church folks believed in pretty much everything we Catholics did—the Trinity, the Incarnation, Transubstantiation. The only problem, as I never tired of pointing out, was that they couldn't do the big magic since they weren't real priests. At the Reformation they'd cut themselves off from the Apostolic Succession, the laying on of hands from Bishop to Bishop down all the centuries since the Apostles which made Catholic priests the real McCoy.

Michael would always go rather pink at this line of argument, which I insensitively didn't realize was because I was saying his dad wasn't a real priest. I could usually bully him into agreeing that the Church of England had indeed broken the line of Apostolic Succession with Henry VIII, but I could never steer him past the big rocks: devotion to Mary, which he insisted on calling Mariolatry, and the infallibility of the Pope, which I secretly sympathized with since the Pope in question was the highly fallible Twelfth Pius. Even when Pius died a few months later it didn't help. The new guy, a jolly old dear called John XXIII, looked like fallibility incarnate.

Conversion of Godless Protestants was just one aspect of a generally reformist zeal I was feeling that year. The most dramatic expression of it was directed at the Corps, the British equivalent of ROTC.

Corps had to parade, or muster, or whatever idiotic militarese was used, once a week. Boys from twelve up were required to wear full British infantry khakis, including blister-inducing black boots, webbing around the ankles, and a web belt. The toe caps of the boots had to be spit-and-polish so that the older boys—the NCOs—could see their pimply faces in them. Belts and ankle-webbing had to be blanco'd (daubed to a dazzling white) with a revolting eponymous paste called Blanco. This process alone took hours; I often stayed up past midnight using several tins of boot polish as I tried to figure out just the right ratio of polish to spit so that the NCO morons could admire their Elvis pompadours in my boot caps. There was something wrong with my spit and I never could buff to the requisite shine—which led to automatic penalties.

On Corps day we were given heavy old World War I rifles and taught to drill. Up and down the playground, in squads, in step, turning right and left, swiveling our eyes, stopping, lining up, standing at attention, sloping arms, presenting arms, and marching along the roads surrounding the school to destinations in the far-off countryside, sweating in the summer, freezing in the winter. There we were given lessons in map reading and identifying topographical features ("bushy-topped tree" has stayed with me for some reason), and every now and then getting lessons in the use of the fixed bayonet and other delicate arts of expressing displeasure with your opponent.

None of which had been used in warfare since the nineteenth century and would not have been of the slightest use when we actually became cannon fodder in the initial exchange 'twixt Yank and Russkie. But that's to grace the process with too much meaning. There was no purpose to any of it except to instill in us habits of craven obedience to the most cretinous boys in the school. As in any military community, the most violent and pinheaded members of the tribe, those who obeyed orders without question and had the lungs to prove it, those with shinable spit, rose swiftly to positions of command.

As one who'd pledged his obedience elsewhere, I couldn't be part of this. There wasn't much an ink-stained schoolboy could do to stop the air-conditioned killers in the Pentagon or the sweaty gangsters in the Kremlin, but I could certainly try to stop war in my own playground.

Before I could take any steps, however, Quarr had to give its blessing. War was a hot topic in the faith-and-morals department, and I wanted to be certain I wasn't on thin doctrinal ice.

My confessor surprised me with the familiar arguments for a just war.

"But Father Joe, the argument for a just war can't hold in a nuclear age, can it? Nuclear weapons are designed to murder untold millions of noncombatants, which is specifically forbidden in a just war."

"I hadn't quite finished, dear. In practice I'm not sure there has ever been a just war. Look at the Albigensian Crusade. Even in the last war, the Allies committed terrible crimes against the innocent. H-H-H-Hiroshima for example."

I'd just devoured William Golding's masterpiece *Lord of the Flies* and had been enraptured by its savage metaphor. For me his schoolboy castaways and their grim evolution represented in microcosm how things all too easily went in the larger tribe of the nation; so too the Corps with its absurd dynamic was a microcosm of the British military, if not all militaries.

"Father Joe, I believe that war is not just some neutral thing that happens, like the weather. War is sin committed by certain people. A certain kind of person will always try to find ways around the Fifth Commandment because of their terrible need to kill. These men are called 'soldiers.' They exist in any tribe, nation, empire, or superpower, and wherever they're found, they're the same murderous parasites. People whose lives can only be fulfilled by crushing the life out of another. They call themselves heroes but they're actually diabolical lunatics who arrogate to themselves the power that belongs to God alone—the power to end life."

"You could be right, Tony dear, about military men and their motives. But you must remember: military men too are children of God, loved by God, candidates for salvation. Even mass murderers, if they want forgiveness and reach out for it, can be forgiven."

"They don't want forgiveness, Father Joe. They hate forgiveness. It prevents war. They're a brotherhood that cuts across all beliefs, all causes, all interests, all politics, all patriotisms. Their greatest enemy is not, as they argue, another nation's military, for it is another nation's military that gives them their raison d'être. Their true enemy is us, people of peace, like this boy called Piggy in *The Lord of the Flies* who resists death and embraces life, who doesn't want to murder or to die. And whom the soldiers of the tribe therefore murder."

Father Joe was silent now, watching me curiously, as if he were seeing some aspect of my character he hadn't quite grasped before. I found this emboldening. I went into the more-or-less rehearsed part of my presentation—the part I hoped would close the deal:

"If we could get rid of the military—theirs and ours—we'd take a giant step toward ridding the world of war for good. That goes for all quasi-military activities as well—like our Corps. In a way the Corps is a metaphor just like *Lord of the Flies.* It shows in microcosm how the military works. It tries to reduce us to unthinking machines so that we can do something we have no right to do under any circumstances: take another life. If I refuse to participate in the Corps, I'm refusing to participate in the soldiers' need to murder others in some future war. Corps is just the continuation of war by other means."

I was pretty pleased with this punch line. But it seemed to have little effect on Father Joe. He closed his twitching eyes and pursed his big lips, in deep message-receiving mode. There was a long beat of silence.

"Tony, dear, you sound angry. Very angry. Like a military man speaking with hate of his enemy. War involves terrible sins, and it arises more often than not from hate. But you can't conquer one sin with another, hate with more hate. It only makes hate stronger. Love alone can conquer hate."

He took my hand between his. The usual warmth flowed into me, and as I relaxed I realized how pumped up I'd been, how cold and hard and alien I had made myself to get my point across. How, in some way I could not discern, dishonest.

"Of course you must leave the Corps if you feel this way. But not in anger. In humility and with mercy. Remember: God's grief at the unspeakable things we do to one another is beyond measuring, but so is his mercy. It might seem a terrible thing to say to people who've lost and suffered so much at the hands of hatred and violence. But true courage is not to hate our enemy, any more than to fight and kill him. To love him, to love in the teeth of his hate—that is real bravery. That ought to earn people m-m-medals."

The Corps was nominally commanded by various masters who, for playing soldier each week, were given an officer's commission—from lieutenant all the way up to colonel. In reality it was run by the iron fist of Sergeant Major Kilpatrick, a rust-faced old blowhard with a military mustache the same color, so rotund he always seemed about to burst every insanely burnished brass button on his tunic. He'd been in the Scots Guards or something and had a Scot's accent you could cut with a claymore. When I told him I was quitting the Corps as a conscientious objector, I tried hard to love him.

"What's that stupid look on your stupid face, Hendra? You look like you're gonna be sick!"

I toyed with plunging into my soldiers-cause-wars speech but decided it would not be wise.

"You can't be a CO. You're a Catholic!"

"Yes, sir, please, sir, but that doesn't mean I believe in war, sir."

"Who's talking about war, you ridiculous boy! You wouldn't know a war if it bit you in the bottom! The Corps is about discipline! Building character!"

"Yes, sir, please, sir, but I don't think carrying guns and obeying idiots builds character . . . sir."

"Who are you calling an idiot, Hendra!"

I threw love to the winds and gabbled out a list of Corps morons with NCO rank. But the damage was done. He sent me to the Headmaster, a formidable martinet named Marsh.

Headmaster Marsh took the same tack. Catholics (except he used the word "Papists") couldn't be COs. Evidently the authorities believed that the Church of Rome either (a) didn't have enough conscience to object to war, or (b) was an enthusiastic non-objector to war on the slightest of pretexts.

But I stuck to my guns, and to my surprise, the school's military-civilian junta caved in. They drew the line at my next move: trying to persuade others to become refuseniks. Converting people to a different faith was one thing; converting them from a belief in militarism quite another, beyond the pale, a sacrilege.

In any case I was soon grappling with a far more pervasive and persuasive enemy: the nascent consumerist society, and in particular the extremely confusing area of adolescent pleasures and possessions. Drinking and smoking, owning a motor scooter, buying cool clothes had no moral pluses or minuses for most of my schoolmates. They were uniformly desirable. But not necessarily for monks-in-training.

The fifties were racketing to an end. While Britain was still extremely broke, but there were hints of a new system that would make you need stuff you didn't need, whether you could afford it or not. Apparently it was all very exciting. Even more exciting, the youth economy was beginning to take off, in clothes, grooming, movies, music. Products in these areas tended to be imported from America or, if domestic, to be conceived and sold on an American model. For the first time, a generational gap opened up, giving the new American-style marketers a clearly defined testing ground for their first shot at national manipulation of consumers.

My friends and acquaintances were tremendously worked up—or were being tremendously worked up—about rock and roll, dancing, drinking, cars, motorbikes, sports, movies, television, clothes, and hairstyles, especially when these products were designed or tailored for Youth.

I took pleasure in many things—music, art, films, decent food and drink when I could wangle it. When it came to such consumer necessities as clothes, cars, hairstyles, and the rest, the teenage monk tended to kick in. But it was hard to avoid the novelty and force of the marketing that pushed them into your consciousness, and I would oscillate wildly between wistful yearning for "just a taste" of such temptations and rigid puritanical rejection of everything the late fifties had to offer.

More significant was that I found myself fascinated by the *process* by which things were sold to people, by advertising and marketing—especially on television—which seemed both morally insidious and creatively brilliant. I asked Father Joe for guidance on the question of possessions.

We started with St. Benedict's Rule and the vows I would one day take:

"Chapter Thirty-three, dear, if memory serves: 'No one may presume to retain anything as his own, nothing at all, not even a book, writing tablets, or a stylus. All things shall be the common possession of all.' "

"Very well, Father. Right now, I'm ready to give up all my worldly goods. Sports jacket, one—handed down from Dad, who's too fat for it. Bike, one—peeling chrome and broken bell included. Flaminaire cigarette lighter, one—designed to impress contemporaries at the Albert Hall during Promenade concerts. But I have to say—this sounds a lot like communism."

"St. Benedict doesn't want your cigarette lighter, dear. And he's not a communist. At least I don't think so. Though now you mention it, he does sound a bit like one, doesn't he? St. Benedict is saying that owning things—something the world takes for granted, in fact insists is a right—has important spiritual consequences. P-p-possessions are extensions of the self, you see. They become the walls of that p-p-prison of the self you talked about once. The more possessions, the less likely will be your release from the p-p-prison. In our community, property is forbidden because it gets in the way of love and trust between its members. If every man had his own private property, the community would just be a collection of individual p-p-prisons, wouldn't it?"

I found this far more persuasive than the puritanical approach (vanity of vanities, all is vanity). Father Joe's analysis of the nature of ownership was much shrewder. The marketer's true target, after all, is the self. Self is the beginning and end of selling. This product will extend your self out into an impressionable world. The more of these fine products you have, the more formidable your self. And of course the more barriers you have set up to clear and open contact with the other. Shop-till-you-drop and true love may well be mutually exclusive.

Father Joe stressed that his analysis didn't mean owning things was wrong, any more than that the pleasures you derived from them were wrong. Which went back to the old principle: *contemptus mundi* was not contempt for the world, but detachment from it.

"It all depends on how you see your p-p-possessions, dear, and the pleasures they give; you must be able to give them up without a moment's regret."

The obligation of detachment led me to a deeper understanding of the pleasures offered by possessions. It seemed clear that however varied were the pleasures to be had from them, the pleasures all had in common that they were fleeting and finite. Pursuing them serially looked like a guarantee of regret and disappointment. It was the nature of pleasure to bloom, wither, and die. Pleasure was the slave of time. I didn't have to be a sage old libertine to know that. Pleasure could be sublime, some pleasure might even be momentary contact with the divine, but it had an inevitable downward curve.

I saw my life as a very different graph—a constantly rising growth curve with no upper limit: self-discipline leading to self-reduction and thence to self-loss. My ultimate goal was zero; the greater my loss, the more I would profit.

I was going in exactly the opposite direction from my contemporaries, the crowd streaming by me on either side as I fought my way back to something simpler and older and, I believed, truer. It included poverty and community, perhaps even a pre-feudal form of socialism. I was skeptical of the value of the pleasures offered by technological society. I believed commercial gratification of my appetites was an impediment to a full and happy life. I had no interest in extending my self through possessions of any kind. It was a good thing I was going to be a monk. As a unit in the coming consumer utopia, I was absolutely useless.

CHAPTER TEN

Then there was sex. Or rather, then there wasn't. But sex was one pleasure dome in which my absence may have gone unnoticed: most of my schoolmates didn't get any either. We were pre-Pill, and rubbers were unobtainable unless you could prove you were twenty-one. Or your dad owned a pharmacy. (On the other hand, you could buy a pack of cigarettes as soon as you were sixteen and drink yourself senseless too. The New Elizabethan Era had its priorities straight.)

Sexually I'd probably gone as far as any guy I knew, and I'd done it three years earlier. I did have one friend, a scrofulous, soi-disant "French existentialist" who claimed to have a "mistress"; but he showed a less-than-Camus-like interest in the dirty bits of *1984,* and I was dubious.

Sex is the elephant in any teenage monk's living room. To tell the truth, though, it wasn't that hard to flee Fornication. The Freudian physics of repression appeared quite erroneous. Once I got into the mental habit of abstinence, sex popped up in the teeming jungle of my brain far less often than in the old pre-monastic days when I'd enjoyed sixty or seventy self-induced orgasms a day. There was the odd dreamland whoops (known in Church parlance by the hideous euphemism "nocturnal emission"), but Father Joe soon set me straight on the rap for that, which was zero.

However, there was sublimation, which always landed me in a briar patch of guilt and scruples. In the fall of my second Sixth Form year we began studying Michelangelo; it was the first time I had ever paid much attention to sculpture. I was hypnotized by the beauty of his statues; they had the same inevitability as Beethoven's music or Shakespeare's tragedies, the final statement on this figure in that space, never to be surpassed, ordained long before Michelangelo existed, waiting for him to be born and to chisel them just that way.

One of his lesser-known statues really got to me: the *Madonna of Bruges.* This Madonna is a very young woman, not much more than a teenager, her eyes cast down as the angel annunciates her destiny.

I had only a few photos to go on, but I fell utterly in love with the *Madonna of Bruges.* I couldn't get enough of that exquisite face, that perfect profile, that delicious eyes-cast-down modesty. I dreamed of her all the time, I couldn't get her out of my mind. All this was platonic. I never fantasized anything sexual about her, not even what might lie under her heavy Madonna gear; but she might just as well have been alive for all the stellar qualities my love invested in her. It broke my heart that I would never meet her, never talk to her, never see that gorgeous face move, those soft lips part, those eyes rise and turn toward me . . . Even if I went to Bruges, even if I spent the rest of my life adoring her, my love would always be locked away in stone.

Unfortunately, the photos in question were in a large art book in the art room and we had Art only once a week. This was long before photocopying, so I had to sneak up there on all kinds of pretexts to catch a glimpse of my beloved.

The Art master, a fat, bald, pseudo-Falstaffian character called

Tanner who looked and dressed as if he might once have painted chunky-heroic Social Realist proletarians but now preferred whining about Tories down at the pub, grew suspicious of these visits.

Embarrassed by my obsession, I made up some story about including Michelangelo in an essay I was doing on the Renaissance. But the *David* was on the cover, and the book had a way of falling open at the *David* section, which of course included many loving close-ups of David's splendid pecs and abs and thighs and buttocks. Tanner became quite convinced that it was Dave I fancied and forever after gave me a wide berth in class, shooting me the kind of disgusted grimaces only red-blooded working-class Social Realists are capable of.

Not long afterward I gave him cause. Almost. For the first and last time in my life I fell for a boy. He was in the Fifth Form—two grades behind me—so I'd been familiar with his sour little mug for years without having the slightest interest in him. He was a small, standoffish, rather taciturn kid who never smiled. Suddenly one day he struck me as having become, at some point when I wasn't looking, extraordinarily beautiful. (Years later I came across a school photo of him at the time, and he was indeed extraordinarily beautiful.)

Again, this obsession had nothing overtly sexual about it. I didn't fantasize about him. I didn't even dream about him. I had no urge to touch him or hold him or see him without his clothes on. Quite the contrary: at one point he made it onto the school field and track team (which I was also on). I got an eyeful of his scrawny legs and mad running style, frenetic and short-paced, like a chicken on speed. Which was almost the end of it right there.

But as with the Madonna, I couldn't take my eyes off that face. The perfectly straight nose and chiseled nostrils, the long almond eyes and dark lashes, the hair curling forward on the forehead, the round chin above the graceful throat, the full solemn lips of the unsmiling sculpted mouth . . .

I was a prefect by now, so it would have been very easy to force myself into his company whether he liked it or not.

But I was uncomfortable about being a prefect—I suspected the junta was just trying to co-opt me so there would be no more sabotage. I hated wielding authority just as much as I'd hated being on its receiving end. So I just gazed on his beauty from afar.

My examinations of conscience revealed nothing in these alarming experiences which I could pinpoint as major sin. There was a whiff of blasphemy about being in love with a Madonna—except it wasn't the actual, factual Virgin. As for the object of my pristine desire, I was completely at sea. I was sex-ed-free, bred to accept legendary "platonic" relationships both in the classical and British imperial periods; homophilia was not even on my radar. I wondered if both obsessions sprang from some rarefied version of idolatry, but that was as close as I could get to a Class A no-no. Still, these feelings must be major imperfections, couldn't be normal, not for a monk-in-training and future saint.

The school workload was getting heavy and it was a while before I could check in with Command Central.

". . . But at least there was nothing sexual about them."

"Of course they're sexual, dear. Whatever's wrong with that?"

"What about chastity?"

"Chastity doesn't involve surgery, does it? We're still sexual beings. Sex is a wonderful gift, a physical way to express the most powerful force in all existence—love. Sex is a brilliant idea of God's, I think. Almost like a sacrament."

"Sex is a *sacrament*?"

"D-d-don't tell the Abbot!"

"There's no sin in having sex?"

"Yes yes yes. There *can* be. But sex is a sin less often than we're led to believe. It's all a question of context. If you have sex to hurt or exploit another, or to take pleasure only for me, me, me, and not return as much or more to your lover . . . then it becomes sinful. We monks make promises before God and the community to remain celibate. For us to have sex would be a betrayal of God and our brothers. It's not the sex so much as breaking the vow that is the sin, just as it is when you break a vow of marriage—the hurt to your partner. They've made sexual sins the worst sins of the lot, haven't they? Because sex is so powerful, people are fearful of it! We must take the fear out of sex as well."

In 1958, with Vatican II just a twinkle in Pope John's eye, a time when the Church's rules, laws, mysteries, sanctions surrounding sex were still harsh and reflexive, such views were remarkable.

I was always somewhat baffled that this monk, who had never slept with man or woman, who had confined himself in a cloister in late puberty, could know and feel so much about a matter he'd taken a strong vow to know not. At least in the sense that the modern world means "to know"—which is to have laboratory evidence, hands-on experience of your subject. He had none of that, yet he got it all. Nothing shocked or surprised him, he always grasped immediately the core of a sexual crisis, he always offered practical solutions. It was a mystery. He completely turned around the old precept of "practice what you preach." He preached—brilliantly—what he could never have practiced.

That same afternoon we revisited the topic, in a rather roundabout way. I had read Eliot's critical essays, through which I'd discovered Dante, and was now teaching myself the rudiments of Italian to get a handle on that glorious terza rima.

In turn I was giving Father Joe a taste of *l'Inferno.* We were kicking through the autumn leaves in the oak woods. He loved the sound of Italian, though he spoke little at the time, and was repeating after me the few lines I knew.

I'd got to Paolo and Francesca, the damned lovers murdered in flagrante, where Francesca speaks to Dante as Paolo weeps in the background:

Amor ch'a nullo amato amar perdona
mi prese del costui piacer si forte
che come vedi ancor non m'abbandona

And Eliot's favorite:

. . . Nessun maggior dolore
che ricordarsi del tempo felice
ne la miseria . . .

Eyes closed, lips working in his word-tasting mode, Father Joe repeated the lines in faultless Italian.

"Spoken like a fourteenth-century Tuscan, Father Joe!"

"Now. Let me try and translate: *Nessun* . . . , 'no greater sorrow than . . .' *ricordarsi* . . . 'remembering'?"

"Yes—"

" 'Remembering a happy time—in misery'?"

"Very good, Father Joe!"

"Thank you, dear—it's the Latin, you see. Haunting. Harrowing. Almost as if he had actually visited Hell."

"Should they have gone to Hell for having sex?"

"For having sex in the thirteenth century? Probably."

"What about now?"

"Probably not."

"Isn't that a bit unfair?"

"Yes, but Dante is quite nice to them, really. Each still has the other, don't they? *Piacer si forte che come vedi ancor non m'abbandona.* 'A joy so strong he still does not abandon me.' There's still that bond, that love between them, you see. Something divine. Even in Hell. Interesting."

"Human love is divine?"

"Oh, I think so, yes! I've often thought true love between two human beings is inspired by the Holy Spirit. Or even *is* the Holy Spirit. Th-th-though I'm not sure the Abbot would agree. Human love can be just as saintly as saintly love. Not nearly enough husbands and wives have been canonized."

"You should talk to the new Pope."

"I will, dear, I will. I'll telephone him when we get back. Now, Tony dear, before I forget. I didn't give you your penance this morning."

I'd gone to Confession that morning about my recent sexual obsessions and indeed, he hadn't given me my penance, though his penances were generally mild. I figured I'd been clean enough to get off scot-free.

"Your penance is: you must go out for the evening with a pretty girl."

"*What!* I'm training to be a monk!"

"It can be part of your training, then. Don't be like us old fogies in here and give up what you never had."

"Is this because I fell in love with a statue?"

"Go dancing or something."

"Just go dancing?"

"And kiss her good night."

"Must I really?"

"Obedience, dear. Saint Benedict's First Rule."

I didn't know any pretty girls. I didn't know any plain girls. I didn't know any girls, period. My mother had been trying various transparent ruses to derail the monastic vocation, like hiring nubile babysitters for the younger kids when she and Dad went out. Conversations with them were stilted. It didn't take a three-figure IQ to question why my parents needed a babysitter with a hulking seventeen-year-old in the house. Was it me they were babysitting?

I did have a bevy of female cousins not far away, one of whom was my age and undeniably cute. Teen functions involving this brood came up quite often; I was routinely invited and I routinely refused. When the next one arrived, as per monastic instructions, I accepted.

Mum went into overdrive. Actually spent money making me look fetching. Got Dad to drive me. She was in a fever of excitement. Where I was concerned, morganatic marriage was no problem. As they got ready in their bedroom I heard her hiss to Dad:

"It's a foot in the door!"

At the dance, her sister, my cousin's mother, hissed to her: "It's a foot in the door!"

My mother's other sisters hissed at one another on the phone next day: "It's a foot in the door!"

My cute cousin had no more interest in getting hitched than I did—in fact I told her I was her date on specific orders from the monastic brass. Being a good Catholic girl, she found this hilarious:

"First time I've ever been someone's penance!"

She plied me with questions about the monastery and we had a few drinks. She taught me to rock and roll, first to Bill Haley, then to a song whose chorus went:

It's late we gotta get on home
It's late we gotta get on home
It's late we gotta get on home

A perfect "out," we agreed. That was that. Penance completed.

In the fall of 1958 I began my second year in the Sixth Form (Americans' twelfth grade) and my final year in school. At the end of this school year I would be turning eighteen.

The academic pressure was considerable. The year culminated in A Levels, exams in your chosen subjects which would determine whether and where you went to college. Most guys also took S (Scholarship) Levels—more advanced exams which could win you a scholarship to a better grade of university. Preparing for both was grueling. Over and above this—for a handful of students—there were the Oxford-Cambridge Entrance Exams, the top of the line.

I'd pledged to Dad that I'd finish my schooling. And I would—which I interpreted as taking the required exams, in my case A and S Levels. Then I would apply to Quarr, and, I was confident, given my hard work, perseverance, and slow but steady spiritual progress, Father Joe would accept me.

If at some point in the future the community decided I had to go to college, I wouldn't have to go—according to my understanding of Benedictine procedure—until I'd taken my final vows, at least three years later.

In Sixth Form I had acquired a ferociously strict English teacher named Mr. Heather. Mr. Heather had told me I was one of his best pupils, but in class and in marking papers he bore down on me mercilessly. "For your own good" he'd say, brush mustache bristling over thin gray lips.

Other, more knowing boys would splutter over the name "Mr. Heather"—Heather being a popular girl's name at the time—though never to his face. He was very buttoned-up, scrupulous in dress, and ruthless in discipline. When he expounded his literary likes and dislikes he was coldly but intensely passionate; everything he said was shot through with melancholy, as if only a sense of duty was keeping him on the disastrous path he'd chosen at some earlier crossroads.

Out of the blue, Mr. Heather suggested that I take the Oxford-Cambridge Entrance Exams that year. I resisted, since I wasn't the least interested in doing it "just for practice." But because I couldn't tell him the real reason—that I had no intention of going to Oxford or Cambridge or any other university—and because he was hugely intimidating, I went along, figuring I had zero chance of winning a place anyway.

One bright cold November day, Dad drove me up the A-1 to Cambridge in our latest lemon. He was ill at ease in Cambridge: to him this was not just a place of public-school and aristocratic privilege, but the stronghold of those upper-crust culture arbiters whose double snobbery he dealt with all the time.

To my surprise I found the old part of Cambridge friendly and familiar: most of the original colleges were built either as monastic houses or on a monastic model. I stayed at Queens College in a room—a cell, really—above a cloistered court and felt quite at home sitting under the arches in my hooded coat, murmuring the Offices of the day.

The exams consisted for the most part of essay questions. The topics seemed vague to me and easy to twist round to anything you wanted to write about. For two days I ripped off a few hundred words on each, feeling a great sense of apartness from the sweating, fearful cohorts of pan-British genius around me. Every one of them cared terribly about the outcome of the exam, the passport to a glorious future that it might give them. I didn't give a damn.

Mr. Heather had advised me not to evidence religiosity in my essays as it would be held against me by the markers. But I wasn't going to Cambridge anyway, so I threw caution to the winds. I arm-wrestled one question around to Dante's *Inferno* and wrote an impassioned screed on why modern secular interpretations of *The Divine Comedy*—like Benedetto Croce's, which set aside Dante's "medieval" beliefs in favor of his poetry—totally misread the whole narrative thrust of the poem. *Inferno,* I argued, was driven by a clear and decidedly medieval message: the moral compromise its actors had made with the "real world" had been *punished.* You couldn't separate Dante's absolute belief in sin and Hell, or, therefore, his grasp of the terrible predicament of its denizens, from either the passion of his poetry or the compassion he shows toward the damned. It went on for twenty pages of white-hot longhand.

I returned to school and resumed preparations for the actual goal of the year: the A Levels. The Oxford-Cambridge exams were history, Mr. Heather was appeased, and the Christmas holidays began. Relieved no end, I went to work at the post office to help with the Christmas rush.

Our house wasn't on the route I covered, so I didn't see the letter. But I did see Dad, silhouetted in the light of our back door, as I trudged down our dark slushy driveway a few nights before Christmas. He'd been there for ages, Mum said, standing out in the freezing cold waiting for me to come down the lane so he could be the first to tell me.

The letter was small and square; inside was a sheet of creamy white vellum embossed in black Gothic script: *St. John's College Cambridge.* Dimly and unevenly typed on a very old typewriter was the information that I'd been awarded an Exhibition at St. John's College to the value of ninety pounds per annum. An Exhibition was a lesser scholarship—not as illustrious as a full Scholarship—but way above a mere place.

For the first time I could remember, my dad took me in his arms and hugged me tight. He had his generation's dread of spontaneity and physical contact—he'd never done anything like this, even when

I was a little boy. I wasn't used to being held against his tubby body, to smelling the day-old aftershave on his jowls, but how could I not respond? The man was trembling with joy, beside himself with it, incapable of speech. I hugged him back, and he seemed to become aware of our contact as something utterly unprecedented. He held me at arms' length: "So wonderful, Anthony! So wonderful! What a Christmas present!"

It was a culmination for him of many things—his own choice to become an artist instead of Something Useful, his political faith in the correctness of socialism, a respite from the downturn of his career now that all the memorials had been painted and the war damage repaired. Wrapped up in the simple giddy joy a parent has in a child's success. He said none of this, but it was radiating from every molecule in his body. It was probably one of the few truly happy moments of his life.

And for me an utter disaster.

What was I to do now? No way I was taking up this scholarship. But I couldn't tell Dad that. It would break his heart. Still, telling Dad a white lie, or simply not telling him at all—call it a white deception—wasn't new. What was new was the realization, dawning over the next few days, that it might not be smart to tell Father Joe either. Probably it would be fine. Probably he'd just tell me to think it through carefully. Probably he'd accept that by the time I entered Quarr next summer I would be eighteen, with all my choices legally my own to make.

Or would he? I was accustomed by now to being upended by his responses. There was an outside possibility that my spiritual dad might have a problem too—especially if he knew what it meant to my actual dad. I couldn't risk that. The thought of not being able to enter after all this time, three interminable teenage years, after all this self-doubt and solitude, all the dark nights when I yearned to be at Quarr and sink gently beneath the surface of the communal peace. No! I couldn't risk that. I couldn't risk even the slimmest possibility of that.

Back at school the landscape had changed. I was now a senior prefect, the School Librarian, Captain of Swimming, and a veteran of the Athletics Team, among other minor honors, like being in school plays. I was also, according to the stats, one of the more academically accomplished students of my year. And unique in one respect: the other brainiacs had few sports credits, and the other sportsoids had few academic ones.

The previous Head of School had won a university place and was leaving before the end of the year. Within weeks there would be no Head of School. I was a possible candidate. I said I wasn't interested—which I really wasn't; it was inexcusably worldly even to consider being the head goon.

Mr. Heather had other ideas. I was his star pupil now, his champion; he would become my academic trainer, toweling me down for the next scholastic bout. He lobbied Headmaster Marsh hard to make me the next Head of School.

Marsh didn't immediately make up his mind. He scheduled interviews with several candidates.

I was first—according to Mr. Heather, the other meetings were mere formalities to avoid hurt feelings. In I went to Marsh's large and lavish office. He was a taut four-square guy who'd served in the Navy in the war and was also a formidable classics scholar. Navy brusque and blunt, and intimidatingly brilliant. A nasty combination.

The interview went like this:

"Come in, Hendra, come in. No need to sit down. This will only take a moment.

"I'm well aware, and I'm sure you realize, that you're the best candidate to be the next Head of School. You're an excellent all-rounder and that's what we always look for in a Head Boy. And I haven't failed to note that your refusal to participate in Corps did not lead to further unpleasantness. A sign of maturity, that, Hendra.

"However, I wouldn't dream of appointing you Head Boy. Why? You're a Papist. We can't possibly have a Papist as Head of a Christian school. You couldn't attend services in the abbey, which would set an appalling example to the other boys and doubtless offend many parents. And of course the Old Boys would be *outraged.* So there we are. I'm sure you understand."

"Absolutely, sir."

"Good man, Hendra. And good luck to you!"

"Thank you, sir."

A fitting conclusion to my first eighteen years. They now wound down to their destined end. The remaining months at school had to be served out; I spent them acquainting myself further with the Roman ruins down the road, swimming, cutting classes I didn't feel like attending, organizing the library on the Dewey decimal system. I took the S Levels in a benevolent haze—they seemed like easier versions of the Cambridge exams; I even recycled the Dante rant. My scores were excellent. Mr. Heather was happy.

Dad was happy too. He'd filled out endless government forms in triplicate—something he usually cursed blue murder about—to obtain the state assistance for me to go to Cambridge. It had been approved and granted. In anticipation of the receipt thereof, a Westminster Bank account was being opened for me at the Cambridge branch. Dad wouldn't have to pay more than a few pounds toward my tuition; it was somewhat conscience-easing that this wouldn't be assessed until after the end of my first year. Since there wasn't going to be a first year, he wouldn't have to pay a penny.

School ended with no bangs or whimpers and few regrets. I turned eighteen without fanfare. I put in a couple of weeks on a quiet family vacation. A bit later I announced my intention of going off to the seaside for a while with a few friends.

Like sixty of them. For the rest of my life.

After all the agony of anticipation, there wasn't much to it. Father Joe asked me no awkward questions about college and I felt no obligation to tell him. Christ, after all, had said that father, mother, brother, and sister all had to be left behind to follow him, and that must apply to their hopes and ambitions for you too. I might hurt someone sometime, but there was a greater purpose.

Dom Aelred, however, wanted to know my S Level scores, and was pleased that they were good. Wouldn't they qualify me for entrance to Oxford or Cambridge? I was ready for his rather dangerous line of questioning. There was a Benedictine foundation at Oxford called St. Bennett's, specifically for monks who qualified to study there. Boys from Downside and Ampleforth (the Catholic public schools) who had vocations to their respective communities went to St. Bennett's, but only after they'd taken their vows as monks. I made the argument that I should proceed in the same way. Dom Aelred appeared to accept this and had nothing further to say about the matter.

Later he relayed a suggestion through Father Joe that I should undertake a period of reflection before actually entering the novitiate; it would be open-ended, maybe weeks, maybe a month or two. In the meantime I could study, attend divine Offices, and work on the farm or on the estate as I was already accustomed to doing in preparation for becoming a member of the community.

It was summer, and I loved working outside. I had an intense passion for the early history of the Benedictines, but never before had had the means or the time to pursue it. Now I had both. I might not have a cell or my black robes yet, but in all other respects, I was as good as in.

The doubts that had plagued me like a recurrent disease for so long abated as though they had lost not just the battle but the war. The joy of my year of light so long ago, my Eden time, did not return: but I knew now that my calf-love for this place had been insubstantial, a glorious mist rising over a meadow that evaporates by noon. Now another kind of joy suffused me—not just the peace of Quarr, but satisfaction that the journey had begun.

Graham Greene says in *The End of the Affair* that happiness is a kind of oblivion in which we lose our identity, and that was certainly how it seemed. Not much changed in my status, but I didn't care. Here things happened on an entirely different timescale than in the outside world. Like no other time I'd spent at Quarr, there was no end.

Before this my visits were measured in days or, if I was lucky, weeks. Now I could begin counting in years. Or rather, there was no need to count at all. Monks thought not in years but in lifetimes; in centuries, not generations; in cycles, not in eras. The Benedictine time-space continuum prevailed, *sub specie a eternitatis,* alpha in omega, in our beginning is our end.

The first Offices of the day—Lauds and Vigils, often said as the dawn light struck across the nave—never failed to bring this home. Every dawn, from every rumpled bed, an entity immeasurably stronger than the sum of its parts reassembled to work yet again at the everyday task of brotherhood. Sixty-odd men, the workforce of prayer, commuted from their dwellings to their place of business and went about their matutinal tasks, skilled, experienced, getting on with the job, unwrapping that formidable engine, the chant, starting it up, turning on the power, recharging the core with quiet purpose.

Whatever dream terrors and night dwellers I had just escaped, my solitude was no longer mine. Like each of them, I was alone, but not alone in being alone.

The certainty I still regretted losing had not been true certainty. True certainty was in the routine, the habit, the Rule, the chant, the obedience to present superiors and past custom, the meaning of the words and thoughts and prayers, the countless thousands of mornings on which this same ritual had been repeated and would be repeated long after all these men—including, soon, me—had been munched and churned and turned by the worms back into the loam that fed our cells in the first place.

The gentle force which flowed into me from Father Joe was not his alone; it came from these men, it flowed through them into him, and thence into me, as ordinary as water and as divine. The supremely peaceful, supremely loving Father Joe was as alone as me, but just like me, not alone in being alone. His true strength was that he was just another monk, an ordinary member of an extraordinary tradition. The gentle strength which bound him to them and each "him" among them to the next would one day bind me too.

I could put my trust in this river of black quietly winding through the darkness; whatever happened, it would flow on through my life as it had through so many others', a river of incalculable depth in which you could sink but never drown, springing, as it always had, from the same million tiny freshets, flowing into the same trackless ocean. I was alone, but not alone in being alone.

CHAPTER ELEVEN

Well, that couldn't last.

I should have known. But happiness is not just oblivious. Happiness is also an idiot.

It was a bright, windy morning. I was getting ready to go to the woods to do something with Frère Louis—my favorite work. Then Father Joe tapped on my door.

I knew the minute the long face came round the door that the game was up. I'd rarely seen that face not smiling. He sat down without a word. Never done that either. He put the tips of his fingers together, making an open-plan church steeple. Was this Father Joe or Mr. Joe, vice president of personnel?

"Tony, dear, is there s-s-something you're not t-t-telling us?"

My mind raced ahead looking for damage control, openings, possible deals. Anything. But I could see little wiggle room up there. I said nothing. Father Joe looked sad—disappointed, I suppose, that I wouldn't come clean.

"Your father telephoned last night. He was wondering when you're going home so you can get ready to go up to Cambridge."

"This is home. I don't want to go to Cambridge."

"Ah, but you must, dear."

"Christ said we must leave father and mother behind to follow him."

"He also spent many years acquiring wisdom and learning."

"Please don't send me away! Please, dear Father Joe!"

"You have a scholarship."

"It was a mistake! I didn't mean to win it! I don't want it! Someone else can have it!"

"That is not yours to decide, dear. It is a gift of God."

There was nothing to be said after that, no appeal, no plea-bargain, no leniency. His quiet severity was unshakable. It was the gentleness with which the sentence was passed that really got to me. The massive door to my future closed with barely a click.

"I'm sorry, Tony dear. You must leave today."

Like Peter, poor weak deceitful Peter, I went out into the garden and wept bitterly.

My room in St. John's was very like the one I'd stayed in at Queens, except First Court was much larger and less monastic and the room was pokier and shabbier. It was sixteenth-century, built after the dissolution of the monasteries, and technically Protestant, but old and beamed and warped enough to provide the right setting for the course I'd chosen. I was going to let Cambridge into my life and into this, my cell, as little as possible. I was here to acquire learning and wisdom, and nothing else. Other than study, I would continue to lead the contemplative life to the utmost of my ability, saying the Offices every day, attending Mass every morning, eschewing the fleshpots and temptations of the great university—except maybe for the odd pint of an evening, which I would drink at the ancient bar next to the college kitchens called The Buttery. I would eat my meals in Hall, which luckily resembled a giant refectory. In short, I would make St. John's my monastery.

My banishment aside, Father Joe had exacted no retribution, offered no rebuke. Nor in the long run would my deceit be punished. He had written me the next day laying out Quarr's conditions: I must complete the three years of an English degree. If I still wanted to enter the monastery after that, there would be no further obstacle. Quarr—and he—would welcome me back with open arms.

When I thought about it in the weeks before Cambridge, it began to look less daunting, less final and catastrophic than at first. I'd already waited for well over three years. What was another three—actually, just over two and a half? I would be sitting at the feet of the finest scholars in the land: C. S. Lewis, F. R. Leavis, A.J.P. Taylor, E. M. Forster, C. P. Snow. I would be bettering my mind—to the eventual benefit of Quarr—and these were my favorite areas of study. A degree of happiness was possible. Happiness made time pass quickly.

In the event, my first year did pass much as planned. Unlike Oxford, Cambridge had no monastic presence, but there was the Catholic chaplaincy, Fisher House. Fisher House was run—and partly financed—by the longtime Catholic Chaplain of Cambridge University, Monsignor Alfred Gilbey.

Gilbey was a one-man social phenomenon. In welfare-state Britain, at an increasingly middle-class, progressive, meritocratic university, at the outset of the sixties, only a couple of years before Vatican II, he cut a fantastic and improbable figure.

In appearance he was every red-blooded English Protestant's worst nightmare—the archetypal Papist priest. He came from a hugely wealthy family with one foot in Spain (they had made their money in fortified wine and spirits), and his mother was Spanish. It showed in his profile, which was irredeemably Iberian, with a powerful El Greco nose, huge sunken dark-rimmed eyes, and a mouth that early-nineteenth-century romantic novelists would have called sensual and cruel. He was not sensual and cruel in the least, but he certainly lived in the early nineteenth century. Tall, thin, and supremely elegant, he insisted on wearing antique clerical garb which he had custom-tailored. Typical morning wear might be an ankle-length soutane, a shoulder cape with episcopal-purple silk lining, a flat round black hat, and black patent leather shoes with solid silver buckles. (He gave me a cast-off pair of these once which I treasured, if for nothing else than that the buckles alone were worth hundreds of dollars. Nominally my size, they were so narrow that I could not force my clodhopping Celtic hooves into them. I felt like an Ugly Sister trying on Cinderella's slipper.)

The *tout ensemble* was outrageously anachronistic, something the revolutions of 1848 ought to have swept forever from the face of Europe: sinister, ultramontane, conspiratorial, beyond reactionary. He summed up everything the British mean by the word "Jesuitical," though he rather disliked the Jesuits and they returned the favor. No one would have been surprised to find a Torquemada in his family tree. When he bustled about the Cambridge streets, dark robes flapping over Regency shoes, he always gave the impression of being on some mysterious, far-reaching mission, possibly at the behest of Metternich or the Duke of Alba, involving double agents and Vatican gold.

It was never clear how seriously he took all this, but he played it to the hilt. He was also blindingly charming and witty, a born diplomat who knew everyone in Oxford, Cambridge, the English Church, and the Catholic demimonde, and had a far-flung network of highly placed friends and relatives from Paris to Istanbul.

When I began showing up at Mass every morning, he took me under his wing, and we became good friends. He did his best to "adjust" my vocation and steer me toward the public-school communities at Downside or Ampleforth. If I had to be a Benedictine, he would murmur suavely, better to be "active" than contemplative, no? Translation: Downside and Ampleforth with their blue-chip social connections were much more his cup of tea than a bunch of Frenchmen in the Isle of Wight moaning chant behind high walls.

But he didn't push it, being far less of an intriguer than people believed. Except in his own interest, that is, where he was ruthless.

Church progressives were naturally scandalized by everything about him and were always trying to dislodge him from the highly visible and influential chaplaincy, but he beat them back time after time. I agreed with them in theory, but in practice he was irresistible, a once-in-a-lifetime character. He was also kind, generous, shrewd, and—provided you were willing to accept where he was coming from, which was, roughly speaking, pre-Enlightenment—very funny.

Through Fisher House, I met a lifelong Catholic friend: Piers Paul Read, future novelist and son of the eminent literary critic Herbert Read. Piers had gone to Ampleforth and was as worldly as I was cloistered. He had a wicked intelligence beneath a deceptive boyish charm which let him get away with all kinds of conversational outrage. He too was tall, elegant, and effortlessly witty; in a different age he might have been a Monsignor-in-training. He was a magnet for women, but had no amorous involvement I could detect; instead, he always seemed to be involved in the love lives of at least two or three women friends, which he manipulated and documented with vast glee. I'd never met anyone this entertaining, but at the outset he both shocked me and made me rather nervous. I wasn't quite sure how we had become friends: maybe my monkishness titillated him, red meat for his mischief.

He would bait me by taking unorthodox or ultraprogressive doctrinal positions and would treat my orthodox responses with amused incredulity: *but surely we Catholics no longer accept the idea of papal infallibility?* I suspected he didn't really hold such opinions, but I wasn't sure what his exact positions were. At best he was toying with the new theology, at worst he saw belief as a parlor game, but I could never be certain, he was so maddeningly nimble, so brilliantly ambiguous. If I challenged him—*you're playing a game! You're saying that to bait me!*—he would smoothly switch manner and become the offended true believer. *Are you questioning my faith, Tony? How dare you?* And smile his boyish smile. It was hopeless. But huge fun. I would say Compline way past midnight.

No meat was redder than my vow of celibacy—our most frequent area of scholastic disputation, the easiest bait of all. Which led seamlessly to his proposing to introduce me to one of his girlfriends. He held out the possibility like a dapper snake with an apple in its mouth. But there was no way. Not this Benedictine.

Of course if had I tried to bite the apple, Piers would have whisked it up his sleeve. The point was to tempt me or even perhaps to watch me fall. Or was it? *How can you say that? Why would I manipulate a friend? This is a completely altruistic attempt to help you, to broaden you. What sin is there in going out with a girl? Unless you're a Manichean. Are you a Manichean, Tony?*

And once again I'd be saying Compline as the bells at Quarr were ringing for Lauds and Matins.

Time shot by; it was extraordinarily easy to bury myself in academic pursuits. The line between the scholarly and the monastic has always been blurred, and the daily rhythm of reading, writing, and researching fit comfortably into the adapted template of Quarr I lived in private.

First-year exams were rolling around; after them was the prospect of summer vacation. Father Joe discouraged me from spending it at the monastery. I had good things to report about my first year—no loss of vocation, voluminous study; he felt I should make the most of my time in the world and take a summer course somewhere.

A friend told me about a British Council program that provided assistance for summer courses; I applied, was approved, and was now set for my first trip to Umbria and Perugia's Università per Stranieri, where there was a monthlong course on Italian art and literature, including *la Divina Commedia.*

On the way I would stop at Oberammergau in Bavaria where a world-famous Passion play was performed at the beginning of every decade (it was now 1960). After Perugia I would head for Spain (another first-time trip) and amble around Benedictine and Cistercian houses there.

I hitchhiked to Oberammergau and saw the Passion play along with twenty thousand other Catholics. It was deadly—like being at a very quiet sports event. I then hitchhiked to Austria where I met up with the Catholic friend of an American author I'd met at Fisher House. He was a well-known English film director; his house was very luxurious and full of young film actors. I stayed a day or two. This gent then gave me the name of a Catholic friend of his, a prominent British Petroleum executive in Milan; I duly hitchhiked to Milan and stayed a couple of days in his magnificent baroque palazzo with some other young men. He was extremely gracious and told me to look up yet a third Catholic Brit in this circle, a well-known designer, if I got to Rome. But I never took up the third invitation as it was time to head for Perugia.

Not until much later did I realize that all my hosts were gay and I'd probably been expected to provide certain services in return for their spectacular hospitality. Being a monk, I'd been too naïve to know this. Being British, they'd been too polite to ask.

As soon as I set foot out of the Fiat Seicento that had given me the ride from Florence, I was in love with Umbria. So those little hills with their scattered olive groves and cypresses in the backgrounds of Giotto and della Francesca weren't idealized images of some loftier Italy inhabited only by saints and Medicis. They were actual landscapes rendered half a millennium ago and still exactly the same. Another blow struck for the great principle of changelessness.

I stayed in the flat of a sweet-faced widow called Signora Carra whose husband had died—pointlessly, she said—at the very end of the war. Her fat, pampered, and arrogant son still lived with her though he was thirty-five and had a perfectly good job in city government. For rent, he treated her like dirt. I had gotten the idea somehow that *carra* meant "hedgehog"; at dinner the first night I tried to break the ice by explaining that this had once been my nickname. Apparently I insulted the family honor; the son flew into a rage, spat on my feet, and stormed out.

So Signora Carra and I became friends. She had no English at all, but taught me more Italian in a month than I've learned since. My bedroom faced the gentle hills outside the city, and in the evening she would come shyly in (*"Scusi Tonino?"*) to catch the *tramonto,* which sounded to me like "between the mountains"; I thought it the most beautiful and poetic word for "sunset" I'd ever heard.

The course was a joke. There were students of every nation from New Zealand to Palestine, but unlike me they all knew (a) that the Università per Stranieri was a party school and (b) how to party. The professor giving the main course taught in Italian with a thick regional accent, Sicilian I think, which was impossible to understand. He was huge and gaunt with wild frizzy hair and looked exactly like the mad uncle in Fellini's *Amarcord* who sits in a tree whenever possible, bellowing, *"Voglio una donna!"* The lecture hall was full for the first few days and empty for the rest of the month.

August in Spain was an unpleasant surprise. I had expected to find lodging at various religious houses, but the clergy and monks were hostile and suspicious when they answered their doors, slamming them in my face when I gave my pitch. They certainly didn't recognize Christ in me. The Rule of Benedictine hospitality seemed to have been suspended, presumably by the Caudillo. This put a strain on my budget: ditches and beaches had to substitute for guesthouses. In turn this meant evading the Guardia Civil, a bunch of thugs as trigger-happy as the religious were unchristian. But Franco's buddies couldn't spoil Andalusia, which gave Umbria a fierce run for its money.

Back in Cambridge I found I'd got a First (first-class honors) on my first-year exams. It was actually better than a First, not all the way to a Double First, but good enough to win a University-wide prize called the Whitman. I saw it as a sign: time to return to the monastic regimen after my wanderings through Europe's garden of worldly delights.

I planned great stuff for my second year, the Provençals, modern theater. Perhaps it was the latter that prompted me one evening, pretty much on a whim, to go see a theatrical revue called *Beyond the Fringe.*

In my general ignorance of Cambridge social life, I was not aware that there was already quite a buzz about this production. Nor was I aware that there was a Cambridge institution called Footlights which put on a comic revue every year, nor that there was a festival in Edinburgh every summer, nor that it had a Fringe—unofficial semi-underground shows that were not in the festival proper, including the Cambridge *Footlights Revue* and its Oxford counterpart—nor that Edinburgh was where *Beyond the Fringe* had got its start.

So I had no idea what to expect when I entered the Arts Theater in Cambridge that night. Onstage were two men from Cambridge, both tall and gangly, Peter Cook and Jonathan Miller, and two men from Oxford, neither tall nor gangly, Alan Bennett and Dudley Moore.

What I saw were two hours or so of "sketches," a generic term covering many different forms: dramatic sketches with two or more characters and a beginning and end, monologues, parodies, musical pastiche, and a couple of long montages, or sequences of various kinds of material, involving the whole cast. One was a non-sensical play-in-miniature which subsumed all of Shakespeare's histories, awash in the incomprehensible references of which the greatest writer in the English language is capable. There was an achingly stiff-upper-lip vignette of the Battle of Britain from a RAF pilot, savaging the hallowed myths of British decency, sangfroid, and wartime bonhomie. There was a speech by Peter Cook as Tory Prime Minister Harold Macmillan, nailing the foggy-minded leader of our foggy nation. Dudley Moore used his grand piano as a scintillating weapon to eviscerate Beethoven and Schubert and Benjamin Britten. A town meeting on civil defense dramatized better than a hundred Campaign for Nuclear Disarmament pamphlets the fatuous illogic of nuclear deterrence. A condemned man on his way to the gallows was "comforted" by hearty, take-your-medicine Prison Governor. Perhaps best of all was a gloriously vacuous Church-of-England sermon from Alan Bennett:

> Life is rather like opening a tin of sardines. We are all of us looking for the key. Others think they've found the key, don't they? They roll back the lid of the sardine-tin of life, they reveal the sardines, the riches of life therein, and they get them out,

> they enjoy them. But you know—there's always a little bit in the corner you can't get out. I wonder—is there a little bit in the corner of your life? I know there is in mine.

What I did was laugh. And laugh, and laugh, and laugh. And as I laughed, I sensed something coming together and something else falling away.

What was coming together here in one place on one stage were many, many strands of cultural and intellectual thought, some connected, some not, that had been growing and creeping across the landscape for years, tendrils of skepticism and irreverence, all having something to do with the postwar realization of just how murderous and ludicrous in 1960 was the idea of Nation and nationalism, all the sanctimonious and meretricious claptrap that sustained in every one of us the false self of national identity, the clown makeup of Britishness.

The four cast members of *Beyond the Fringe,* which was about to become a phenomenal success in the West End and on Broadway, consistently downplayed critical glorification of their masterpiece, insisting it wasn't satire, and even if it was, of minor social significance. But for those who heard and saw what they had to say, the social significance was impossible to avoid. No one had ever gathered in one place the sacred goods of the scepter'd isle—Parliament, the Church of England, V-day, the BBC, Shakespeare, the Royal Family, the Courts—and asked just what it was all worth, considering the damage that had been done in its name over the last couple of centuries. And no one had done it so gloriously, so dazzlingly, so unforgettably.

What was falling away was my vocation. I didn't realize it at the time, because nothing negative was taking place, there was no cataclysmic conversion, no thunderclap on the road to anywhere. On the contrary, the experience seemed all of a part with my habitual ways of feeling and perceiving, not unlike the very similar sense of wonder and community I felt in the dawn light at Quarr—except that this was its reverse side. It wasn't even that different from a religious service. We were sitting in the same formation as in church—though the pews were a bit more comfortable—attending a kind of ritual in which four black-clad young priests, albeit in the vernacular and without a shred of reverence, dealt briskly with sacred matters.

There were a few huffy exits, seat backs banged in protest, walking sticks and handbags swinging their outrage up the aisles. For the most part there was elation, release, celebration. The theater was full of crazed joy, helpless, transfigured faces, laughing at things they'd probably never laughed at before or had never been allowed to laugh at before, perhaps things which had never been laughed at, at least not for a hundred years or more.

I loved it. Not just what was being said, but these waves of demented delight, this wild energy surging through five hundred people, connecting us all for a timeless instant when truth flashed, then flashed again and connected us again. The laughter was magical, mysterious, pure, an irresistible force. Where did it come from? How did you conjure it up? How did you *do* that?

I wanted then and there to learn what Cook, Miller, Bennett, and Moore did so effortlessly; to have an audience bound together in this delicious way, united by this ethereal stuff. It didn't strike me as a temptation, as a worldly pleasure dangled in front of me; in fact the laughter presented itself as something akin to holy, something with awesome transformative power.

I went into that theater a monk. I came out a satirist.

Save the world through prayer? I don't think so.

I'm going to save it through laughter.

Part Two

CHAPTER TWELVE

Outside the vast picture window, the evening mist was gunmetal gray, sluggish as the heaving, oily ocean. The setting sun glowed through it, tinting the conflicted waves the glistening orange-red that beef goes when it's beginning to turn.

My first wild, whirling day in L.A., years earlier, I'd been stunned by how depressing the Pacific sunset was. I'd driven west down Pico to see it, and as I hit Santa Monica I just came crashing down. The girl I was with said I must be bad-tripping, because the Californian sunset was the most fantastically groovy thing in the whole world. But it wasn't drugs. I didn't do drugs in the sixties. Too scared of them. No, I was clean and sober—and there it was, a mighty flame-gold/episcopal-purple/hot-pink light show spread out across the ocean, and all I could think was *this is the end. This is as far as you can go. After this it all starts over again.*

Every L.A. evening from then on it was the same, however "up" I'd been all day, however well the meetings had gone, however officially magnificent the mountainless *tramonto.* I would just come crashing down, down into the depths.

De profundis L.A., *clamavo ad te Domine.*

The house was pretty sumptuous. Belonged to Robbie Robertson or Levon Helm or someone. Someone from The Band. But there was nothing to do, nowhere to go, no one to call. I didn't want to turn on the TV because Reagan would be on it, and I didn't want to start ranting to myself about Reagan—Reagan, the putrid-meat Pacific sunset, the end, as far as you could go, beyond whom there was nothing . . .

There you go again. Same useless drivel you've ranted to yourself a hundred thousand times in the two years since he ascended to the throne, loved and admired by all for his fantastic acting talents and brilliant election strategy.

It was the emptiness of the Malibu night. There was nothing to do but obsess. No doubt at this very moment—just a few miles up the Pacific Coast Highway—Joan Didion was obsessing about something too.

But it was impossible to get Reagan's face off my internal screen. Those simpering, wattled features: "Face looks like a scrotum," Ritchie Pryor once said. The face would even chuckle its way into my dreams—enter their narrative—however hard I resisted, with all the exotic resources dreams give you. There it would be, rising from the plane wreck, appearing out of the snake-strewn dreamscape, always with the same murmured message: *c'mon, I'm not as bad as all that, am I?* Which was the whole problem with Reagan. He was as bad as all that and worse, but the face made it just fine.

I was in L.A. to kill two birds with one stone: (1) promote my latest publication, a parody civil-defense manual called "Meet Mr. Bomb!" and (2) start shooting another, very different parody, a low-budget comedy.

"Meet Mr. Bomb!" was a cheery pamphlet, purportedly put out by the Futile Preparedness Agency, detailing all the futile things you could do to (not) survive, before, during, and after the winnable war our plucky, battle-hardened commander in chief was proposing. It had been written by humorists like Bruce McCall and Kurt Andersen; as its editor I was pretty proud of it. I'd privately dedicated it to the cast of *Beyond the Fringe* in honor of their seminal civil-defense piece.

It had a shot: other parodies I'd edited with much the same team of writers—like *Not The New York Times* and *Off The Wall Street Journal*—had between them sold almost a million copies. *Newsweek* had enthused over their advance copy of "Meet Mr. Bomb!" They were thinking about putting me and a couple of colleagues on their cover. My publisher felt we were being cautious in printing two hundred thousand.

Our newsstand distributors in L.A. were the biggest newsstand guys in Southern California, and Southern California had been a good market for parody. Naturally, in my outdated seventies naïveté, I assumed that anyone who made their bottom line from newsstands would have to be live-and-let-livers, realists, subscribers to the principle that you can make a buck from anyone's point of view. You'd have to be to display *The Nation* and *Hustler* and *Commentary* side by side, wouldn't you?

Wrong. Our distribution company—or rather its boss—was not remotely interested in live-and-let-live or realism or probably even a free press. He was a razorback Reaganite and had quite disliked "Meet Mr Bomb!", describing it, in his most restrained assessment, as "treason." According to my publisher, who'd called minutes earlier, Ronnie's boy had shredded the hundred thousand copies we'd shipped to him and refused to shell out a cent of the hundred thousand dollars he normally would have had to pay for the privilege. The project was effectively bankrupted. The local radio and TV interviews I had planned for later in the week had been canceled.

Through the smog, the sun was low and red and tiny. Like a naked emergency bulb outside a hospital you'd tell the ambulance to drive by. ("Hit me with the morphine and try the one in Long Beach.") This was the end. As far as I could go. Beyond this there was nothing. The question was: after this, would it all start over again?

Far worse than the fact of Mr. Bomb's demise was its meaning:

we were in a new, barren, Babbitt-ridden landscape. Our little publishing venture might not be able to function in it. I was interested in—perhaps qualified to do—only one kind of project. Stage, page, or screen—I didn't much care how it got to the public—it had to be about something that mattered, a funny statement on a vital issue, a small but painful bullet in the posterior of an odious power structure. Most important—something that might make the powerless laugh at what they weren't supposed to. Lenny Bruce told me that backstage once: the best laughs come from things you're not supposed to laugh at.

I'd butchered a few holy cows over the last decade or so: Woodstock and the Movement (when they were still pretty sacred ruminants), American historical icons, the Kennedy murders, Vietnam, cancer, political meat on the hoof by the cartload, other people's religion (not as much as I would have liked) and my own religion (a lot).

Not the Benedictines, though. Not yet. In the pasture of my soul there remained one lonely cow I'd never laid a finger on. Her name was Joe.

My abattoir had been the *National Lampoon,* where I'd arrived in the summer of 1971, though I'd been writing for the magazine since its first issues in early 1970. The magazine was very shorthanded at the time, so I went to work at a variety of editorial chores. That fall, on one of those washed-clean, windswept, dazzlingly sharp mornings peculiar to Manhattan, when the light makes everything glitter with the promise of something utterly new in the course of human events, Cofounder Henry Beard invited me to become the *Lampoon*'s first managing editor.

It was glorious. For the only time in six years of wandering across America as a stand-up comedian—or rather, a sit-down comedian: my partner and I used stools—in a haze of unaccustomed consumer gratification, half-understood mythology, insincere nostalgia for my British homeland, and bitter disappointment—this *wasn't* Camelot or the New Frontier or the Great Society—a strong, uncomplicated feeling blazed forth. This is the place. I spent the next seven years of my life dreaming up the most scabrous things I could about its leaders and history and customs and beliefs, but it was at this moment that I fell unconditionally in love with America.

I hadn't come close to doing what I set out to do that night in Cambridge more than a decade ago—the night I heard the holy laughter. It had been far easier to make a very comfortable living sucking chuckles from those whom Abbie Hoffman was calling "Pig Nation," to settle into the soft trap of conformity: at work write one thing for those who control the means of TV production; at home write the other, more honest, possibly world-changing thing—and keep it in a drawer.

Keeping it in a drawer had to stop. I owed that much to Father Joe. I'd abandoned one vocation for another and then, in effect, abandoned that one too. Father Joe, far away across the Atlantic, was not so constantly in my thoughts as before, but he had shaped my sense of vocation and the obligations that went with it. The *Lampoon* was giving me the chance to make up for my decade of torpor by dedicating myself to a new community, this one inspired by the Unholy spirit. To take a new set of vows: of disobedience, stability of satirical purpose, conversion of the easy life. And, given the *Lampoon*'s felonious salaries, of poverty.

Nothing I'd done comedically so far was currency here. Fine by me. There was a heady lack of respect for the Movement with its glib maxim, "If you're not part of the solution, you're part of the problem"—which had always seemed to me problematic. Habituated to the sanctimonious solons of San Francisco and lugubrious lefties of L.A., for whom the Hollywood Ten were still a hot-button issue, I found this disrespect hilarious and liberating. There was no line drawn—as there always had been in TV or teach-in—beyond which things were "just not funny, Tony." The *Lampoon*'s humor worked because it was about things that were off-limits to all sides. That old Lenny Bruce yardstick. Radical, yes, but the radicalism of the White House—and of the White Panthers—demanded radical humor. Extremism in defense of levity is no vice either.

In these, its glory years, the magazine expressed and nurtured the internationalism that typified the seventies and so maddened the patriot Right. Various other Brits were involved at various times, like Alan Coren, editor of *Punch.* Several French comic artists were in the extended *Lampoon* family. A South African, Danny Abelson, became an editor. One of India's most prominent journalists wrote a parody of *The Times of India* which doubtless reduced four or five readers to helpless laughter. Most significant, the magazine included several brilliant Canadians. Primus inter pares was Sean Kelly, a Jesuit-trained college professor, small and wiry with a huge, wiry brain and a Celtic knack for things that rhymed, from rock lyrics to T. S. Eliot.

Sean and I, severally or together, were responsible for a number of satires on Catholic themes. With another Canadian, Michel Choquette, Sean wrote the best known: a comic starring the Protestant superhero, Son O' God aka Jesus the Messiah. His mission here below: to combat the Scarlet Woman of Rome and her lover, the diabolic Antichrist in the Vatican, whose slogan is "Power to the Papal!"

The Catholic, or ex-Catholic, aspect of the *Lampoon* was anomalous. Comedy and humor writing had long been dominated by Jewish giants like S. J. Perelman, Lenny Bruce, Mort Sahl, Woody Allen, Mel Brooks . . . the list is endless. Although the *Lampoon* had significant Jewish talent "Catholic humor" was a breakthrough area. Reflecting the convulsions the Church was going through, it got enormous response.

One of the very first pieces I did for the *Lampoon* was a kiddie version of the Gospels, taking the feminist attack on the Church to its logical extreme—a female Messiah (or rather *Ms.*iah), Jessica Christ: "At Her Last Supper, Jessica took bread and broke it and gave it to Her Apostles saying: 'Take, eat, for this is my body.' 'Hubba! Hubba!' said the Apostles."

Blasphemy was a novel experience. On one level it was oddly comforting. It had been years now since I'd practiced my religion, but it was still a deep vein of my identity. I felt at home creating mayhem in places where I'd once been so dutiful. It even bought me some group acceptance. I was still tentative about American political and cultural referents, but Catholicism was an area where no one could challenge me. Plus it was international—the idiocies of growing up in the One True and Universal Church had been the same for us all, in the U.S., the U.K., or Canada.

Except it hadn't been the same for me. Unlike Sean Kelly (or for that matter, my friend George Carlin), I hadn't kicked against the pricks as a kid. I'd been a monk in all but habit. So what was going on?

I suppose I took it on faith, as did many others, that doctrines of any kind—not just of the Church, but of patriotism, capitalism, and socialism, of art, education, psychology, moviemaking, golf, sex, embroidery—deserved to be torn down just for *being* doctrines, along with the guilt or intellectual inertia that had kept us beholden to them. That was the sixties for you. (Or rather the seventies, when for most people the sixties actually took place.)

But blasphemy and nihilism aren't quite the same. This rationale didn't really answer what drove me to blasphemy. Perhaps it was that blasphemy is practically an occupational requirement for your average apostate. Look at the Goliards, look at Rabelais, look at Luther. Luther actually wrote *satires.*

Nothing explained the giddy, scary laughter that blasphemy induced in me, the sense of being cut free, floating in a seductive void, with no idea where I was going and no concern about it either, a kind of high, really. As if blasphemy was my drug of choice.

There was often a kind of guilty hangover to the high, and when I came down, a shadowy misgiving. Lingering fear of damnation? Were we quite sure Hell was over? As Sean Kelly used to say: a lapsed Catholic is someone who no longer believes in Hell but knows he's still going there.

For me the issue was more personal. The real question was: what would Father Joe think of Jessica Christ? His reactions never failed to surprise me, but even he, I felt, might balk at Jessica. Was that my

whine that was beginning to creep into everyday English. It was also a half-truth, not totally answering the question. I thought it was because I hadn't absorbed the road map, couldn't remember the answer I was supposed to give. But it wasn't that.

Something was going on between us. Some kind of force was flowing between four equals, an instinctive understanding of the context, something about the music we all shared but had never quite voiced and was now coming out. It was all about rock and roll, every cut of that cow no longer sacred, fat and flatulent, with udders as dry as beef jerky, but which, way back when, we had all in some way loved, even believed in. And the characters these guys had chosen to be needed this character that had come out of me. Not that I'd chosen it—not the way they had theirs. It was more as if they had drawn it out of me. It was their character, not mine or me. And at that moment, I was very happy not to be me.

Cut! I didn't want to cut. I didn't want it to be over. That would mean I had to be Tony again. With this other guy, there was a ray of hope. Happily, it wasn't over. Whatever we'd done was good but could be better. We did it again and then once more and that was a print.

I'd tried to prepare for this. One has to be professional. I'd dipped into the "Good Book" of improv, Viola Spolin's *Improvisation for the Theater,* and read up on her son Paul Sills, cofounder of Second City. I'd solicited Second City friends and veterans for help. I'd reconsidered the many times I'd been in improv theaters and witnessed that near-miraculous process when a cast is on, the two, three, or four actors shaping a common experience whose outcome is as yet unknown, discovering, as they proceed, the others onstage and each of their uniquely skewed worldviews. The scores or hundreds of audience members also guiding the experience by reacting (or not) to the choices made by the performers. A communal journey of discovery for everyone in the theater, usually comedic though not always (a couple of nights chez The Committee at the height of Vietnam had been anything but comedic but were no less powerful and memorable for that). The whole a completely unique experi-

aim? To sever the bond with him at last? To break free of the gentle stranglehold he'd had on my soul? Or whatever souls become when you don't believe you have one anymore?

Right after *Beyond the Fringe* I couldn't go to Quarr—or even write. I was too confused and excited about my coming plunge into the world and what its fallout might be. I didn't want my new mission to weaken my bond to Father Joe. On the contrary, I wanted his approval—but without his catching on that I foresaw the possibility of a new vocation. When I did finally write to him I settled for a subtle blend of evasion and preemptive self-defense. The letter became longer and longer, more and more convoluted, veering between self-justifying apology and scholastic rationales of satire, all of them extremely unfunny.

Father Joe wrote back soothingly.

I made it into Footlights with several others, among them John Cleese and Graham Chapman. Graham and I launched a comedy team (the only time in my career as a comedian that I was the straight man). I fell in love (with a friend of Piers', of course). We heavy-petted a lot, went to Italy to maybe have sex in a tent. Didn't. Broke up.

At each stage I wrote to Father Joe.

And he wrote back soothingly.

Footlights took over my life completely. I was cast in the annual *Footlights Revue* and met my future wife, Judy Christmas, who was a big cheese in the Cambridge theater world and hung out with the likes of Trevor Nunn and Ian McKellen. I stopped going to Confession, since Confession was typically on Saturday night and Saturday night was the best night to sneak into Girton College and Judy's narrow undergraduate bed where we had serial sex until dawn. At least I wasn't committing the mortal sin of using birth control. Since it was hard to sneak *out* of Girton College on Sunday mornings, I soon stopped going to Mass as well. No problem: it gave me time for a couple dozen more orgasms.

I graduated, my degree having plunged from quasi–Double First to a 2.2, the last-from-bottom grade. At this point, my plan since time immemorial had been to return to Quarr where I would be welcomed with open arms by Father Joe and become a monk.

I was so embarrassed I couldn't set pen to paper.

Father Joe set pen to paper frequently. And soothingly.

A baby girl soon appeared—out of wedlock. There may have been rejoicing in the Vatican that another future Catholic had defeated the Satanic forces of contraception, but there wasn't much cheering in the scuzzy end of Hampstead where Judy and I were now shacking up.

I had a new partner, Nic Ullett, another alumnus of Footlights, Graham Chapman having decided to become a doctor. We appeared at clubs like the Blue Angel and Peter Cook's Establishment, now passed from his hands into those of a highly satirical Lebanese honcho named Raymond Nash, one of Christine Keeler's legion boyfriends.

At their insistence, Judy and their new granddaughter soon went to live with her parents, the Christmases. Understandably, they were not at the time evincing much good cheer at our tidings of great joy. I slunk away to Quarr to try and get my bearings in this crazy new landscape. Father Joe was far less alarmed, far more serene about the situation than I or Judy or my non-in-laws. He urged me to think only of the baby and Judy. *Be unselfish, be loving, be patient, be with her whenever you can.* The Christmases didn't agree, didn't ever want her to see me again, would ring jingle bells only if I jumped off Tower Bridge.

So, like most wayward British swains down the centuries, I went to America.

Father Joe's soothing letters over the next few months persuaded me that the right thing to do, despite the opposition, was to return to England, marry Judy, and bear my new family back to New York. It would have to be a civil ceremony, given the situation with the in-laws. Father Joe didn't care and gave it his blessing. It meant Judy and I would now be living in permanent sin. But never in all this mess had he ever used the word "sin"—or "wrong," or "guilt," or even "should have." He said he would put the three of us in his prayers. Soon he had to make it four.

Reluctant fatherhood is no way to raise children. I had as an excuse for my absences our comedy team's relative success in the U.S.—our manager insisted we were going to be "the Beatles of comedy," which kept us constantly on the road and, when in New York, out at clubs till the wee hours. Any remaining free time was needed to entertain the comedy demimonde.

Thanks to America's amber waves of gain—beer, whiskey, fries, pork, pancakes, biscuits, smoked fish, corn dogs, cheese balls, johnnycakes, apple pandowdy, deep-fried Heath-bar sandwiches with caramel sauce, etc., etc.—stretching in terrifying abundance across the fruited plain, I exploded from 170 to 250 pounds. Since my partner had the build of a stick insect, this made us officially funnier, backing into the archetype of Laurel and Hardy, Abbott and Costello, Gleason and Carney. More success meant more freedom from paternal duties; my massive fatness also guaranteed my reluctant fidelity. I have a shot of myself and Nic hosting the Advertising Awards of 1967 in which, though fatter, I look indistinguishable from my father, who in that year was fifty-six.

I had almost no contact with my parents during this time. Vaguely, from my sister's letters, I pieced together that Dad's career had collapsed entirely, in part because his traditional approach to stained glass was out of favor in the sixties, but mostly because there just wasn't much ecclesiastical work to be had. The attention of post–Vatican II Catholics was certainly not on church adornment. He'd had a couple of humiliating jobs using the engineering skills he'd acquired in the RAF; Mom had gone to work quite happily at a local chemical factory, the source of the severe pollution in my beloved River Lea. Her first purchase with her earnings had been a fridge. I can't remember exchanging more than a few words with Dad before I left for America, other than to tell him that he was a grandfather. I was so desperate and distracted at the time that I didn't really register his reaction. Only much later did I remember that it was utter delight.

Our performance schedule left time for little more than occasional mad dashes to Europe. I got to Quarr perhaps once or twice a year and then only for a day. On one of these visits, not long after emigrating, I felt compelled to confess to Father Joe that I no longer practiced the Faith. I'd been very uneasy about making this revelation, but he seemed to consider it no more worthy of note than a passing spell of bad weather.

Whenever I came to Quarr, despite my lapsarian status, some gem would always emerge from our chats which, though it would be a Christian and Benedictine gem and I no longer viewed those templates as having much relevance to my life, always had some immediate application to it.

There were frequent letters in one direction or the other. The rush I'd get from the Isle of Wight postmark and his spindly copperplate was always startling amid the constant mêlée in which I now lived, of planes, motels, and rental cars, of dates and running orders and rehearsals, of deals and meals and interviews, of New York openings and L.A. studios, the pressure for new material and—worst pressure of all—the endless rows of placid white ovals out in the darkness of clubs and concert halls and gyms, waiting to be jump-started into laughter.

That envelope from Quarr held the promise of something exquisitely out of place in this world, a flash-cut of a chestnut grove leading down to the sea; it held the prospect of an old-fashioned weekend surrounded by familiar faces that would need no help to laugh. After I read his letter, I would always feel cleansed and renewed, as if my sweaty, pendulous new body had slimmed back down, its protective layers vaporized by his warmth.

In 1968, soon after starting another menial job, Dad died suddenly. Collapsed down the stairs one cold fall morning, his dinged and dented Cornish heart rebelling at the prospect of more disappointment, signaling its surrender in his empurpled face. My little brother caught him as he fell, his last words, typically by now full of sad self-knowledge, resigned to failure and death: "Perhaps I should have taken better care of myself."

I rushed home from some standard-issue excitement in L.A. My mother seemed quite chirpy and appeared to have disbursed as little as possible on the funeral arrangements. I was angry at myself for not having been there on the spot, in a position to have done better. Most of all, I was horrified at how little I felt about my father's death.

After the funeral I went down to Quarr. It had been a while, and Father Joe was delighted to see me. Even at this mournful moment, we fell without thinking into an easy dialogue, like two old jazz musicians picking up on each other's licks. Then it came home to me why I'd found it hard to weep for Dad. Despite our rapprochement and my pride in his artistic integrity, he'd never been as much my father as Father Joe. "My Two Dads" had been a defiant adolescent formulation, inaccurate despite the truth at its core. One man was far more my dad than the other—the one I thought of all the time, with alternating love and relief, with simultaneous guilt and anger and bafflement at the way bonds between men evolve.

That was when I cried for Dad, because he must have known. He was a smart and sensitive guy. How lonely and desolate to discover that his firstborn—war-born—son had found another father. Worse still that he'd never had time to find a path to me, nor I to him. It was too late when I left home and too soon when he died.

The *Lampoon* changed everything. Slowly, subtly, but inexorably. A few months into my tenure as managing editor, I realized one night that I hadn't thought about Father Joe or Quarr for weeks. Like many things I was experiencing at the magazine, it was a new and not unpleasant feeling. Until quite recently, hardly a day passed that I didn't brood upon the road not taken, how things would have been if "upon completion of my studies" I had turned my back on it all, whatever the cost, and returned to the banks of that river of black.

A letter came from Quarr and—I couldn't remember ever doing this before—I didn't open it right away. There was an aura of obligation about it now, like a letter from home when you're away on holiday that you know is going to remind you not to swim too far from the beach. When I did open it several days later, I scanned it quickly to see if there was any cataclysmic news, but registered only the usual keywords: "God" (several times), "love," "unselfish," "Father Abbot," "community," "blessings," "wonderful," "dear" (many times)—"dear" everywhere in fact. Father Joe's usual tone, letter writing of an earlier age, chatty but formal, following a set formula of greeting, apology, news, counsel. Normally I would be waiting for that point in every letter where the formality cracked a bit and I would hear his stuttering, question-ending sentences, nothing like the full-strength Father Joe but unmistakably his voice. Which had always made me want to jump on a plane.

Now, in the initial flush of my *Lampoon* passion, learning its ropes and applying its lessons, all that crossed my mind was: *I bet I could write a great parody of a Father Joe letter.*

I almost sat down and did it. I didn't, of course. What would be the point when only I and sixty-odd monastic non-subscribers three thousand miles away would get it?

But that wasn't quite why. I'd already learned (and repeated to *The New York Times*) the routine *Lampoon* defense of even its cruelest parodies: you only parody the things you love. (We rarely went as far as admitting the next step—and the truth—that you only parody what you once loved and now loathe.) I certainly didn't loathe Father Joe and never would, but I knew I'd passed a milestone. *I have him down,* I thought, *I can do him.*

Parody is also a way of owning and containing what once you were in awe of.

For me, the *Lampoon*—and I was not alone in this—was a kind of delayed adolescence. Partly the "normal" adolescence I never had, partly the metaphorical adolescence all immigrants go through, in which the basics of work and sex and community are learned and the social reflexes and instincts that swim just below the surface of the collective consciousness are absorbed. I was doing this backward, having become a parent first, but now finally I was flexing my muscles, spreading my wings, shouldering aside the only father I'd ever acknowledged.

Small wonder blasphemy made me giddy. It was a very specific truancy, a very private rebellion. That whisper of misgiving, that shadow of fear, was neither guilt nor fear of Hell. They were natural reactions to letting go, loosing the ropes, jumping off the cliff, the momentary hesitation before you embrace independence. Blasphemy was the symbol of the larger hopes I had for the *Lampoon* and of an attitude toward other institutions than religion, in fulfillment—long delayed—of the epiphany I'd had a decade earlier in the Arts Theater.

For the first time since I'd met him, sixteen years before, I felt I didn't need Father Joe to navigate the waters ahead. There were other, more experienced sailors from whom to learn. Not just how to survive, but how to be the terror of the high seas, how to sail like the pirates of New Providence in their nimble sloops, up under the stern of some vast galleon of corrupt and bloated empire—and sink the bastards at the waterline with a single shot.

CHAPTER THIRTEEN

Pirates like . . . Michael O'Donoghue.

O'Donoghue was extraordinary, the plutonium rod at the core of the *Lampoon,* as remarkable and devastating a personality as Father Joe was pacific and self-effacing. But they had a few things in common.

Stringy chestnut ringlets surrounded a fierce white face with blood-red lips, death cell of countless Virginia Slims. He wrote with incredible precision, each perfect word set in its perfect place like a razor blade concealed in a mouthwatering *amuse-gueule.* He had a unique gift for drawing humor from things that normally make people recoil. He was the funniest of the group; laughter followed him everywhere. But yuks didn't do it for O'Donoghue; making people laugh, he said, "is the lowest form of humor."

Within weeks of my arriving at the *Lampoon*—to my utter surprise—we hit it off. We began collecting material for the *Lampoon*'s first comedy album, to be called *Radio Dinner.* For economic (and ecological) reasons, Judy and the girls were now ensconced in an ancient stone house near the Delaware Valley which I'd bought several years earlier when my paycheck—and I—were considerably fatter.

It was a bus ride of several hours. As a New York base, O'D offered me a couch in his vast drafty SoHo loft. It was packed with bits of late Victoriana that had odd or disturbing purposes: a gout stool, mannequin limbs, a silver grape-peeler, deceased dolls, stuffed animals, things that might be shrunken heads or long-dead rodents, sinister daguerreotypes, and everywhere card files, each card containing a comic haiku of exquisite horribleness.

He had a small-town background—Rochester, New York—and a similarly humdrum education, but he soaked up crucial phrases and ideas from countless sources: Kafka, matchbook covers, old copies of *Life,* the original *Nosferatu, The Book of Common Prayer,* flotsam and jetsam of every subculture, violently juxtaposing them to produce a poetry of humor. He spoke in brittle, slashing phrases that gave new vigor to the cliché "verbal fencing": he really did thrust and cut and lunge, and his word choices had the sharpness of fine steel. You parried at your peril. Attack was the only way to keep up with him.

I soon realized that the incessant verbal contest was teaching me to think and talk and write in American. It was sharper, harder, quicker to the punch than the more oblique forms I'd grown up with: "You're circumlocuting again, Hendra. I believe 'circumlocution' means removing the foreskin from an otherwise healthy joke?"

What he saw in me I wasn't sure. I was a rarity in his circle, the downtown Velvet Underground crowd: a man his age with kids. Kids and parents intrigued O'Donoghue mightily. It drove his strongest work—like *The Vietnamese Baby Book,* which he did for my first issue: a saccharine-sweet baby-blue memento of baby's first year, except the baby was one of those machine-gunned at My Lai. Or his *SNL* character Mr. Mike, the ultimate *loco* in *loco parentis.*

In the spring of 1972 we produced *Radio Dinner,* which contained, to our knowledge, the first parodies of folk and rock icons Bob Dylan, Joan Baez, and John Lennon. Of these, Lennon was far and away the most sacred. When I first heard of O'D's intention to do a Lennon parody (which he called "Magical Misery Tour"), it actually gave me pause. "Magical Misery Tour," a montage piece in the style of "Yellow Submarine," had appeared in the magazine. Parodying Lennon on an album—his medium—was quite another matter.

I had no qualms about Lennon's being too sacred—not after hanging out with O'D for the better part of a year—but I wondered whether attacking the most loved and admired rock singer on the planet mightn't blow up in our faces. (I thought this privately; articulating it to O'D I would risk being pinned to the woodwork like a bug.)

The Lennon parody was an object lesson in O'D's MO. He had no interest in the fallout from it; the more furious the reaction, the better, even if people threatened to kill us. (Someone actually did try to blow us up while we were recording the album, by sending us a parcel of unstable dynamite. So this wasn't out of the question.)

The limitless love and respect people accorded Lennon were what attracted O'D to his target. It wasn't malice that drove him, though many people thought it was, but rather a fascination with the absolute, with pushing things far, far beyond all normal, reasonable limits into a void where sacredness, veneration, respect, decency, any kind of social norm would not register, had no measurement or meaning. He was a friend of that void. There was something mystical about his attraction to it. If he had any belief system at all, it was that there existed a mirror image of the sacred, an absolute not-sacredness which he was always striving to attain and to improve his ability to attain. He had total satirical *contemptus mundi.*

He had no interest in Catholicism (which presumably was somewhere in his Celtic family tree), but this single-mindedness struck me as ferociously Catholic. I was reminded of those fierce Spanish saints that had terrified me as a teenager.

Lennon was tough, himself no slouch in the satire department. "A Day in the Life" was one the most unforgettable musical compositions I'd heard since *The Rite of Spring.* But he'd exposed his flank. In 1971, deep into primal scream therapy, he'd given a series of interviews to *Rolling Stone* in which he ranted with primal frankness about his genius, his childhood, his hatred for his fellow Beatles (and the Stones), his role in history, and much more good stuff.

For *Rolling Stone* these were the Words made flesh. They ran the interviews verbatim. All O'D had to do was take the choicest bits and arrange them into verses, and we had our lyrics. Music? Enter an old *Lampoon* hand, Chris Cerf, who set them to a driving "Imagine"-style piano accompaniment. Perfect. Now all we needed was a singer.

Our new young vocal genius Christopher Guest opted out; it was not his thing. There were those who could do it but were nervous about professional retribution. We put off recording it again and again, desperate to find the right voice, until we finally ran out of studio time. Came the night when we either had to do it or dump it. O'D had the vocal gifts of your average bivalve. So it had to be me.

Though I'd sung in the comedy act, I hadn't the slightest talent for impressions. But when I got into the booth and Cerf went into his piano intro, something took me over. A voice I barely recognized, but which sounded a lot like Lennon's, began pouring out of me, screaming out his words in a ferocious tumble.

It wasn't me. It was some superior—or inferior—being, an angel or a dybbuk. It felt like being possessed. For the hour or so it took to record, I dwelt in O'D's dimension of not-sacredness, someone else entirely, someone without limits or boundaries, transfigured into a para-Lennon. It was glorious, hilarious, and as close to a mystical experience as anything I'd ever had at Quarr.

Radio Dinner was a success and, according to the powers that be, helped the magazine significantly in the areas of advertising and circulation. They wanted another album—and more of those rock parodies, please.

In truth neither O'D nor I was very conversant with rock music or rock lyrics. Sean Kelly, however, was a master of the form. Live albums were all the rage at the time, so he and I put together an album called *Lemmings,* a full-scale parody of Woodstock and its icons, with a few non-Woodstock icons (like Jagger) thrown in. We cast Chevy Chase, John Belushi, and Christopher Guest in their first major stage roles in the show, which was to have a limited run at the Village Gate for the purposes of recording. But even in previews we were turning away hundreds of people. The *Times* and *The New Yorker* came to the opening night and gave us money reviews. We decided to extend the run beyond recording, and before we knew it we had another hit album—and an Off-Broadway smash.

But I was missing the magazine. That sleek, supple monster inside whose opaque folds and curves flashed constant arcs of brilliance; which—as Harold Ross once said of *The New Yorker*—"went down in the elevator at 5 P.M." to split into smaller buzzing, sizzling organisms, sliding into the night, across the city, continuing to probe and play and conceive and laugh at the dazzling connections to be made between wildly disparate terminals, the fun to be had at the expense of greed, corruption, hypocrisy, power, and stupidity.

No genre of successful creative effort I'd been involved in to date—no sketch that brought the house down, no well-reviewed TV show, no record on the charts, no theatrical event that got standing ovations—ever gave me as much satisfaction as the heft in my hands of a new issue of the magazine, fresh from the printer's. Product of that brilliant monster, it both represented the goal I'd embraced in the lobby of the Arts Theater and fulfilled the need for community I'd felt all my life. It wasn't the community I'd envisaged, exactly—for one thing, it was on the banks of a river of yuks—but I was happy to dedicate the rest of my life to it.

Visits to Quarr settled down to a pattern which would continue throughout the decade: one every year or so. A trickle of letters continued, but more to me than from me. It was becoming very much a driven-male-in-his-thirties/aged-parent relationship. Swamped as my brain was with projects, premises, concepts, and absorbing the information to feed them with rapidly evolving skills and habits of perception—not to mention having to survive the murderous politics of any successful magazine—I had entered the obligatory phase of my love for Father Joe. The only difference from a normal parent-offspring modus vivendi was that there was never a breath from him of "you never come, you never write." He remained as serene as ever, as changeless.

What had changed was that these qualities were no longer virtues in my world. Serenity to Manhattanites is likely to be interpreted as catatonia, changelessness as cluelessness, and both as indicative of a background in the boonies. A city whose true coat of arms is a wrecking ball rampant on a field of Sheetrock has zero patience for the monastic virtues. This toxin had entered my bloodstream.

Two visits in particular brought this home. On the first, I had made a flying detour to Quarr in the process of tearing through London promoting the *Lemmings* album (half of whose targets were British).

I had a pleasant enough chat with Father Joe, said hi to Dom Aelred, ate lunch. As I hurried away down the driveway, late for the ferry, I was suffused with an unfamiliar emotion: relief. It disturbed me enough that I fought it down, deeply ashamed, but the feeling was strong and real.

For almost twenty years, after every visit I'd made to the abbey I would turn as the Portsmouth ferry headed out into the Solent, look back for that funny round elf-hat spire sticking out of the oaks, and say a silent good-bye. Often, in recent years, with a twinge of regret.

This time I felt nothing. My silent good-bye brought no twinge of anything—except that I suddenly found the spire dated and ludicrous. What on earth were the lines of Cordoba or Byzantium, whatever the hell it was, doing on the Isle of Wight? The era it came from, the decrepitude of Edward VII, was the most culturally bankrupt period in recent British history. Wherever had my affection for it come from? *Ugly, man. One ugly church.* As if depressed and diminished by my thoughts, the spire slid quickly behind the trees.

The second time was worse. Father Joe's charisma, his funny tic-ridden face and body language were still there, but that was all that was left of Quarr's charm. His world, bounded by pink and yellow brick walls, hemmed in by the greater walls of history that loomed around the place, depressed me to no end. Quarr seemed small, irrelevant, and insular, its activities futile. Again I felt relief as the taxi sped toward the ferry, but this time I made no effort to resist it, happy to be returning to my exciting, stimulating, fulfilling modern life. When the ferry hit open water, I didn't even turn to seek out the lumpy spire. The ferry had a bar now, and I needed a drink.

Nineteen seventy-four was our golden year. Monthly circulation hovered just under a million. O'Donoghue, inspired by *Lemmings,* began the *NatLamp Radio Hour,* which also starred Guest, Chevy, and Belushi. When O'D quit, Belushi took it over, bringing into the cast Gilda Radner, Bill Murray, and others—in effect, with himself and Chevy, assembling the bulk of *Saturday Night Live*'s first cast.

There were a few trifling clouds in the sky. Nixon's resignation turned out to be a bit of a letdown. In the 1972 election we'd run an item about a new PAC, Satirists for Nixon-Agnew, with the slogan "Keep them in office and us in business." Now we realized it hadn't been entirely a joke. We'd actually achieved our goal. We'd bitten the hand that fed us. Were things really going to get better? God forbid.

A desire for change had always been implicit in the savagery of the *Lampoon*'s MO, though the editors would have died rather than admit so straightforward an emotion. Not change for its own sake, nor for missionary goals. We only wanted to save the world from people who wanted to save the world. The one thing we did believe was that we could accomplish this; our cynicism was still in its first sweet innocence.

Now a pair of criminals—one a convicted felon—had been removed from the White House. The military and its vile war had been properly defeated, the stranglehold of Big Money on the affairs of the nation appeared to have been loosened. And we appeared to have been part of it. Many years later Carl Bernstein told me that not only was he a huge fan of the magazine, but that "if it hadn't been for the *National Lampoon,* Nixon would never have resigned." He was only half joking.

The savagery mellowed. There were many jokes about food that year. There was more unalloyed comedy—a lot of it about animals, notably the best known cover we ever ran: a cute mongrel with a huge .44 Magnum in his ear and the legend "If You Don't Buy This Magazine We'll Kill This Dog."

The group had mellowed too. The magazine was approaching its fifth year, its circulation higher than that of most magazines that could be regarded as competitors (such as *Esquire*). We had our chops down. We were no longer brash new kids on the block. A subtle shift was evolving, both conceptually and editorially, toward restraint, a savoring of, a playing with absurdity rather than ripping it to shreds. There was every expectation that we could become—were already—an institution, the humor magazine of America.

These dreams were never fulfilled. In its fifth year, the magazine was convulsed by an internal buyout agreement which led to the departure—several million dollars richer—of one of the founders. Kelly and I became coeditors and ran the magazine for the next three years.

We had serious competition now from the show we had in several ways helped spawn: *Saturday Night Live.* In much the same way the English TV hit *That Was the Week That Was* had taken the wind out of *Beyond the Fringe*'s satirical sails, *SNL* gave viewers a version of *Lampoon* attitude—if not its content—each week for nothing. It was bound to hurt circulation. Eventually we held steady at about three quarters of a million, still very respectable for a general-interest magazine in a bear market.

In 1978 the success of *Animal House* (at the time, the biggest-grossing comedy in Hollywood history) convulsed the magazine yet again. Though the editors saw the movie as a mainstream *Lampoon* satire of American higher education (the Nixonian Dean Wormer; the Young Republicans of Omega Theta Pi; its military; the ROTC; and Neidermeyer, the ROTC's psychotic student-Patton, all brought low by the Deltas' anarchic sixties insurgency), its satirical force was largely ignored by reviewers. The film was lumped with the mid-seventies revision of the fifties and pre-assassination sixties as a better and "more innocent" era (a form of propaganda best expressed by *Happy Days*). In conventional cinematic wisdom, *Animal House* went down as the first "gross" movie.

Eyeing the cool millions "grossness" was raking in each week, management demanded more of the same in the magazine. Kelly and I refused. Another editor, P. J. O'Rourke, was happy to oblige. He became editor in chief, the first person in the history of the magazine to arrogate the title to himself. In two short years, between 1979 and 1981, he turned a multimedia operation of phenomenal breadth and talent, capable of producing genuine comedy classics, into a monthly catalog of masturbatory, automotive, and racist fantasies, defanging the magazine completely and presiding over a collapse in circulation from which it never recovered.

Now, on this sad Santa Monica evening, the black saltwater fields beyond the deck stretching away to eternal night, well and truly into the dark decade Peggy Noonan would soon preposterously dub "Morning in America," I realized what others had no doubt realized years before: the long moment of skepticism and sanity in America had come to an end.

The Big Chill, they called it—a movie inspired by the death of Doug Kenney, one of the *Lampoon*'s cofounders. Or was it Belushi's death? Or Lennon's? Death was everywhere.

I ought to have known. Father Joe had drummed it into me long ago. The *Lampoon,* that raucous, riotous brotherhood, and its laughter, the demented force that bound us for one glorious nanosecond of truth, would pass, as all things must, like grass before the wind.

I found some of The Band's vodka. I gulped it to keep the elevator on my floor, to hold it from plunging down into the chasm which opened on so many nights now but which I could ignore for a while with enough to drink or snort.

My marriage was in ruins—if it had ever been constructed

enough to fall into ruins. My beautiful, gifted wife, whom I knew from the start I hadn't loved, nor she me, except she was too polite to say so, was roaming the rubble, working at unfulfilling jobs, her promise and talent long shelved and forgotten. And it was all my doing.

Once when the kids were small we'd gone to see a hypnotist somewhere in L.A. and she'd wound up onstage as a volunteer. The guy was a sadist, putting his subjects under, then telling them they were animals or working at bizarre jobs. The crowd loved their antics, the more so because none of them remembered what they'd done when he brought them round. He hypnotized Judy and told her she was a ballet dancer. (A previous woman subject had brought the house down with her "Dying Swan.")

Judy went into an ethereal pas de deux with an imaginary partner, sweeping across the stage, her leaps and pirouettes so intense and elegant that the house was riveted. You could hear a pin drop in that theater, and there must have been a thousand people in it. What magnetism she had, what stage presence she could have commanded if she'd ever had the time and freedom to train as the actress she'd wanted to be . . .

The hypnotist was furious. He'd lost the crowd completely. He ran after her as she floated around the stage, the audience beginning to titter—but at him. Eventually he caught her and brought her out and tried to get a round of applause as if she were just another clown. The theater barely responded. The people around me were silent; they knew they'd seen something special and beautiful.

Every guy who was anyone in Cambridge theater had wanted her. Not just because she was beautiful, but because they all knew she had a big future. I wanted to love her; who wouldn't when having her with you made you look so great? But I didn't really, and she didn't really; it was one of those affairs that are approved and defined by others. When Cambridge ended, there was nothing left to keep us together, but by then it was too late, a sweet little girl was on the way—and then another—whom for most of their childhoods I largely ignored and certainly resented because I had to be a father, which prevented me from fucking as many hippie chicks as everyone else appeared to be.

Be unselfish with her, Tony dear, his letters always said. Not "don't be selfish," but "be unselfish." *I know you will be unselfish with her and your beautiful little girls.*

No father could have been more selfish—treating his family like props, possessions, inconveniences, mostly forgetting them completely in his precious mission to save the world through laughter.

The airheaded heathens in whose company I passed my time had more morals. Sure, they exploited each other, sure, they unwittingly caused pain, but most were blindly seeking good, boring their way like moles up through the dirt to the light. Figuring out on their own that love and peace were the only worthwhile currencies in life.

Whereas I who had been given the keys to the kingdom, had held the pearl of great price, had dropped them in the mud, ground them in with my heel, and headed downtown to score.

What had happened to that far-off boy, murmuring his ancient Latin words, humming his ancient music, full of hope, hankering for the infinite, all agog for sanctity? Yes, he was gullible and naïve, yes, what he thought were ecstasy and despair and faith and God were just neurons firing in his synapses, just proteins coursing through his brain, yes, his beliefs were phallic fantasies, anthropomorphic projections, ancient archetypes implanted in his psyche over centuries, whatever the theory was this week; but he'd been a better, sweeter soul. He wasn't what I'd become. Not at all. He was someone else entirely, who had died tragically young.

Far away across the Rockies, the *tramonto,* across drowsy, sleeping states, across the jagged teeth of my hometown, across that other eternal night of an ocean—thousands upon thousands of miles away—was the man who once had been the center of my world, my calm harbor, my sheltering wing. A tiny lighthouse on a tiny island, blinking his faith into the night. Here comes the beam again, sweeping round, a pinprick in the darkness, sending out its simple tiny message. *Love. Love. Nothing but love.* There, now it's gone again.

I had failed him. I had failed my vocation. I had failed my family.

I had failed, period. I had nothing of worth. No hope, no faith, no God, no intellectual resources, no desire to use them if I had. It was all gone forever, as irretrievable as the wind.

I fingered the bottle of Valium. I hated downers. They made me lose control of my body and therefore of my heart. I had to stay alert, sometimes awake all night, to stop the only thing Dad bequeathed me, his lousy heart, from sneaking up and murdering me too. If I was going to die, I had to be in control.

I'd never seen Valium before. The pills were rounded yellow triangles. Tiny trinities the color of cowardice.

I shook a dozen or so into my hand. How many would it take? I swigged a mouthful of vodka and tossed down . . . two.

I knew that wouldn't be enough, but I couldn't quite bring myself to do them all at once. Okay, two more. Hit the vodka.

I stared out at the dark Pacific. Was I looking at Japan or New Zealand? Have to look it up tomorrow.

What tomorrow?

Not even drowsy. Fuck it, take another. Five now. That should do it.

What if there was a Hell? Was it too late to get a stomach pump? Did they bring it with them? How big was a stomach pump?

Was I doing anything that merited Hell? I'd confessed, sort of. At least to myself or to . . . whatever. This was a pretty tough penance. Say three Hail Marys and kill yourself.

What I was doing was fine and worthy. Saving the world from myself. Get it over with.

I drained the vodka bottle, raised the half-dozen remaining pills in my hand slowly to my lips, composed myself for death, closed my eyes as if in prayer . . .

And fell asleep.

I woke twelve hours later. I ought to have had the hangover of all time, or at least a skull-cracking headache, but I had neither—as far as I could tell. Mind and body were utterly numb. Like frostbite all over. I had no identity, no self I could detect. I wasn't relieved to be alive. I wasn't disappointed not to be dead. Just—nothing.

I knew only that I would try again someday soon. And next time I wouldn't wake up. Not now that I'd had some practice.

I got up and drove to the location. I was hours late for my call but it was the first day of shooting and no one had noticed.

I don't remember which scene it was. I think it was in the limo or perhaps it was the coffee shop. The director explained the rules. They were terrifying. All I needed to know was the "road map" of the scene—a couple of sentences outlining what had to be accomplished during the three minutes or so it would run. It was up to me to improvise the lines. They could be whatever I liked. Mundane or not, funny or not, just so long as they made the scene clear.

I had no background in improv. In the sixties I'd sat in on a session or two at Second City in Chicago and its more radical offshoot The Committee in San Francisco, but always cheated, using lines from existing material. I'd been in awe while directing Belushi and Chevy and Chris Guest in *Lemmings* at how the words just flowed out of them and fit together and weren't banal blather either, but hilarious stuff, as funny as anything you could write and rehearse.

There were the other actors now in their fright wigs, with—collectively—a couple of decades of improvisation under their belts. "Intimidated" does not begin to cover the way I felt. I was a complete and utter fraud. I couldn't do this. If I'd had any feelings at all inside me, instead of a quart of whatever vodka and Valia become after a night of interaction, I would've just balked right there and said "I can't do this" and gone back to New York with my tail between my legs and a few dollars poorer but with my pride intact. But who cared about pride anymore?

Action! They were in character! They were brilliant! None of them was British, but they were doing flawless Brit accents. And funny. Understated, super-real, hilarious. Normally I would've been helpless with laughter. But I had no intention of laughing ever again.

One of them asked me something and I heard a voice replying. It was sort of like mine but with a touch of the nasal middle-class

ence which could happen only at one time, in one place, with one collection of individuals.

The advice I'd gotten from every source, if I wanted to arrive at a similar apotheosis, was: listen. Listen at every level: to the words, the emotions, the intent of the other or others. Be completely open to them, bring nothing preconceived or prepared to the moment. Listen and then speak only to what you've heard. Do that, and you can't go wrong. Improv is not just a means to entertain, it's also a process that is an end in itself, a way of knowing, of grasping the nature of another, the reality of the other's existence, an aspect of the truth of the matter under discussion which you thought you knew but didn't until this moment.

Which is also why a successful improv is exhilarating, uplifting, enlightening, renewing.

That first night after we wrapped I did feel rather exhilarated and uplifted—if not yet enlightened and renewed. There'd been only two short scenes and my role was pretty secondary, but something remarkable had happened both times, and that simple advice had done it: listen.

As I pondered this, a memory was suddenly standing in the far shadows of my mind: hadn't Father Joe twenty or more years ago said an almost identical thing?

The only way to know God, the only way to know the other, is to listen. Listening is reaching out into that unknown other self, surmounting your walls and theirs; listening is the beginning of understanding, the first exercise of love.

None of us listen enough, do we, dear? We only listen to a fraction of what people say. It's a wonderfully useful thing to do. You almost always hear something you didn't expect.

We must listen because we are so often wrong in our certainties. When we pass a motion in the chaotic debating chamber of our heads, it's never completely right, or even, most of the time, half right. The only way to edge closer to the truth is to listen with complete openness, bringing to the process no preconceptions, nothing prepared.

No question that there were startling parallels between what the fathers of improv and Father Joe had to say. Between Second City and the City of God.

How seldom, in fact, did I listen. I brought to almost every encounter with another human some preconception of people or issues, none-too-subtly intent on getting mine out before the other guy. New York was a city of non-listeners.

Long years now since something Father Joe had said had fit so immediately and precisely into my life. Perhaps I was ignoring a great resource, a resource to whom I'd once turned at every opportunity but to whom I had, quite simply, stopped listening.

The next day of shooting was the same, and the next. The understanding didn't falter, the listening and the flow continued, the work began to have bulk and shape. More and more as it proceeded, the movie rekindled my faith in the precious stuff of laughter, in the miraculous manner in which it was generated and the unpromising landscapes from which it could be mined—so long as you were willing to listen. My urgent need to off myself became less urgent, was postponed and, in the weeks that followed, quite forgotten.

So I suppose I can say—in a way that others who've claimed the same perhaps can't—that rock and roll saved my life. At least rock and roll as played by Spinal Tap.

CHAPTER FOURTEEN

It sounds to me, dear, as if your satirist is a bit like a monk. They both take a rather dim view of the world, and both try to do something about it."

"Thank you, Father Joe! I think I knew that once, but I'd forgotten. *Contemptus mundi.* We both have contempt for the world."

"You p-p-persist in your error, my son. *Contemptus* does not mean 'contempt.' It means 'detachment.' Are you detached from the things you satirize?"

"I am now. I'm unemployed."

It was two weeks before Easter 1984, a year of some significance to the satirist. We were back under the mighty Benedictine oaks of Quarr, where we'd walked when I was young and he was not yet old. The gray-green leaf clusters were beginning to sprinkle the massive limbs and trunks of the trees, beneath whose rugged skin I still fancied I could see huge muscles slowly flexing. The oaks formed gnarled, unstately arches through which the sullen Solent heaved, gray, blue-gray, charcoal gray, the colors of school uniforms.

The face was much the same, long and raw, deeply creased but still unwrinkled. Father Joe never seemed to change physically or in any other way. When I'd first met him I couldn't peg his age, and if this had been my first visit I still wouldn't have been able to. Fifty? Eighty? (He was seventy-five.) He walked with a slight stiffness, his sandaled feet still as flat and turned out as a character in Astérix comics. When I'd arrived I'd told him this. He chortled.

"I love Astérix! Can't get enough of Astérix!"

"You read comics at Quarr now?"

"Good heavens, these days we have a hi-fi. With h-h-headphones."

That drew me to his ears, which had grown as old men's do—or do old men shrink everywhere but their ears? Anyway, they were Dumbo-sized jobs by now, with lobes like mud flaps.

It was almost four years since I'd seen him—the longest Joe-less period ever. In the second half of the seventies, I'd started to visit Quarr more regularly again—once a year or so. For some reason the discomfort of the early *Lampoon* years had passed. There was an element of filial duty to these visits, but as New York, off life support, plunged into bicoastal wildness and my post-*Lampoon* freelancing took off—these two things usually blending in the bathroom of Elaine's and involving hundred-dollar bills—Father Joe also became my counterintuitive little secret, something no one else could boast. Others had to buy their self-improvement in a book. I had, in the flesh, my very own Maharishi, Lao-tzu, Mr. Natural.

We'd take a pleasant walk, having very much the same conversation every time. It proceeded on parallel paths rather than really connecting. I would enumerate and explain my various projects, this book or that TV special, a movie I was writing in Paris, plans for a new humor magazine. I never knew how much he understood or absorbed of all this, but I suspected it didn't matter: I figured he was content to hear the distant Muzak of my activity.

On his side—though he knew how hostile or apathetic I was about the Church by now—he'd chatter on about his old friend God, quite unself-consciously, not at all in that defensive, half-missionary tone the pious adopt when speaking to the impious. I didn't find it grating as I once had. But nor did I absorb all of what he was saying. It was just soothing and cleansing to be around him. I might be of the world, but there's nothing to beat a hefty hit of monastic peace. We had reached a certain stasis, neither advancing nor regressing, saint and cynic side by side.

On this visit, though, it wasn't stasis or comfy chats I was looking for. I needed something that I could get nowhere else, least of all in New York. A Confessor. A shrink who knew right from wrong: one who would talk while I listened.

I had a lot to get off my chest. I wanted advice, I wanted comfort, I wanted guidance, I wanted . . . I wasn't quite sure what. I planned to stay as long as necessary.

The proximate cause of the visit was my latest enterprise—a British comedy series called *Spitting Image.*

It's a pretty good rule of thumb in showbiz, as in marriage and foreign policy, that you keep making the same mistakes again and again. Trouble is, you never realize it's the same mistake until you've well and truly made it.

While still at the *Lampoon* I'd come across a pair of brilliant British caricaturists named Roger Law and Peter Fluck. (They called themselves "Luck and Flaw," to further confuse employers already confused by the treacherous name "Fluck.") Their trademark was sculpting from Plasticine (a British kiddie product rather like Silly Putty) brutally funny life-sized caricatures of the great and famous, which they then costumed, propped, placed in outrageous environments, and photographed.

I hired them to do some work for the *Lampoon* and we became fast friends. They were both huge guys, especially Law, who looked like a Cornish pirate, topping six foot five and twenty stone (280 pounds), a red bandanna permanently enclosing his balding monastic pate.

They were working-class lads who had grown up in the Fens around Cambridge, met while attending art school there, and made extra money serving tables in—of all places—St. John's College. At some point they had probably served me my dinner or cleared it away. Though I was just as much a prole as he, Rog would frequently refer to me, with much tugging of nonexistent forelock, as "the young master."

After I left the *Lampoon* we began talking about making their caricatures into life-sized puppets that could move and talk and perhaps star in a TV series. The Muppets were all the rage on both sides of the Atlantic, so this was not that far-fetched. Thanks to Jim Henson, the technology existed to make large puppets talk and move on camera. I began paying regular visits back to the U.K. to help develop the project, which by the early eighties—with the infusion of some capital from pioneer tech entrepreneur Sir Clive Sinclair and the recruitment of a hot young TV comedy producer named John Lloyd—was looking feasible.

I'd first met Lloyd when he was producing the hit BBC2 series *Not the Nine O'Clock News.* He broke the ice by confessing that he'd stolen the word "Not" from me (the first known use of this hoary parody prefix having been *Not The New York Times*). Lloyd was also an alumnus of Cambridge Footlights, so we had that link as well. He was thirteen years younger than I (and Rog and Pete), he already had a British Academy Award, he was the golden boy of British TV comedy, and he was fascinated by the puppets. He looked like the right man to get our show off the ground.

"You've never told me much about satire. How does it work?"

"Good question. First of all, it's cruel and unfair. It hurts people and it's supposed to. You take on the coloring of your target's thoughts and beliefs and exaggerate them mercilessly. But you can't just do it arbitrarily, without knowing them. You have to be inside his skin. Or, in the case of Maggie Thatcher, her hide."

“Good heavens. It sounds horrible.”

“It’s not a pretty business.”

He walked thoughtfully for a dozen paces. Much twitching of lips and eyebrows. Setting lobes aflutter.

“Tony dear, by ‘inside’ Mrs. Thatcher’s, er, ‘hide,’ do you mean that you’re thinking the way she does?”

“Part of you is, yes.”

“And that would be the unpleasant or unkind side of her. The side you want to criticize with your satire?”

“Absolutely.”

“So that would mean that you have an unpleasant or unkind side too?”

“Well, er . . . no, not necessarily.”

How had we got here so fast? I was supposed to be the expert.

“It’s a question of mimesis,” I explained. “You’re just mimicking her cruelty or hypocrisy or whatever. It’s like a kid walking behind an old man, copying his limp.”

“You don’t mean that satire is childish, of course.”

“Nope. It’s serious grown-up business. I think of it as a branch of journalism. The inspired lie that’s closer to the truth than any number of carefully researched facts.”

“I’m sorry, dear—did you say satire was a lie?”

“Only in the sense that all art is fabrication.”

He walked for some distance, head down, concern in his busy brows, thinking this over. The silence between us grew so long that I was on the brink of saying something, when he stopped.

“You don’t think, dear, that if you do a great deal of, er, mimicking cruel or hypocritical people, it won’t have a bad effect on you eventually?”

“Satirists do have a way of turning into what they satirize. But it’s a risk I’m willing to take—if you can bring the bastards down.”

“Does satire often ‘bring the bastards down’?”

“Alas, no.”

* * *

The year before, back in the United States, there'd been more ominous signs of a sea change. *Newsweek* for the first time put parody on its cover, in the shape of Sean Kelly, an actor named Alfred Gingold who'd written a best-selling parody of the L.L. Bean catalog, and me. Being on the cover was dandy, but the cover story was rather negative, suggesting that parody was something of a cultural parasite—a view I didn't entirely disagree with, if its targets were trivial and the parody was of style, not substance. Sean and I made that point by immediately publishing a parody at Ballantine called *Not the Bible,* which included texts previously unknown to biblical scholars such as "Christ—The Early Years." In fact it was less a parody than a frontal satirical assault on Christ-free Pharisees like Messrs. Falwell, Bakker, and Robertson; nonetheless it was the Cardinal Archbishop of Boston who stood up for Jesus. His Eminence gave *Not the Bible* a loud *non imprimatur* and asked that it be taken off sale. Rather than nail the prissy Prince of the Church to the First Amendment, Ballantine stopped shipping the book. The scrofulous boneheads from the Knights of Columbus and the Catholic League of Decency—whom Sean and I had held at bay ten years earlier—were now calling the shots.

Things had to be better in the U.K., given its tradition of irreverence and experimentation, *That Was the Week That Was* and *Monty Python* to name but two. Plus they had a genuine left-wing opposition, not like our mildewed and compromised Democrats. Here some truth could be told to power, some real pain inflicted on the high and mighty.

In reality the Labour Party was being led by the doddering Michael Foot, who made Fritz Mondale look like Rambo. And Ronnie's girl Maggie, with the miners and the Malvinas under her belt, was at the zenith of her power. Rog and Pete and I were also ignorant of a subtler problem, one to which the antennae of the politically adroit and superambitious Lloyd were acutely tuned. There'd been a long history of tension between politicians and broadcast authorities (especially the BBC) over the airing of political satire on British TV; it went all the way back to *TW3* two decades earlier. There was plenty of experience on both sides of how to "deal with" political satire. Lloyd had already navigated these shoals with *Not the Nine O'Clock News.*

We made an excellent deal at Central TV (the arm of ITV in Birmingham) with ample creative legroom, mainly because Central's director, Charles Denton, was politically in our camp. But for those very reasons we were all going to be watched like hawks by the far more conservative ITV Board.

"You seem very worried about the effect satire has on the satirist, Father Joe."

"Well, this business of mimicking evil . . . But I suppose you're not *committing* it in any way. I think St. Augustine applies here. In his *Confessions* he admits to sin, to a knowledge of sin, even a longing for it. We all have evil in us. To admit it is essential. Perhaps your satire is a way to admit the evil in you without giving in to it."

"That's comforting. Still, I'm more interested in the effect on my targets, of changing people's perception of those in power."

"Can you give me some examples?"

"For *Beyond the Fringe*: the Tories, the Church of England, the romanticizers of World War II. For Voltaire: the Jesuits. The U.S. military for Stanley Kubrick."

"So the point of satire is to change the way people think about the Tories or the Jesuits or American military men?"

"There is usually a certain Us-Them attitude. Satire is one weapon the powerless have against the powerful. Or the poor against the rich. Or the young against the old."

"Satire always divides people up into two groups?"

"I suppose that's often its dynamic, yes."

"Is that a good thing?"

"It's the way the world works, Father Joe. People think in teams. We're good, you're evil; we're smart, you're dumb; we're upper-crust, you're vulgar. I think most humor works that way. Even the most basic jokes. The English tell Irish jokes. In America the most notorious jokes are Polish jokes, because the Poles have been stereotyped as stupid."

"Tell me a Polish joke."

"Okay. What has an IQ of two hundred twelve?"

"I don't know, dear."

"Warsaw."

Father Joe gazed at me expectantly.

"Is there a joke coming?"

"That's it. The entire city of Warsaw has a combined IQ of two hundred twelve."

"Oh. But the Poles are a rather sensitive people, aren't they? Tragic and poetic and long-suffering. Look at Chopin. Or even the Holy Father."

"Okay, Chopin and John Paul the Second are not Polish jokes. But the dynamic holds for jokes about Tories. Or blondes. Or the French."

Father Joe's eyes brightened.

"Tell me a joke about blondes."

"You display immodest eagerness, Father."

"I like blondes."

I told him a fairly clean blonde joke.

He didn't get it. I explained about dumb blondes. He still looked puzzled.

"To say people are stupid when they're not—isn't that a little cruel?"

"I think it's basically harmless, really, a safety valve—letting off ethnic or sexual tensions."

"I see what you mean."

We walked quite a way in silence. He was frowning now, pursed lips pouting and unpouting with the regularity of a diaphragm.

"You see, dear—I think there are two types of people in the world. Those who divide the world up into two kinds of people . . . and those who don't."

* * *

One thing I'd told nobody was that I badly wanted to come home to England. Come home at the top of my game with an original and controversial hit, bringing together everything I'd learned in the U.S. and all the wit and flair and innovation of British TV. British TV, after all, was the best in the world. British TV guys told us so all the time.

Even if it failed I wouldn't mind, so long as we went down in a blaze of glory. That ought to get me started in my new base, the place I belonged, where I really spoke the language, which didn't feel like a foreign land the way the U.S. was beginning to. Dear old England, land of the creatively free, home of the artistically brave.

And yet, and yet . . . in truth I had little deep feeling for England. I'd always felt like an outsider growing up, which was probably why I split at the first opportunity. I was aware too that I was no longer, in a cultural sense, very English. An entire generation which was being born as I was leaving had grown to adulthood. They had innumerable points of reference, memories of things great and small I couldn't tap into at the reflex level you have to if you want to make people laugh.

The country looked different from the place I'd been young in, whether it was the hideous new motorways carving up the lovely countryside or the Cockney accent emerging from an exquisite Asian face. Complaining about the one, being delighted by the other, meant nothing to the English; these things were deeply woven by now into the fabric of normality, beyond unremarkable. That I noticed them only re-marked me—as an outsider.

Just as the teenage monk had, I was going in exactly the opposite direction from my contemporaries. The crowd streaming by me on either side—British performers, writers, directors, producers, musicians, agents—couldn't wait to get to the U.S., to New York, or, better, L.A., hungry for its wealth and potential for self-extension, if possible the ultimate self-extension of stardom.

So I was swimming against the tide. So what? They could have

New York and L.A. I wanted the U.K. I had not been this up about a project since I joined the *Lampoon.* Rog and Pete were two of my closest friends and easily the funniest. They thought I was brilliant. Lloyd had the Midas touch.

A down-and-dirty pilot we'd done had floored everybody who'd seen it. This was the one. A TV show you wouldn't have to apologize for behind its back. On the contrary, the funniest, hardest-hitting TV show ever produced.

Same mistake. Over and over.

"You remember, dear, when you used to come a few years ago and you'd tell me all the wonderful things you were doing in America?"

"Fondly. I lived for those walks."

"And once, as you talked—I think it may have been the last time you came, my memory isn't what it was—there were such a lot of things you were doing. There was a film in France, I think, and a new magazine, and a book about the eighties before they happened . . ."

I'd thought my chatter had been just white noise, and he'd taken in every word!

"You were very blasé about it all. I remember thinking: what a shame he isn't enjoying it more. I hope he hasn't lost his soul."

"I'm not sure anymore that I have a soul."

"Even an atheist can lose his soul, dear."

"Funny, your bringing that up. Last night after our walk I began to, well, examine my conscience. It was your 'two kinds of people' theory that set me off."

"Which k-k-kind are you, do you think?"

"I do tend to think in black and white. Even though I know there are a hundred shades of gray. I've trained myself in paths of thought—'ruts' might be a better word—that reflexively denigrate certain people. People I don't agree with or have contempt for or whose motives I suspect. I must admit I haven't considered for years what effect that might have on my own moral state."

"It can hardly be a good effect, can it, dear?"

"No, but most people I know have the same reflexes. Editors, journalists, writers, TV and movie people. We all share pretty much the same assumptions. They're considered morally neutral. They're how you generate material. Some journalists would say that suspicion and skepticism are professional obligations."

"Is anything morally neutral, Tony dear? Suspicion, skepticism, contempt? They don't *sound* like virtues."

"No one uses words like 'virtue' anymore, Father Joe."

"But these attitudes must have the potential to hurt, no?"

"Yes, but with the likes of Reagan and Thatcher running the show, there are things we need to fight for. Defend the Bill of Rights. Stand up for minorities. Try to stop the military from murdering quite so many people."

"Do you and your friends succeed?"

"We're not chalking up a lot of wins right now."

"Then why do you continue?"

I thought about this. A simple enough question. But when had I ever asked myself: why *did* we continue? Were my "friends," or was I, really defending anything? Bernstein said the *Lampoon* helped bring down Nixon. Of course it was really him and Woodward. But what had been their ultimate purpose? To put Woodward and Bernstein in the White House and do a better job? No, to put Woodward and Bernstein on the map. Secretly we were sort of happy with the status quo. So long as we got a piece of it.

"Well . . . the truth is, Father Joe, what we really do it for is—attention. We all jostle endlessly to be on talk shows, get items in columns, or columns in papers, or books on the best-seller list, or green lights for our pilots and our movies, to . . . how did you used to put it . . . to extend our selves out into . . . other people's awareness."

He considered this, looking out at the Solent.

"Needing attention is a p-p-powerful force in the world, isn't it?"

"Absolutely. Most people would think of it as a very natural need. Almost a right."

"By 'natural' you mean 'm-m-morally neutral'?"

"Touché."

"Without God, people find it very hard to know who they are or why they exist. But if others pay attention to them, praise them, write about them, discuss them, they think they've found the answers to both questions."

"If they don't believe in God, you can't blame them."

"True, dear. But it still makes for an empty, unhappy person. I'm sure Mrs. Thatcher wasn't always the way she is. As she came to power and got more and more attention, she began to be more and more what people wanted her to be. But that's not the true Mrs. Thatcher. The Mrs. Thatcher God wants her to be."

"I'm not sure Mrs. Thatcher would see the distinction you do between herself and God."

At least I got a smile out of him.

"Are you saying, Father Joe, that in the matter of motives, or even morally, there's not ultimately much difference between me and my targets?"

"I'm afraid not, dear. If the result is that you only have a personality other people shape. If you really exist only in other people's minds."

"I think you've just described celebrity."

"I've just described pride, dear."

The show went into production in the fall of '83 amid great media excitement, a lot of overhyped press, and rumblings from Maggie's mastodons. We'd made no secret of our intentions: Rog and Pete and Rog's wife, Dierdre, were quite visible in left-wing activist circles, my track record was hardly Reagano-Thatcherite, and Denton's sympathies were well-known. We'd also acquired a hard-driving executive producer, John Blair, a South African exile with impeccable leftist credentials (he'd produced the first documentary on the Soweto uprisings). Blair and I hated one another on sight; he quickly made it clear to the other principals that he thought there were too many captains on the bridge.

As the great actor Edward Kean said on his deathbed: life is easy.

Comedy series are hard. *Spitting Image* had the added burden of being topical (making scripts hard to stockpile), and the actors were both actors and puppeteers, holding over their bodies three-to-five-foot-tall puppets whose actions they could only track on TV monitors and who were based on living people whose voices had to be mimicked well enough to be funny, usually by an off-camera impressionist who had to lip-synch to the puppets' mouth movements. No one had ever attempted a show this demanding.

I insisted that the three "originals," Rog, Pete, and I, keep script control; it was the only way we could guarantee that the show would not "go television." That meant me, as Rog and Pete had their work cut out molding rubber oligarchs.

Lloyd was responsible for everything between script and final air tape—rehearsal, the studio, the edit suite. Plus it was his ass on stage, his golden-boy reputation at stake.

To make script production easier I developed several mini-sitcoms, segments with more or less the same characters each week. Ron and Nancy (and Ed Meese) would appear in "The President's Brain Is Missing"—Reagan's walnut-sized brain having escaped from his head and gone on the lam. "Number 9 Downing Street" had Maggie's next-door neighbor, a silver-haired eighty-something German gentleman named Wilkins, clearly Hitler in retirement, giving her political advice over the garden fence. A third was "Ex-Chequers," a retirement home for doddering ex–Prime Ministers like Wilson, Macmillan, Callaghan, and Alec Douglas-Home.

Lloyd hated these. They were "too political" and "too long." He preferred quick sketches and lots of *Laugh-In*-like jokes, the shorter the better and plenty of them so he could discard the ones he didn't like on the studio floor.

"Are you happy doing what you do, dear?"

It was the third day. His hip was acting up, so we were sitting in the garden. He had taken my hand in his, resting them on the wooden bench between us.

"Let's see. I'm happy at the beginning of a project and at the end, but rarely in between. I suppose I'm happy when things succeed—though however successful they are, it never seems to be enough. I'm happy when I'm writing—if it's something funny."

"Is it the writing or that it's funny?"

"Writing by myself rather scares me. I suppose that it's funny."

"So being funny, Tony dear, having people laugh at you all the time, or at what you write, makes you happy?"

"Yes, but I worry a bit when I see what often happens to funny people. You'd think that constantly making people laugh, being around laughter all the time, would have a very positive effect on a person, right? But quite the opposite seems to be the case. Perhaps it's constantly looking for the failings in people, to get a laugh out of them."

I told him a story about Jerry Lewis. Years before, my partner Nic and I had been on Jerry's telethon. I was waiting to go on, standing beside Jerry off camera. It was twenty-odd hours into the show and mine host was well into his *n*th bottle of the good stuff. One of "Jerry's Kids" was on camera, a severely disabled young teen who was desperately trying to pick out a solo on his guitar. The noise was excruciating. Jerry had turned to the floor manager and snarled: "Get that fucking cripple offstage!"

At this punch line Father Joe flinched as if someone was about to hit him.

"Sorry about the language."

"No, no, it's not that. Did the poor boy hear him?"

"Luckily, he was making too much noise."

"Perhaps it was just a momentary lapse because Jerry—er—Lewis was so tired."

"Maybe. To tell the truth, I've never met a funnyman, or funnywoman, who wasn't crazy, unhappy, vindictive, untrustworthy, screwed up—and that's just the normal ones."

I had another example for him: Jackie Mason, the man who'd found me and Nic in the Blue Angel in London, who invited us to

America, got his manager, Bob Chartoff, to manage us, and sponsored us for green cards. Before he became a comedian, he'd been a rabbi-in-training—not unlike me, bred in many of the same traditions. After twenty-five years of probing other people's failings he had orange hair, wore a corset, and had an endless string of girlfriends.

"Jackie's funny as hell, but happy? Or, more to the point—good? As good as when he was a young ex-rabbi? I don't know. Would he still help two young men come to America?"

"Do you think you're becoming a J-J-Jerry Lewis or J-J-Jackie Mason, dear?"

Was I? Would I end up with orange hair and a corset and my own pet disease? Was I already halfway there? I was one of the craziest, unhappiest, most vindictive, least trustworthy people I knew. Yikes.

Pre-production started in the fall of '83. Immediately tensions began to build. Lloyd, backed by Blair, demanded "final cut" on the scripts; I refused. He loaded up Rog and Pete with dozens of new puppets over and above obvious figures like the Royals, Thatcher and her Cabinet, etc., almost all of them inane British TV personalities. Ominous—with these puppets we'd end up doing TV about TV, precisely the kind of comedy we wanted to put in its grave.

What could make things more tense? Ah yes, cut costs by transporting the entire show by rail each week to Birmingham—armpit of England—compounding its massive logistical, design, and performance problems, driving everyone to a fever pitch of fear and insomnia. Blair flourished in this atmosphere and began promoting the notion that "Hendra's scripts" were the root cause of all the chaos.

Things shot from bad to worse to appalling at warp speed. Never in my experience of American TV or the *Lampoon* or any other U.S. enterprise had I come across the level of viciousness these Brits displayed in their infighting. The archetype of unflappable Britishness had disappeared with unscarred countryside and gnarled old Cockneys. No one seemed to have heard of stiff upper lips. Frothing fits, screaming fits, cursing which you needed a medical degree to understand echoed down the corridors till dawn.

I'd been struck before by how crazy Brits were for their TV: not surprising, really, if you're watching the best in the world. Whereas Americans became slack-jawed and narcotized by TV, as if it were a giant light-emitting Quaalude, Brits became jumpy and hysterical, as if it were bombarding them with neutron-sized hits of crystal meth. Now I wondered if this hysteria was somehow endemic to the British version of the medium, since it was the order of the day on the production side as well.

"I remember long ago when you saw that show in Cambridge, you wrote a wonderful letter about it."

"You remember everything. How can there be any space left in there after seventy-five years?"

"In your letter you said laughter was holy and capable of changing the world."

We were rounding Quarr's great farm from the other direction than our accustomed one. It was less steep this way and he was moving a little slowly. In the early eighties he'd developed asthma, and he had to stop once in a while. There were whispers at Quarr that it was psychosomatic.

In 1964 the last French Abbot had resigned, and there had been an election in which the only viable candidates were Father Joe and Dom Aelred. Dom Aelred had won and made Father Joe his Prior, or second in command. The head and the heart, the Holy Odd Couple, worked well until, rather abruptly in 1980, the Abbot demoted Father Joe to Sub-Prior. The excuse was that the monastery needed younger, newer blood.

That was when the asthma started.

Joe told me none of this, of course. As far as he was concerned, the situation was sweet. Fewer duties, and his newfound disease meant he could pop off occasionally to balmier climes: France and, best of all, Italy.

His current wheezing suggested it was time to call the travel agent.

"Dear oh dear, I shouldn't be flagging. I don't think I'm going to make old bones, I'm afraid."

"Don't say that, Joe! I'll tell you when you can die. It won't be anytime soon."

"I think you're quite right to think of laughter as holy, Tony dear. And I don't mean just at holy things. Laughter's a kind of s-s-safety valve, isn't it? It's very good in Chapter, when a man's being really tiresome or far too serious and someone else just can't stop themselves giggling. Oh, I like that! I join right in!"

"What I loved about you when we first met, Father Joe, was that you were the only priest who'd ever made me laugh."

"Well, there you are! And I hope I always shall. We should laugh at priests much more often. When you think about it, laughter's a very important thing. Life is full of little pretenses and pretensions, and when we laugh at them, we get at the truth behind them for a moment. That's very good for all concerned, I think."

I remembered the time long ago, when I was almost one of them, that yes, they did, they laughed and smiled and joked and played pranks. Apparently even in the greater silence they found ways to crack each other up.

"We don't think of God laughing, do we? Yet if God is happiness, God must be laughter too. Do you remember that wonderful passage of Meister Eckhart you found once?"

For the life of me I couldn't remember who this German guy was. It was twenty-five-plus years ago. Yet Father Joe had it verbatim:

" 'When God laughs at the soul and the soul laughs back at God, the persons of the Trinity are begotten. When the Father laughs at the Son and the Son laughs back at the Father, that laughter gives pleasure, that pleasure gives joy, that joy gives love, and that love is the Holy Spirit.' "

* * *

The first air date approached. The frenzy, panic, cursing, fear, frothing, loathing, and throwing of fits reached unscalable heights. This was comedy? I spent most of my time and energy trying to calm people down. Forget it. No one wanted to be calmed down.

The show went on the air. The puppets were lumbering, badly blocked, woodenly shot. Editing appeared to have been done by a blind amputee. The mini-sitcoms dragged. The sound was awful. The reviews were execrable. There were questions in the House of Commons. The Royalists were furious at a segment in which the Queen made fun of Thatcher's sleazy pretensions. The piece clearly took the inbred old parasite's side against the rabid grocer's daughter. No matter; they objected to reducing the Head Royal to rubber.

But all the signs were there. We had the potential for a huge hit. The puppets were a new dimension in the medium. You couldn't take your eyes off them. They were intrinsically hilarious. They didn't need week-to-week building up, as most series characters do; they were instantly recognizable news figures. Best of all, they made the right people furious. We had only to make them move better, write shorter lines, establish relationships between them, and *Spitting Image* would take off like a cruise missile. It might take a month or three, but we were sitting on a revolution in TV satire.

John Cleese wrote me a note that night saying how brilliant he thought "whatever your show is called" was. He found some of the puppets and voices weak, but the scripts were strong; he particularly liked the mini-sitcom "Ex-Chequers."

I took his note with me the morning after the première to show to my colleagues. When I got there I didn't bother. The level of frenzy, panic, fear, and loathing had achieved the impossible: it had increased. No one seemed to have seen, or to have the slightest confidence in, the TV breakthrough that had occurred the night before. At this point I knew I was not long for this loony bin. The endgame began.

* * *

"Have you changed the world at all, dear?"

"No, Father Joe. Not one tiny bit."

There were a couple of occasions in the late seventies—at least I think it was a couple and I think it was the late seventies—that dawn moment when the euphoria is as distant a memory as the coke and you know you're not going to sleep till noon, when the rising sun strikes across Upper Manhattan from East Side to West, turning the ziggurats of New Jersey into fiery bronze and Ur of the Chaldees lives again in Weehawken, but all that this sublime urban vision does is depress you further . . .

Then I'd call him. It would be lunchtime at Quarr, so he could talk awhile, which he did in the wary, overpolite manner monks have on the phone. I who had been up all night in fast and furious coke-monologue, listening to no one and making everyone listen to me, would just slouch there, silent, as he hurried and stuttered on, burbling away with news of the monastery, interpolating "are you still there, dear?" and dropping a few gems of loving wisdom. The post-coke shame would fade and I would have a brief fantasy of faith and hope: *someday soon, I'm going back and my faith will make me whole and I will finally, finally be a monk . . .*

"The world is hard to change, Tony dear."

"I thought we were having some effect once. But no. The dogs of war are back in charge. The poor are being told poverty is their own fault. The free market rules."

"Whatever is the free market? A market where everything's free?"

"Au contraire." In a few pithy words I explained the gist of Reaganomics.

"Let me see if I understand. What it boils down to is: my self-interest is in your interest?"

"That's pretty much it."

"Sounds like p-p-p-poppycock."

We were rounding back up to the monastery, having taken a shortcut through the garden. He was leaning heavily on my arm by now.

"Work is so important, isn't it, dear? Work works in unknown ways. If work is done well, conscientiously, joyfully, I think it has an effect far beyond what's actually made or grown or sold."

"Laborare est orare."

"Very good. You do remember."

"I thought that only applied to monk work."

"I don't see why. *Laborare est orare* doesn't mean we actually mumble prayers while we work, does it? You'd drive the other chaps barmy. The work itself is prayer. Work done as well as possible. Work done for others first and yourself second. Work you are thankful for. Work you enjoy, that uplifts you. Work that celebrates existence, whether it's growing grain in the fields or using God-given skills—like yours. All this is prayer that binds us together and therefore to God."

"My work is prayer?"

"Why is the work you've chosen less valuable than mucking out the cows?"

He nodded toward a monk who was hosing out the cattle pens.

"I guess I muck out sacred cows."

Finally! I got a real laugh.

I thought about work as prayer. Driving a truck? Logging a forest? Slinging hash? Selling cars? Teaching school? Working as a GS12, or in the IRS or the DMV, or a fire department? All this done joyfully, thankfully, unselfishly, conscientiously becomes . . . prayer?

Why not? Not in the pious sense of nice, polite requests floating up to a capricious Godhead; rather a force, vital and alive, part of the quotidian fabric, producing—at a depth unknown to pollsters, spin doctors, demographers, and other calibrators of human emotion—widespread outcomes throughout society? Innumerable small acts of generosity and goodwill, binding us closer, motivating us, giving us little boosts of hope and faith in each other. Changing the world, even.

Why not indeed? For a man who didn't see the everyday world as separate from the sacred. Who saw God everywhere, shining out from the down-to-earth and battered and untidy and defeated. Who was a commonsense saint, a saint of what could be done, not should be done, a practical saint, a saint of imperfection.

How I exited *Spitting Image* doesn't matter much. There was a lot of red-in-tooth-and-claw politics and supremely unfunny hand-to-hand combat. With the completion of the first series (six shows in the U.K.), I resigned.

Lloyd got his script control and turned the show toward more harmless, quick-fire material—a lot of it TV about TV. Several of my contributions survived, notably the adventures of Reagan's tiny brain and a long-running segment with Thatcher terrorizing her obsequious Cabinet. Despite the appalling script job I'd supposedly done, the first season's series was nominated for a British Academy Award, which in the U.K. are given for TV as well as films. It didn't win that year, but it did the next. Dear old England. Land of the creatively fairly free and home of the artistically quite brave.

Spitting Image was a massive hit in the U.K.; it ran on ITV for ten years, making many reputations and clinching Lloyd's. It was widely imitated elsewhere in Europe, and its clones are still running there. It continues to make the right people furious. The Canal+ version is an enduring factor in French politics, including the seismic French elections of 2002. Vladimir Putin imprisoned the producer of the Russian version.

The day I resigned was one of the worst of my life. My dreams of return: the modest but prestigious success of the series establishing me in the smart, tasteful milieu of British popular culture, securing my place as a bona fide member of the sixties humor generation . . . the thatched cottage in the West Country with the paddock and orchard and pair of green wellies by the wisteria-choked back door . . . the English Rose girlfriend—or three, or ten—one morphing eventually into a second wife . . . the Land-Rover (or two), the son (or two), the getaway place in Tuscany with the tenth-century cellar (for the wine) . . . the thoughtful but irreverent columns in the *Observer* . . .

History. Down the tube.

"How about atheists? If they work in the spirit that you're describing, would that be prayer?"

"Of course. God loves atheists as much as he does believers. P-p-probably more."

"Comforting for us atheists."

"What you must ask yourself, Tony dear, is this: do you do the work you've chosen with joy and gratitude? Do you do it conscientiously? Do you do it for others first and yourself second?"

The questions hit me like a flurry of hooks to the solar plexus. He could not have known how on-target he was.

The ferocious, unfunny fight I'd just put up, standing like some fundamentalist preacher at the church door against the forces of levity and triviality? My argument with Lloyd being, at the end of the day, that long, tendentious jokes were politically and morally superior to short, silly ones?

Never in a quarter century of the work I'd chosen had I had so humorless a humor experience as during the last six months. How much of that was me? There'd been no joy, no gratitude, no uplift in my work; "conscientious" wasn't even on the table. Others first? Forget it.

Perhaps it was the string of disappointments after so many successes. Perhaps humor was more a creature of fashion than I believed, and the fashion had changed. Perhaps Father Joe's theory of prayer was correct and whatever prayer's evil opposite is had come back to bite me.

I had arrived at the end of one phase of my life. I hadn't known it when I came, but Father Joe had. With consummate skill he'd led me step-by-step to the realization that I had become a rather unpleasant person, that it was time to move on to a second phase, but without rejecting, as I was prone to do, everything I'd so far accomplished.

If he'd come out and said any one of those things I would have bristled or resisted or just run away. Instead he'd used his own code—prayer, God, and so on—and what he had to say was unerring.

"How do you do it, Father Joe?"

"Do what, dear?"

"You live inside a cloister, itself cloistered inside this pink and yellow pile. You have no driver's license. You have no TV. I assume you don't get out to the movies much. You live by a Rule that was written a little under fifteen hundred years ago. Yet you have an uncanny ability to grasp the essentials of the most worldly things, in this case what I do for a living. Have you been seeing other satirists?"

"You're the only one I know, dear."

"Know what you are, Father Joe? You're an innocent savant."

The next leap off the cliff had to be faced. I knew what it was. One I had been putting off and putting off. Because it scared the bejesus out of me. No more hiding behind editing and collaboration. I had to learn to be a writer.

Over the next couple of years I did write my first book. It was a history of American satire over the previous thirty years ("Boomer humor," my editor made me call it) titled *Going Too Far.* Some was semiautobiographical; I knew many of the people it covered; so it wasn't much of a cliff I plunged off. But it did force me to reexamine many preconceptions I had about laughter, satire, the whole business of being funny.

The central discovery—which I couldn't avoid, given that I was reviewing some of the best comedy of the twentieth century, an extraordinary generation of comic genii—was most unwelcome. While I worshipped laughter and those who made it, on stage or page, I just wasn't that funny myself.

I didn't possess the glorious madness that I loved in others. Lenny Bruce, Zero Mostel, S. J. Perelman, Mel Brooks, Peter Cook, Terry Southern, Peter Sellers and Spike Milligan, Jonathan Winters, John Cleese and Graham Chapman, George Carlin, Lily Tomlin, Ritchie Pryor, Michael O'Donoghue, Doug Kenney, John Belushi, Eddie Murphy, Gilda Radner, Dan Aykroyd—all had that ability to induce helpless hysteria in people. My theories of attack and changing minds would never produce more than appreciative chuckles. Great comics did attack sometimes, did direct laughter at targets—Cook at Macmillan, Lenny at racists, Pryor at Reagan, Carlin at the Church—but even then, what you really laughed at was *them.* The madness within them, their openness to their own weirdness, a complete admission of their own surpassing imperfection.

I had talent, perhaps. But I came to think of the word as an attempt to diminish the wild uniqueness of the truly funny, lumping them all together into one impersonal commodity. Talent was for the second string, a dim reflection of the real gift. A bathetic word when applied to the hard-edged one-and-only presence, the *haecceitas,* of the true comic genius. That mysterious quality that you know the second the performer comes into view, which has you spluttering before she's said a word, before he's done *anything.* Then the demented god on the tongue, the delighted electricity rushing through the audience, the crack and rolling thunder of the laughter. We know it intimately, that quality, but no one has ever explained where it comes from, what it is, why you can't learn one iota of it even if you study it for a lifetime. For the truly funny, making people laugh *is* the highest form of humor. It comes first. Changing an audience's mind about something—my life's mission to date—comes a very distant second.

A bitter moment unearthing this truth; though I'd always known it, not so deep down. Often, afterward, I wondered if somehow in the vast reservoir of his intuition Father Joe knew it too, and was gently trying to tell me: *give it up, son, you're wasting your time.*

Truth has its comforts. If I had not found through him the

wherewithal for this new conversion of life, had not written the book, I would never have arrived at that realization—might have gone on slogging away forever at Changing the World through Laughter.

Talented guy. Sorta funny. You believe that hair color? And why the corset?

There were other compensations. To my surprise, the solitude of writing was sublime after so many years of collaboration. The arctic blankness of the page which I'd so dreaded melted like spring thaw. Writing was a new countryside to wander in, a new boyhood of discovery, a new green shade for new green thoughts. I got lost in it as I hadn't been able to, in anything, for twenty-five years. I owed this man all that. How could I ever have thought him—irrelevant?

We talked endlessly for the rest of that visit, *Spitting Image* already forgotten. We talked more about laughter and we made each other laugh. I told him jokes that he actually got. Some he laughed at.

We were speaking as equals, as friends, the way fathers and sons do when age begins to lessen the gap between them. I regretted the preceding years of first dependence, then distance, of obligatory love and grudging duty, that awful feeling of relief I'd had as I walked away from Quarr. But those feelings had been felt, and perhaps they'd had to be. Otherwise we would not be here.

The day before I left, we went for our last walk. I was leaving early in the morning for Heathrow, where my girlfriend and I would fly to Crete and the ruins of four-thousand-year-old cities.

He asked me about her.

"She's Italian. Or rather, Italian-American. Very beautiful."

"Is she a blonde?" Again the brightening of the eyes.

"No, she's extremely smart."

He still didn't get it.

"Are you going to marry her?"

"Never. Once is enough."

As we came under the shadow of the monastery, something struck me—so simple it made me laugh. The wonderful new English life I'd hoped *Spitting Image* would deliver to me was not just a fantasy but a delusion. The reason I'd been so passionate about returning to England was the old man limping along by my side. Father Joe was my England. I didn't ever again want to be as far away from my little lighthouse as I had been on that night in Malibu.

When we got up to the monastery, he let go of my arm and hauled himself over to a gallery-like area under one of the wings. Then, to my surprise, he began stomping up and down as briskly as he could, his big old Astérix sandals slapping on the cement.

"They told me to do this for ten minutes each day to strengthen my hip."

I watched him slog back and forth. He didn't look happy.

"What you need is a marching song."

"Good idea! What do you have in mind, dear?"

"There's an old World War Two song my dad taught me. First the melody . . ."

I whistled the "Colonel Bogey March." He picked it up right away, of course.

"Okay, now here are the words . . ."

Hitler has only got one ball
Goering has two but very small . . .

Father Joe laughed louder than I'd ever heard him laugh.

Himmler is somewhat sim'lar
And poor old Goebbels got no balls at all.

Father Joe was bent double, helpless, slapping his knobbly knees with delight.

"Oh my goodness! My turn to sing! Help me now!"

He began marching up the gallery, picking up the pace, straightening his seventy-five-year-old back, bellowing at the top of his lungs:

"*HITLER HAS ONLY GOT ONE BALL!* Who?"

"Goering."

"GOERING HAS TWO BUT VERY SMALL!
HIMMLER IS SOMEWHAT SIM'LAR! That's my favorite part!
AND POOR OLD GOEBBELS GOT NO BALLS AT ALL!"

He sang the entire thing six more times at full volume.

CHAPTER FIFTEEN

Her name was Carla and her Italian blood was immediately apparent: dark lustrous hair, *castagna*-brown eyes the size of golf balls, skin the color of young *vino santo.* I first saw her in the fall of 1981 across a crowded room of young neoconservatives from the University of Chicago. What was I doing in a group of young neoconservatives? Being hired. (I work for the side that pays me the most: at the same time I was also being paid by some anti-Shah, anti-Khomeini—but not pro-American—Iranian exiles to edit and translate a tome called *The Sayings of Ayatollah Khomeini.*)

The U of C group was led by Peter Cohn, son of legendary agent Sam Cohn. They'd decided that their postgraduate tribute to their Amanuenses Milton and Rose Friedman would be a full-scale parody of *The Wall Street Journal.* Through Sam, who was my agent, I had been suggested as the editor of this enterprise.

Carla was a graduate of U of C—Phi Beta Kappa, in fact—

though not, happily, a neoconservative. She was strikingly beautiful and quite voluptuous—she'd worked as a model in L.A.—but that night, had a sullen, depressed demeanor, which I took to be boredom at the entrepreneurial prattle of her classmates. It turned out to be that and more: a defense mechanism protecting great insecurity, odd considering her intelligence and accomplishments, but which led people to underestimate her. This may have been why the role foreseen for her in the coming parody was general dogsbody.

She turned to me with a bored, heavy-lidded look, gave me the once-over, and smiled a conspiratorial little smile. I decided then and there that working for these Reaganite sprats might not be quite as obnoxious as it was beginning to sound.

Of them, Cohn was by far the most aggressively neocon and monetarist. In fact the whole enterprise, unlike the abysmally (and unintentionally) nonprofit *Not The New York Times,* which was its model, was supposed to make money for its investors. (It did, though not, as usual, for its creators.) Cohn also had incoherent notions that it would somehow promote the lifework of Uncle Miltie and Auntie Rose. I had to explain at length and frequently that in that case he should have chosen a nonmonetarist publication to parody. Hard to do a funny *Journal* parody without being adversarial about the causes it championed and the pro-corporate policies of the administration it supported so enthusiastically.

The fascinating thing about Cohn and his group was that they saw themselves as a new humor broom, an anti-*Lampoon* swing of the pendulum. They dressed like, spoke like, and were proud to be preppies, arrayed against and contemptuous of permissive, hairy peace-and-love loonies with no dress sense, like me. They were all, Carla included, fifteen or so years my junior, and it was startling to be, for the first time, not the young insurgent but the establishment fogy who had to be dealt with for the moment because of his contacts and know-how, but who would be swept away, once these skills had been learned, by the counterrevolution.

More mundanely, Cohn and his group were rich kids. Cohn's fiancée—Carla's best friend—was the daughter of movie giant Eric Pleskow, the genius behind first United Artists and then Orion, a man with fourteen Oscars in his dining room and the bucks to match. (And, in a truly Shakespearean twist, Sam Cohn's sworn enemy.)

Carla wasn't a rich kid at all, and neither was I. This was our first bond, and making fun of the "young masters" our second. She had a sharp, sour wit and, just as important, was a good audience. She also turned out to be a sensational manager, holding together all aspects of what became a mammoth job (twenty-four broadsheet pages with no paid advertising, every word and image of which had to be written, researched, photographed and/or retouched, copyedited, typeset, changed at the last minute, paid for, printed down to the last agate stock listing, and five-point classified . . . and, of course, funny). She showed the first hints of a management style that would eventually make her a top-echelon executive: an ability to get things out of people under great stress in a patient, nonconfrontational way that didn't leave them bruised and resentful as prevailing Darwinian corporate practices did. At the time, businesswomen tended to be either low-echelon drones or highly visible trapeze artists like Mary Cunningham; Carla was an early bird in a more solid and influential wave that would transform corporate management over the next two decades.

What I did notice was that despite her beauty and obvious talents, she couldn't accept compliments. She would deflect them or make some self-deprecating rejoinder or even challenge them as if unconvinced of their sincerity. Both this insecurity and her management skills may have been the result of growing up in the midst of an unusually large family.

Catholic? Of course. The twist was that it was her German-Irish father, Mr. Meisner, who was the devout Catholic, not her all-Italian mother. Carla's mother was from the other end of Italy than the usual Neapolitan or Sicilian American—her family had deep roots in Piemonte—but she had been raised a Methodist. Like my father, she had agreed to raise her children as Catholics, and the result had been seventeen pregnancies, fourteen of them successful.

So large a family was a kind of demographic subset in which could be found almost all the various tragedies, comedies, and tragicomedies that afflict modern American life. One boy had served in Vietnam, one girl had died senselessly in a mundane teenage car collision; one child had leukemia, two were dedicated advocates of the downtrodden (one a public defender, the other an immigration attorney); one was a pediatrician, another a nurse. Two had been in the Air Force, not so much from militarism but as a way to get a college degree at public expense, one graduating from the Air Force Academy, the other becoming an airline pilot. One worked on Wall Street, one was a professional concert violinist, one was becoming a big wheel in the California wine business. The only areas they hadn't got to so far were showbiz and the media. I could cover that.

The more I got to know the Meisners and their growing number of spouses, the more it struck me that they weren't the usual stuff of American family/dynasty stories: on the one hand insufferably rich egomaniacs you're supposed to admire, on the other impossibly saintly poor people who are supposed to inspire. They were neither particularly rich nor poor, neither obnoxious successes nor spectacular failures. They were the middle stratum of Americans, active in a huge range of activities, kind and generous and rather self-effacing, noisy and funny, politically neutral, tolerant of others' weirdness, remarkably accomplished—almost all the girls, including Carla, played classical piano at an advanced level. Though most had been born and raised in the Northeast (in Connecticut), the majority had ended up living in the South. Almost everything that happened to members of the extended family was both typical of some larger trend and too individual or idiosyncratic to be dismissed as "typical."

Unlike Carla, not all of them looked Italian, though the girls all had their mother's huge Madonna eyes; you didn't have to scratch the surface much to find that their Italian mother and her ancient roots were what united them, held them together, made them survive as a family.

It certainly wasn't Catholicism. The procreative progenitor raised them to be good Catholics, but the Family Meisner denied the Church success in the hidden agenda of its birth-control policy: to populate the earth with Catholics. Only two practiced, one of whom tried hard to make up for all the rest, for a net generational gain of one.

I loved that Carla was Italian—all Italian as far as I was concerned; I loved that she was smart and resourceful, I loved that she was young and beautiful. I loved that we shared ex-Catholicism. In short, I loved her.

My first marriage was by now a completely dry well; whole weeks went by when Judy and I didn't exchange more than ten words—all of them polite. My elder daughter had left for Barnard, my younger would soon be off to Sarah Lawrence and spent as little time as possible at home. Our NoHo loft felt like an abandoned subway station through which the ghosts of long-dead commuters would sometimes drift, looking for things they had dropped in the 1920s.

Judy's nose seemed to be getting rather large.

Office affairs went against my grain—I'd been seriously burned at the *Lampoon* by an intramural fling and watched several other people turn brown and crispy. But one thing led to another, and when *Off The Wall Street Journal* came out and was a hit, I had a funny, sexy lover to take to downtown parties, fly around the country with, and help me pop champagne from minibars in provincial presidential suites.

Our first few months were a blur, but one moment stuck out. Judy and I had to spend a weekend in our country place in New Jersey, to take care of some business. Though we hadn't split up yet, everything we did by now had an ominous finality, as if by unwritten consent we were wrapping things up. I'd promised to call Carla in the morning but didn't feel right doing it from home. I drove down to the highway and a dreary little mall where there was a pay phone. It was a rainy winter morning, outside a convenience store called

Pop 'n' Stop or Chick 'n' Chek or something. I called Carla, and after many rings she answered. Her voice was very small and young and faraway and slurry with sleep.

A chilly spasm shook me from head to toe, a bit like the old elephant-stepped-on-my-grave feeling but with far more foreboding, as if something seismic were happening to my life, not necessarily pleasant but impossible to avoid, ineluctably ordained.

At the time, I put it down to adultery in New Jersey in the rain. It wasn't adultery in New Jersey in the rain.

Fling turned into affair. I could deceive poor Judy no longer, came clean, and moved out. Affair became arrangement as Carla and I passed beyond the first fine flush. We fit together in all kinds of ways and were capable of major good times. In common we had classical music, books, food and wine and cooking, old places and things, travel.

I'd always been a European penny-pincher, reluctant to splurge, fearful of debt. Carla was more American with money. She bought me stylish clothes and lavish presents and made me travel to places I'd only dreamed of, like St. Barts and Crete and Rio. She got a job and began shooting up the corporate ladder. She revealed a brilliant flair for design and decoration, transforming the places we lived. My kids took to her, especially my younger and more volatile daughter, who called her "the wicked stepmother." For her part, Carla, nearer in age to them than to me, who knew their music and could talk their language, acted as a kind of ambassador, allowing me to begin trying to repair some of the damage I'd done.

But the more involved we became, the more often we fought.

One reason—according to Carla—was that we shared an ingrained sense of inferiority and insecurity. She put it down to our shared Catholicism. A more immediate reason: I was not used to living with someone so emotional and intuitive. My habit was to provide reasoned explanations for my moods and behaviors to Judy, which she would accept as sincere and accurate though we both knew they were hardly ever either. It wouldn't have been polite to challenge me. As for emotion, we barely remembered the meaning of the word.

Carla couldn't have been more different. She had an uncanny way of sensing not just evasion but any unaccustomed tick in my thought process. There was one enormous thing that I was holding back—rationalizing, paradoxically, that I didn't want to hurt her and lose her: I would not remarry. The clearer it got, as one year became two and then three, that this was where things were headed, the harder it became to hide. I never really came out and said it. Foolishly, I said the opposite: *yes of course I want to get married—just not yet. Let's wait till such-and-such is over.* I'm sure she sussed that out as an evasion, but . . . she didn't need to call me on it.

I was out of the country often, and then all the time, with *Spitting Image.* I didn't confide to her my yearnings for the homeland, any more than I did to my partners. The yearnings did not include marriage to her; despite my fantasy of the English Rose in green wellies, they didn't include marriage to anybody.

I was in a bind. I'd said I would, but I knew I wouldn't. It wasn't that I wanted to play the field—there was no need. Nor did I have some pea-brained notion of freedom or independence like some of my pals who'd broken up with their wives and now had younger girlfriends but wouldn't marry them. Who the hell wants independence as you approach the half century? Only a hermit or a serial killer.

Marriage became unthinkable after *Spitting Image.* I would not repeat any more mistakes. That eerie roadside frisson that had shaken me so, right at the beginning, became my rationale. A warning, a foretaste of more misery at my hands for yet another woman—this time one I loved.

Carla was becoming more and more successful. She would be thirty in 1986—a woman who adored children. A born competitor whose siblings and in-laws were spitting out babies like buns from a bakery.

Things came to a head. We'd gone for the weekend to Atlantic City. It was 1985; it seemed a very eighties thing to do. We had a great silly time, as we always did when we were babes in the wood, the wood in this case Trump's Taj Mahal. We laughed for hours, losing a couple hundred bucks in the process. And so to bed.

Next morning we awoke in high spirits and headed back to New York in a car she'd rented, chortling over the hideous denizens and torments of Donald's pleasure dome. As often happened, our high spirits turned dark and cancerous. By the time we hit the New Jersey Turnpike, we were in a fight as bad as any we'd ever had. It started with my nervousness at what I took to be her typically American driving style, tailgating the car in front while casually multitasking, looking for a map in the door pocket, fiddling with the radio, checking her makeup in the rearview mirror.

This segued into *It's my FUCKING car, I'll drive any way I FUCKING want!* A sensitive point. I was in the middle of my book, and though the advance was okay, the initial chunk was gone. She was now in effect supporting me. Which in turn segued into why wouldn't I agree to get married? *EVER?* (I'd said we'd deal with it when the book was finished—the latest of many deadlines.) She said she was calling me on this. Right then and there.

"It's now or never. Say yes or it's all over. I can't go *ON LIKE THIS!*"

I yelled back: "That's *RIDICULOUS!*"

She screamed: "No it's *not!*" and screeched to a halt on the median.

"Either you agree to marriage *NOW*—which you did years ago, by the way—or *GET OUT OF MY CAR!*"

"I'm not agreeing to marriage with a gun to my head!"

"THEN GET THE FUCK OUT!"

"We're in the middle of the fucking *TURNPIKE!*"

She reached across me furiously and wrestled open the door. I didn't move. She shoved me hard, punched me a bit. I thought *what can she do if I get out? A standoff. She'll have to let me back in when the troopers show up.*

I got out.

She took off up the median.

I ran after her. She swerved into the roadway, nearly ending several marriages. Then she disappeared up the turnpike.

I was dumbfounded. I had no money (it was my last two hundred bucks we'd lost). I was way down the turnpike in the Pine Barrens. It was Sunday morning. There were no cops, and no one in their right mind picks up hitchhikers from the turnpike median. What was I going to do?

The big one began to sink in. She meant it. She was going to New York. She wasn't coming back. I'd lost her. She was a decisive corporate bigwig now, used to making up her mind and moving on. I was totally, totally fucked.

I sat on the metal median divider, disconsolate. I couldn't go back to England. I had no money. It would be months before I even finished the book, let alone got the next advance. It was too late in the year to start a garden in New Jersey. How would I eat? How would I pay the mortgage? I'd have to sell. Jesus, I was going to be homeless!

"Hey, fuckhead!"

It was Carla, going about three miles an hour in the fast lane on the other side of the divider, cars blaring at her as they swerved desperately into the center lane.

"Changed your mind?"

"Yeah, yeah, yeah!"

She speeded up, did a triple-illegal U-turn at the end of the divider, and pulled up behind me, spraying dirt.

I went over to the car to get in. The door was locked, but the window was down.

"Open the door."

"Uh-uh. Not till you agree."

"Fuck, Carla."

"By-eee. Have a nice day."

The car began to move.

"Wait!"

I leaned into the car.

"Will you marry me?"

"Yes."

She popped the lock. I got in. She screeched out onto the roadway at seventy, checking her eyelashes in the rearview mirror.

"Carla, you're an asshole."

"But an effective asshole."

And so on the twentieth day of September in the year of our Lord 1986, in the sixth year of the reign of Ronaldus Caesar, a civil ceremony, not recognized by the Church, was celebrated in the garden of my (soon to be our) New Jersey home. A gratifying number of people showed up, including several regiments of Carla's brothers and sisters. On a whim I'd invited the only two lefties I knew anymore. One was Carl Bernstein, whom I'd always liked for two things: *All the President's Men,* of course; but also, his front-page lead in *Not The New York Times,* written in about five minutes after hearing of the death of John Paul I: POPE DIES YET AGAIN; REIGN IS BRIEFEST EVER; CARDINALS RETURN FROM AIRPORT.

The other was Abbie Hoffman, whom I'd gotten to know—though I can't remember how—when he was on the lam from the FBI and living in the Thousand Islands as Barry Fried. It was Barry, not Abbie, who, when we went up to the islands, tried strenuously to seduce Carla, believing her to be Jewish and far too good for a goy like me.

The old lefties met the very Republican mayor of our township, a silver-haired and -bearded three-hundred-pound ex–U.S. Army colonel given to quoting Aristotle in township meetings. He married us with quiet eloquence. One of my best friends from the *Lampoon,* playwright John Weidman, was my best man. Carla's father read Gerard Manley Hopkins' "Epithalamion" in an intense, lyrical Pittsburgh accent. In every way it was a gloriously American afternoon, the day I married my American wife. And she was breathtakingly beautiful.

We traveled to England for our honeymoon—the first time I'd set foot in the country since *Spitting Image;* my little sister gave us a second wedding party at her sixteenth-century farmhouse in Derbyshire. And so to the tiny Piemontese hill town of Perosa where we nailed the Italian part of the deal by spending a week with my new mother-in-law's family.

The current *nonno* and *nonna* of the clan were the most hospitable people we'd ever met; we were family, so they had to give us their finest room, *quella col letto matrimoniale.* When we woke the first morning it was to hear the pigs who lived in the sty below awakening to their breakfast. I thought I'd never been so happy.

No sooner had we returned than the fighting resumed. We held nothing back, now that we'd tied the knot for the rest of our lives. The worst came on Christmas Eve, with the two of us stalking each other through the house, screaming uncontrollably. Later she cried uncontrollably. For the first time I noticed that her nose was rather larger than I'd thought.

Friends helped us patch things up and we vowed to do better. We stumbled through 1987. I got very busy finishing and publishing my book and staffing a ghastly CBS morning show starring Mariette Hartley. She seemed smart and charming when she interviewed me, but on air turned out to have a limited supply of marbles. The other regular, Bob Saget, and I got through the ordeal by becoming good friends. Between ourselves we called the show *Diary of a Mad Housewife. Spinal Tap* had now become a solid video hit; for the first time in my life I was recognized regularly in public. Work flowed like cheap wine.

Busy was good, but not very deep down I had a feeling that history was repeating itself. For the second time I could not help thinking *I've made the mistake of getting married to save a relationship.* Or, more accurately, getting married because I couldn't think of where else the relationship could go if it wasn't going to end.

There's a second, related mistake people who've made the first often proceed to: having kids to save the marriage that saved the relationship. Which we now did.

For me it wasn't the first time either. As the end of my first marriage had neared, Judy and I experienced a rush of regret and a resolve to salvage something before it was too late. We had decided to try for another baby.

The mission warmed things between us. She was almost forty, but she happened to be working on a book with an East Side ob-gyn to the rich and brainless. This twerp assured her she'd be fine. She wasn't. She became pregnant and not long afterward went through a life-threatening ectopic pregnancy. I came home one evening to find her gone from the house.

It got later and later, but we were in the habit of leaving one another to each other's devices and I assumed she was busy working with her author. Finally the doctor's office called. I found out she was in the hospital and why. I was at first desperately disappointed; then, to my horror, relieved.

The ob-gyn gave me little idea how serious the situation had been. She would be fine and home in a day or so. Since I have a near-psychotic terror of hospitals, I didn't go to visit her that night. For that, she never forgave me.

Here I was a few years later, not learning from history, doomed to relive it.

As before, resolving to have a baby had a calming effect. In due course a period was missed and a pregnancy confirmed. Christmas of '87—our fifth together—was as quiet and sweet as any I could remember. Carla and I began to talk of the son who was coming, the little golden boy grinning up at us, running through the garden and along the trout stream just a couple of summers from now, holding us together in renewed love.

Very early one rainy Sunday in January she woke bleeding, in terrible pain. All I could think as I helped her to the car was *this can't be happening again!* And again too, that wicked little spike of relief.

I hit ninety tearing to the nearest medical center down our local state highway, a two-lane killer that had the highest fatality rate in the Northeast. I flashed my brights, blared my horn, crossed the double yellow line at will, Carla curled beside me in a fetal crouch of pain. I didn't really care if we head-on'd with someone. It didn't matter. There was no baby. There was no marriage.

They rushed Carla into Emergency and did what they do. At least it wasn't life-threatening. Soon she was comfortable, though lost and distraught. The nurse who'd attended her said the baby had been about three months old. She couldn't really tell at that age, but she thought it was a boy.

CHAPTER SIXTEEN

Quarr was changing.

On my first walk down through the grove of chestnuts, mature trees by now, to the little promontory overlooking the Solent where I'd once seen Father Joe's knobbly knees, I came upon a monk I didn't recognize. He was standing with his back to me on the promontory's edge, the wind whipping his skirts, loading a handgun.

His body language didn't suggest he was about to end his life, so I stepped behind an evergreen bush to see what the firepower was for.

He cocked the gun and peered out over the breakers. A lone seagull cruised into view, tacking against the gusts, looking for its lunch. The monk took careful aim at it, fired, and missed.

"Shit!" He shook his cropped head in disgust.

He recocked the gun and fired again, the gun making a pop like a silencer. This time he hit the bird and it fell into the surf, flapping wildly in its death throes.

"Got ya, ya bastard."

His accent sounded South African, instantly evoking the odious Blair. I tried hard to flood my heart with charity. Hopeless. I hated him. Maybe he sensed this. When I greeted him, he turned without counter-greeting.

"See that? I got the bastard."

"But . . . why?"

"Hate the bastards."

Not South African after all; British, back from some Commonwealth outpost. Mea culpa. He seemed to think a layman might need an explanation for the gat. He waggled it in my direction, his finger still on the trigger.

"When you enter the monastery, they let you keep one thing."

"Oh, I see."

As far as I could remember, sidearms were not mentioned in St. Benedict's Rule. But the shooter had lost interest in me. Another victim had appeared, checking the lunch menu.

When I mentioned the matter to Father Joe, he looked uncharacteristically judgmental and pursed his long untidy lips. There was more than a hint of Mary Poppins.

"I'm sure God has some purpose in mind, dear."

After we lost the baby, Carla and I stopped fighting. At first that seemed a good thing, whether it was out of respect for the dead or a mutual understanding that what we fought about was always trivial and losing a baby was not trivial. There was emptiness too, which for a while also seemed natural and good, an intrinsic part of mourning, a little dark void where there had been a little glow of promise.

But as the silence and the emptiness continued, another conclusion started pecking at my brain: there were no more fights because we had nothing left to say to each other.

Fighting was one of the ways we connected; the clue was that rank though the fights could get, they never were terminal. Sometimes they were even foreplay to great tenderness or wild activity. They were a bruising way to let the pent-up frustrations of our relationship release themselves and fly away, a regular cold shower of secret truths about the other which piled up inside each of us until the pressure got too great. Other couples had other ways of releasing them: teasing or venting to shrinks or harassing their kids. Fighting was ours. No harm done.

But now—nothing.

Was it the baby's death that had stopped us from fighting—or was it that we'd arrived at a point where the only utility we had for each other was to collaborate on the making of a child? And that once that proved impossible there was nothing further to be done or said? Or fought about?

Once this thought entered my mind—though it was quite evident where it led, and I was not ready to look down that path—it would not go away. With it came another, even more poisonous thought, seeping through me like the lethal chemicals spreading through a condemned man's body.

Punishment.

I believed in no agency capable of inflicting so intangible a punishment. Years of watching others commit moral mayhem at least as bad as mine and get rewarded with only more and greater success had convinced me of that. There was no retribution for anything outside of Felony One in front of witnesses.

Yet on the old principle that he who knows the sin is the greater sinner, I couldn't quell a fear that this death, in some higher court, might be infanticide. Had that tiny scrap of stillborn innocence, bearing within him the seeds of self, been denied his shot by virtue of my vices, aborted by thirty years of selfishness and apostasy?

We lived high. Illegal substances had traveled through various bodily passages. A lake of legal ones had gone much the same way. It made no difference whether you chose the medical or the religious approach. They were just different routes to the same destination: fault. Was it my fault? Was it our fault?

In the old days of our relationship, these weapons of mass destruction could never have been contained. They would have exploded into the mother of all battles. And yet, still, nothing. The two of us went about our business, sharing few words and fewer actions. We were even courteous to each other—a terrible sign. Politeness rang deafening alarm bells in my marital memory bank.

With Carla there had been great love. But something else had always lain beside our love, plotting its murder. We had never been able to get rid of our unwanted partner, our Iago, our Unholy spirit.

The conflicted sinning Catholic writer and his beautiful dark-haired American lover had reached . . . the end of their affair.

I began to feel the tug of Quarr as never before. Not the customary run-to-Father-Joe-in-a-crisis either. There was something much more elemental about the impulse this time, something irresistible.

When I came up the driveway, gray with jet lag, the great looming evergreens dripping with winter rain, the monastery looking shabbier and less inviting than I could ever remember it, one thought came into my head and kept running through it, in time with my sloshing feet:

Home. Home. Now you are home. Home.

"I want my faith back, Father Joe."

"I can't give you that, dear. But the fact that you are here, seeking faith, is itself an act of faith."

"Why can't I believe even that? Why can't I believe in *something*? I'm so tired of believing in nothing."

"Would you like . . . to try going to Confession?"

"Weird! I was thinking about that on the plane. I have plenty to confess. But honestly—I didn't know if you guys still had Confession."

" 'We guys' do. These days it's called the Sacrament of Reconciliation. There's less call for it, I find."

We were in my room in the guesthouse. I hadn't stayed in the guesthouse for decades. Utterly unchanged it was; the same drab paint along the corridors, the same worn carpets and rickety armoires, the same smell of piety in the halls. *Home.*

He sat. I went to kneel, forgetting his preference. He gestured me up and into another chair and took my hand and placed it on the arm of his and put his big warm hand on mine. Utterly unchanged.

His face still moved in the same patterns, twitching and screwing itself up to gather the energies within, but more slowly than of yore. He was seventy-nine and had just gone a few rounds with prostate cancer. Not one of Nature's athletes, always frail, he looked little the worse for wear. Apparently he was in total remission, the cancer having recognized a life force when it saw one.

"Now, dear, how long is it since your last Confession?"

"Twenty-eight years."

"And what would you like to confess?"

I'd thought about this a lot. I hadn't been able to go to sleep on the plane, thinking about it. I'd thought about it for the last two days. Now my mind was blank.

"Well, er . . . I've been drunk many times and done a lot of drugs. Had sex with many women, um, some pretty weird things there. Do you want to hear details?"

"No. I'll imagine."

"Okay, um, I've committed many acts of blasphemy . . . written many things that hurt people, haven't always worked as you said, unselfishly and thankfully, er, pride, pretty bad pride, and gluttony, um, anger, rage, lots of that. Did I say blasphemy?"

He squeezed my hand gently to stop me.

"That's very good, Tony dear. I know you're out of practice. Have you hurt anyone? Have you taken anything of value from anyone? Have you committed any crimes?"

"All of those things. Father Joe, I think I killed our baby. Carla and I were trying to have a baby and—we lost it. I'm sure it was the drink and the drugs and just the . . . sheer unending malice inside me."

"Alas, women lose babies all the time, dear."

"But it's not the women. It's not the first time. I did the same to Judy with another baby. He died too. Two deaths, Father. I'm the common factor."

"You're too harsh on yourself, dear. You always have been. It is not a virtue."

"Wait till you hear this. Both times, when I heard the baby was dead, I was happy! I can't believe that. I so wanted a little boy. I still do. I dream about it. And then when the little boys die, all I feel is relief! What kind of person have I become, Joe? I was going to be a saint once."

He checked some incoming messages, eyes still closed.

"These are great imperfections, dear. But they're not what you really want to say, are they?"

He was right. He was listening, but I was not. There was something, but I couldn't quite reach down far enough to find it.

"Say what's in your heart now, dear."

"I seem incapable of love, Father Joe. Utterly incapable of feeling it, even thinking it. Even wanting it. No, that's not true. I want to love, terribly. But it won't come.

"I'm really good at hate. Expert at that. First with Judy. Now with Carla. I just don't know what part of me that comes from. Two kinder and more generous souls there couldn't have been, and I'm sure they loved me. Yet I cursed them and hated them and resisted them. Not once but twice—just in case you think the first time was an aberration. Uh-uh. That's the way I am. I hate love.

"It *feels* the way a sin used to. Like when you got a present as a kid and for no reason at all you'd smash it into little pieces . . . and you'd be put somewhere alone, because alone is how the wicked are punished. You said something like that once, didn't you? Hell is being alone for all eternity? Alone, unloved, unloving?"

I realized my tears were falling on his hand. *God, what a self-pitying, fuckhead asshole.* It took me a beat to realize that I hadn't just thought this, I'd said it out loud.

He didn't seem to have heard. He was absolutely silent. His face was at rest, eyes still closed, in reception mode.

"Tony dear, you will only be able to love when you understand how much you are loved. You are loved, dear, with a limitless . . . fathomless . . . all-embracing love."

He didn't say by God. By whom then? Himself?

Like a tidal wave overwhelming the breakwaters of common sense came the thought that this slowly shrinking, mud-flap-eared old elf of a man was . . . God.

Or a body God would from time to time inhabit.

But I didn't believe in God.

He whispered the words of absolution. I closed my eyes as he formed a cross on my forehead with his thumb, and time rewound to a fourteen-year-old boy sitting in this same spot, in this same room, being absolved by this same man with the same cross and the same long thumb. With all that I now knew would happen to that boy unknown.

Father Joe replaced his hand on mine and we sat in silence.

His hand was older, the skin slacker, as big and bony as ever and as warm. I sat there a long time, feeling its peace flow into mine and through my aging frame.

I hadn't been to daily Offices or Mass in years. When I came to Quarr it was usually just for the day. If I stayed overnight it would be in a hotel. The abbey church and the guesthouse always panicked and depressed me. The echoes of my boyhood still hung in their rafters. The road not taken still stretched beyond the locked door of the cloister. The most disturbing thing was not how distant all that seemed but how recent. As if everything I'd done between then and now was trivial, forgettable, not worth recording. "Fleeting" is the old word, and it's a great one. Time collapses as it flees.

The same night that I went to Confession for the first time in twenty-eight years, I decided to attend Compline in toto for the first time in twenty-eight years. I was curious to see how it felt after so long.

It was late February and it had been dark for hours. The church was pitch-black except for the tiny red light glowing far away in front of the Blessed Sacrament. The Savior is . . . IN. The altar boy's joke. Last time I thought that, I was twelve.

The bell summoned the community, and in it glided. Or flapped and limped. How small it had become. When I last attended Offices regularly, there had been sixty-odd monks, of all shapes and sizes and ages. Now there were no more than twenty-five, and a preponderance were old and gray and stooped. This place needed recruits.

Nothing hit me like the Psalms. Gone were the sonorous Latin cadences, replaced by the flat complexities of English. And not the King James's glorious poetry either; another, more modern translation which fell into a very large crack between the mid-nineteenth and late twentieth centuries, unable to decide whether it was an early Methodist sermon or dialogue from a soap opera. The chants still sounded Gregorian, but since the melodies had been designed for Latin there were odd discrepancies with the English; at the end of verses, the nasal Nu-Brit accent of the younger monks sometimes protruded.

Not having kept track of the convulsions the Church had been going through since Vatican II, all this was new to me. My first thought was that in some obscure ecumenical gesture the place had gone Protestant for a while.

Quarr was indeed changing. On the whole I preferred monks packing heat to this travesty.

Evidently the community was still in the bosom of the Church. Toward the end, the Office reverted to Latin. The final hymn to the Virgin was not the *Salve* but that of the season, *Ave Regina Caelorum,* serene and intense. It soared into the arches, this half prayer, half ballad, addressed to the spiritual mother and, who knew?—in the secret places of their hearts, the lover—of these quiet men.

Something in me came alive, like the glow of a pilot light, a match lit in the distance at dusk.

I went outside. I was the only guest staying at the monastery. The entrance area outside the church was empty and unlit, the guesthouse dark except for my room and the common room.

I looked up at the night sky the wind was sweeping clean.

It wasn't an éclat as once long ago. The universe up there, all around me and within the atom, seemed no less impersonal, no less immeasurable.

I listened. The way he'd once said: *just listen, dear.* In the roaring silence was a voice; my voice, it seemed, but then it always does seem to be your own voice:

"Reconsider what you dismissed so long ago. Reconsider what you've grown accustomed to dismissing without a second thought. That's all you have to do. Rewind to zero and start again."

It came less as a revelation, more as something plain and obvious, a thought quietly edging through the door of my mind. The stars shining in the black cupola of the universe could not be there now—any more than I could be here, or the little lump of cooling rock I stood upon, nor any atom it contained, nor the forces that bound them together—were they not *maintained* in their existence. By something. Some fundamental principle or force or thing beneath all other existent principles, forces, and things.

Otherwise there would be nothing. Why not just nothing?

Wittgenstein once said: *the mystery is, why does the universe exist at all?*

Like many people of my age and milieu, I'd arrived at a vague, emotional rather than reasoned, conclusion that the questions of the origin of the Universe and therefore of existence had been pretty much settled. The sheer weight of research and discovery, of the various theories postulated, forced questions like "why not just nothing" to the far horizons of the scientific agenda.

I even felt a bit proprietary about all the progress that had been made, the great mind I once sat behind, Stephen Hawking, having been so central to it. I can't have endeared myself to the great mind by making him do my homework, but still, for a moment there, I'd been on his team and he on mine.

In light of the inconceivable age and vastness of time and space and the inconceivable smallness of its quanta, a question like "why not just nothing" didn't need to be answered, or at least could be postponed. Why matter, energy, time, and space exist, what brought them into existence and maintains them in their existence, are now largely meaningless questions. The universe simply *is*. The observable fact that matter, energy, time, space, and the forces that govern them exist is all we know and all we need to know.

On the other hand, I did quite enjoy bugging scientifically inclined friends by maintaining that the big bang theory, once you started picking at it, was as loopy as any other creation myth.

Example: how did we know that the Ur-lump of super-dense matter was the size of a baseball (as confidently asserted by popularizers of the theory), not a golf ball or a watermelon? How exactly did this baseball create within a short time (three minutes to be exact) ninety-eight percent of all the matter contained in our current universe, an entity at minimum trillions of light years across?

Or take the issue of time. If the big bang occurred, as was generally accepted, 13.7 billion years or 5,000,500,000,000 days ago, wasn't that instant an actual moment in time, a specific date? As measurement techniques got more sophisticated, you would soon be able to place the big bang on a specific day of the week. How then could you say that before the big bang, time did not exist? If there was an after, there was a before. Was the big bang theory really very different from Bishop Usher's seventeenth-century calculation that the creation of the universe began on October 22, 4004 B.C., which we all found so hilarious?

Say you preferred the more sophisticated notion of the inflationary universe in which these questions were avoided by calling the baseball a "singularity" containing within it not just all matter, but also the space, time, and energy in what would become the universe. If energy did not yet exist, how did it explode? What did it mean that after the initial bang, the singularity spewed space as well as matter through nothingness so that the material universe would have somewhere to spew through? Didn't "creating space in nothingness" sound like semantic nonsense? And if there was nowhere before that, where was the singularity the instant before it exploded? When was T=0, zero time, the moment when all this was supposed to take place? Was T=0 a non-moment that existed before time began? If so, when did time begin? The instant after T=0? If so, what started time ticking?

Juiciest of all was the response that none of this had to be explained because there'd been a previous universe which had flown apart just as ours is doing, reached its outer limit (wherever that was), and then somehow collapsed back down to a baseball (or a singularity) and started all over again. This explode-expand-contract-explode daisy chain would go on forever, or was "continuous"—the modern cosmological term for "eternal." Which sounded ominously familiar.

If you stood back from a blind belief in the ability of science to explain everything, these notions started to sound no more plausible than giant snakes arising from the sea to mate with giant elephants, or an inexplicably motivated deity slapping the universe together in a Judeo-Christian workweek. Could the reason for the implausibility be that the first person to postulate the big bang was Georges Lemaître, a Belgian Catholic priest?

But these were just dinner-table games. Though the game was exhilarating, I'd always end up feeling grim and sad. The implausibility of the theories was just another blind alley, another nonanswer to the agonizing conundrum of why and how we are here. I hated being so close to the questions, to having them even pass through my mind, leaving their fog of depression and despair.

Now, gazing up not at some word in a game but at a suddenly tangible and real universe, a new idea flooded my brain with the cool simplicity of water irrigating a drought-stricken field.

What if the big bang theory was not a rather loopy theory but exactly right, the correct account of something that happened a specific if uncountable number of days ago, and not only exactly right, but the final horizon of knowledge beyond which lay the next and only logical conclusion: the intelligence, force, principle that conceived it?

What if the super-dense baseball or the Fabergé egg of singularity didn't come magically, absurdly out of nowhere and magically, absurdly happen but was triggered by an immeasurably ingenious, lucid, and resourceful intelligence? And even if the continuous explode-expand-contract-explode universe was the correct template and the big bang was not a birth but a resurrection, why should that not be purposeful, making absolutely fundamental to existence the dynamic of birth, death, and resurrection? In short, what if this force behind all forces, this light behind all light, this mind behind all matter, existing in time beyond time, was not some obscurantist rubbish or sublimated primitivism or desperate clinging to some collective Freudian blankie, but an obvious and inescapable conclusion of all that science had discovered?

What if the same were true of the impossibly small as well as the impossibly large? How fine was it, how limpid and perfect a creative idea, that everything that existed should be based on one infinitesimal building block—the atom—each of the inconceivable number of atoms in the universe existing for all time, endlessly constituting and reconstituting itself with an inconceivable number of its fellow atoms into everything in the universe, from galaxies to Galileo to me? How glorious was that? That some part of us, some of the atoms in my flesh-and-blood body had actually been part of a star or a stegosaurus or Dante or the first fish to crawl on dry land, or for that matter, the Buddha or Jesus of Nazareth? That I was, we were, not just spiritually but actually, factually one with everything?

What if the elusive grand unified theory which every physicist dreamed of was right in front of me? That force beyond forces effortlessly uniting the inconceivably immense with the inconceivably minute? This G.U.T. did not nullify three centuries of coruscating scientific genius, the staggering revelations made by cosmologists, astrophysicists, quantum theorists, subatomic researchers, those whose Nobel Prizes were nugatory compared to how immeasurably they'd deepened our understanding of the universe and all that's in it—how beautiful, how simple, how vast, how small, how awe-inspiring and superbly conceived. No—their work and all that remained to be done would be ineffably fulfilled.

Perhaps "why not just nothing" was a question science could not answer. It could only prepare one to answer it. "Why not just nothing" was above and beyond the random uncertainties of the material. A question that could be posed and be understood only by those who study and calibrate that unique aspect of the human mind: the ability to consider its own existence. A question that can be answered only by a poet—or a saint.

I had no idea what this force or principle that suddenly seemed so real and present was—whether it had a presence in the sense of a person or in the sense of a truth present in the universe. It was obviously what people meant when they said God, but no formulation of God I'd ever heard, in terms of person, parent, or gender, had made sense to me, even as a metaphor.

I felt no love for, or from, this force or principle. I made no connection between it and what I'd witnessed going on inside the church, beautiful or moving or spiritual though that might have been.

Father Joe would connect it for me somehow, sometime. I had utter confidence in his ability to do that. This was his field of study and he was a world-class scholar.

But that could wait till tomorrow. Right now, I thought, the God-force-principle-thing would like me to pop down to the pub and celebrate.

Which I did.

CHAPTER SEVENTEEN

Father Joe didn't think of it as his doing. He was not a cheerleader. Success and failure were not in his lexicon. They imply an end point, and he'd always been more interested in a process—of eliminating the self, of finding the principle or force which he called God, loving it, listening to it—a process that had no end point, nor any point at which it could be measured and success or failure declared.

He was happy beyond telling that I might be started back down the path of faith. But it had been mine to find, and now that I could see a possible way—not much more than a deer track, but still a way—through the undergrowth, he took no credit—though I showered him with it. He only gave thanks. I would never be a check mark in some spiritual score book.

I had known this man now for thirty-three years, more than half his career as a monk. In a few weeks it would be his sixtieth anniversary. Sixty years, that is, since his profession in 1928, at the age of nineteen, writing out his solemn vows of stability, obedience, and conversion of life on a sheet of parchment and depositing it on the altar. St. Benedict's first and shrewdest Rule: put it in writing.

With the exception of the Great War, which he was too young to be aware of, he had bypassed just about everything in this terrible, grasping, murderous century. Where did he spend the Depression? In poverty. Where did he spend World War II? At peace. Where had he spent the Cold War, with its bloody capitalist tyrants and bloody communist revolutions? Loving his enemies.

Even now, that absurd conflict was winding down—thanks to men of peace like John Paul II and Mikhail Gorbachev, thanks to the stubborn populations of Europe—my contemporaries and their parents—who for all their manifest mindlessness and endless tribal squabbles had remained a generation of peace, refusing to buy Reagan's fatuous cartoon of the Russian people or be cowed by his cowardly weapons of mass murder. After all the terror and threats and nightmare scenarios and brinkmanship, the most pointless and dangerous face-off in the planet's history was being ended without a single shot. *Pax*—the simple, timeless word that was at the heart of the Benedictine tradition, that had endured through all of Europe's travails and convulsions from Charlemagne to Churchill, had won the Cold War. The spirit of Father Joe was coming out on top in the worst century in human memory. Perhaps his faith in the force of prayer was not so far-fetched.

I had sometimes wondered—a common pastime of my generation—what would have happened if the Nazis had succeeded in overrunning England. They certainly would have swept away Quarr, and Father Joe with it. The Nazis exterminated Catholics—Catholic clergy in particular—as efficiently as any of their other victims. But the Benedictines would have gone on. Other Father Joes would have arisen from the river of black to build other Quarrs. Down the centuries other Nazis had overrun other nations; monks had been slaughtered and monasteries burned for the very act of refusing to fight, for sheltering the helpless, for meeting hate with love.

Those mighty empires, and the greed and violence and hatred that are the lifeblood of any empire, had all passed like grass before the wind. Where were the Visigoths and Vikings, the Golden Hordes, the Spaniards, the Venetians, the Moguls, the invincible British Empire on which the sun never set and never would? Where were those great peoples upon whose works the mighty looked and despaired—and whose names even scholars now had trouble remembering? The Abbasids, the Franks, the Lombards, the Saracens, the Magyars, the Ottomans? All gone.

And here was Father Joe, mighty in his meekness, still surviving and thriving after fifteen hundred years of other Father Joes.

Over the years my focus on my old friend, on not losing sight of him however much I lost my way, had shouldered out my once intense feeling for the great tradition in which Quarr had its place. In my apostasy, or atheism, or—more honestly—plain indifference to the divine, he had remained an exceptional human being, whose wisdom and quiet charisma transcended the religious and monastic terms in which it was couched. But Quarr I had put aside.

Now, like someone rummaging in the attic and coming upon long-forgotten treasures, I began to recall how deeply excited I'd been by the discovery of changelessness, that some institutions did not pass like grass before the wind but endured, acquiring a profoundly thrilling aura by their very refusal to succumb to the never-ending pressure for change. By the related discovery that history was not simply a catalog of the dead and buried and benighted, but rather a vast new world to be pioneered; that if you approached the past generously, so to speak—its people as humans, not facts, as modern in their time as we were in ours, who thought and felt as we do, the dead would live again, our equals, not our old-fashioned, hopelessly unenlightened, and backward inferiors. Humanity, to be fully known, had to be seen as changeless as well as ever changing. Quarr and the Benedictine tradition had been my gateway to these discoveries, a specific living example I was part of and which made history vibrate with life.

* * *

In the days that followed, I read as much as I could about what had happened to my Church while I'd been away. It was pretty bad.

The mighty chain of events and people stretching back over almost two thousand years, which even a pimply teenager like me had once thrilled to, had been not just shattered but thrown on the garbage heap. As if only certain links in it mattered—the Church's official lapses and sins—not the hundreds of millions of other links: kind and generous people, clergy and laity, hard-striving souls full of faith and good works and humor—and of failure and frustration and sin and tribulation. These had been the Church also—for two thousand years. But they appeared to be without merit for our doughty reformers, nothing but a millennium-long death dance of superstition and gullibility.

As far as I could tell, the reformers who had taken charge after Vatican II—mostly my contemporaries or slightly older—had indulged enthusiastically in one of our generation's most deadly flaws, nurtured, no doubt, by growing up in the rubble of World War II—a willful lack of any sense of history.

I'd been doing no reforming, but I was not without blame. Like my contemporaries, I'd for years bought into an attitude that went well beyond Henry Ford's reprehensible "history is bunk." In our version, history was far worse than bunk: it was suspect, the enemy, invariably evil, a repository of constant failure and deadly delusions and appalling role models. History was when all the mistakes were made, all the atrocities committed, that time before we knew better. History was before we were born again to the One True Faith: only change, with its benison of the new and the now, can lead to salvation.

There was an object lesson here that went beyond the chaotic state of the Church. To reject any vast group of one's cultural ancestors in the cause of some current theory is not just arrogance; it's posthumous mass murder. It's the same kind of thinking that makes genocide possible. The masses (albeit the dead masses) and the pathetic little lives they lived are irrelevant compared to this greater purpose we have at hand. Write them out of the record. They never existed.

One very concrete result of these "reforms" could be seen in the choir stalls of the Quarr Abbey church. If you brought the next generation up to despise history, especially the history of their own Church, pretty soon you'd have only one third the monks, the old farts or young kooks who *liked* singing unhummable thousand-year-old chants and following an unempowering, self-negating fifteen-hundred-year-old Rule.

Quarr was not changing. It was being changed. Why? What on earth had been wrong with it? A more serious question: if it was shrinking at this rate, could it survive?

I mentioned my misgivings to Father Joe. He was less concerned about what looked to me like wreckage.

"People are always changing themselves and their world, dear. Very few of the changes are new. We rather confuse change and newness, I think. What is truly new never changes."

"You speak in riddles, aged progenitor."

"The world worships a certain kind of newness. People are always talking about a new car, or a new drink or p-p-play or house, but these things are not truly new, are they? They begin to get old the minute you acquire them. New is not in things. New is within us. The truly new is something that is new forever: you. Every morning of your life and every evening, every moment is new. You have never lived this moment before and you never will again. In this sense the new is also the eternal."

Unless change generated newness of this sort, he went on, it was pointless change, undertaken simply for the sake of change. That did not mean that every so often it wasn't necessary to clear away bad habits, deadwood, and outdated customs, to adapt to new information. That was necessary to return the Church to its essentials.

That in turn did not mean fundamentalism, the recurrent urge of all reformers to sweep away everything and return to the way it had been "in the beginning"—in the Vatican II reformers' case, "the early Church." Wisdom and genius and sanctity undreamed of by the early Church had been acquired along the way since then. It had to be preserved too.

It was the oaks that drove his point home.

The autumn before, in 1987, terrible storms had invaded England and Western Europe, sweeping in from the Atlantic and devastating, among much else, its magnificent forests. The great oak woods of Quarr now looked as if they'd been carpet bombed. The mighty trees had toppled one on the other into a gigantic rat's nest of gnarled and tortured timber. The choppy gray sea could be seen everywhere through the tangled web woven by their dead branches. The proud skyline of the woods, the billowing shapes of the trees which used to form a majestic gray-green cloud bank in summer, an immense rood screen of exquisitely delicate tracery in winter, was gone forever. But what was "forever"?

Oaks had been here eight centuries ago, when Quarr Abbey was down the hill. Some might be the grandchildren of trees that had been growing in much the same places then. The children and grandchildren of these, standing tall amid the carnage, would spawn and propagate. Quarr's oaks would still be here, as sturdy, safe, and reassuring, long after I was gone, after all the sad and violent and stupid and laughable experiments of the twentieth century were not even footnotes. Those were the fallen trees, the ones whose roots were not deep enough, or were deep in treacherous soil.

One could not judge things by the brief span of one's own lifetime. That was at the core of modern arrogance: only my lifetime counts. My lifetime is "forever." Time before it and time after it do not exist. Everything of importance must come to pass in *my* lifetime. This is what drives the frenzy for change.

And that's really how the idea started. The idea was at first mostly practical: I could do something to stop this rot of newness. Just one person I might be, but you had to start somewhere.

Which is why Father Joe and I came to be walking along the edge of the devastated woods.

I was chatting about how I was getting back into the rhythm of the Offices, despite how disturbed and repelled I was by the new forms, telling him that some faint whiff of faith was beginning to seep back into my soul. I could hardly say that my belief in every Catholic doctrine had returned; many of the old doctrines seemed to have disappeared anyway, making the Sanctity Aptitude Test rather easier.

But that wasn't what I wanted to talk to him about this morning.

The idea had grown into a certainty in the week or so after it first came to me. The more I looked back on my life and behavior over the last twenty-five years, the more it seemed to be what I had always been avoiding, the nose-on-my-face obviousness of it now ridiculously clear.

The idea also made sense of the time that remained to me. Because it had always lived within me, *in profundis,* I had held back through both my marriages. What had lain in our marriage bed had not been an Unholy spirit, an Iago. On the contrary, it had not been evil or murderous at all.

My idea could not have occurred to me before. But now I had reached the culminating point of my life, the moment of decision to which I had been heading all along. I could stop running. Escape was not the answer.

At a particularly appropriate point, on the edge of the derelict woods with a magnificent view up over the bosom of the field to the pink and yellow mass of the monastery, I stopped. It was very early spring, hard and blue and chilly. I wanted to remember this moment; and I wanted him to as well.

I turned the rounded old shoulders toward me. He was quite a bit shorter than I now, squinting up at me, a twitching smile on his lips, relishing my air of mystery, the surprise I had planned for him.

"Dear Father Joe, I've thought about this long and hard. It's why I'm here and why I'm being led back to faith and, well, there are a hundred reasons we can go into later . . .

"I'm twenty-six years late, dear Father Joe, but I've never been known for punctuality. I wish to present myself once more as a postulant to the community of Quarr Abbey. This time, I'm ready."

Over the last week I had seen it in my mind's eye a hundred times: the old face turning in surprise, creasing bright with joy after all these years. After so much sin and apostasy, the lost sheep is found. The prodigal returns. The father embraces his long-lost son and gives thanks to the Lord, and there is great rejoicing in that house . . .

What I actually saw was an old man suddenly look very weary. He sank down on a huge newly cut oak stump and patted the stump. I sat down beside him.

"Dear Tony. We've known one another so long. You have been such a joy in my life."

Every crease of his face radiated tenderness. For once it was at rest, rapt, serious. His sharp old eyes searched mine. He was silent for a while.

"You know, dear . . ."

He paused a long moment and sighed.

". . . almost from the first moment I set eyes on you, I knew you would never make a monk."

Never in my life had a few little words hit me with such force. I had to gasp for breath.

"Often I resisted this knowledge. I would think *perhaps I'm wrong.* You never know. One must be humble. And you were so dedicated, even after your terrible vision of Hell, so certain of your vocation . . . I was confused."

Father Joe was gazing at the ground, hands clasped as if he were in Confession and searching his conscience.

"Sometimes I tried to push you away. Sometimes through my selfishness I encouraged you to persevere. Because I love you, dear, and always have, and wanted you very much to become a monk here. That's why I kept you in the guesthouse all those weeks, Tony dear. I could not bring myself to present you as a postulant. Although I wanted to—oh yes. That was what *I* wanted, you see. That was not what God wanted."

I wasn't listening. His self-examination had given me a moment to regroup.

"Father Joe—wait! Is this because of my marriage? My marriage is—"

"No, there is no canonical barrier to your entering Quarr. The Church recognizes neither of your marriages."

"So then surely it's not your decision. It's mine!"

His eyes had moistened. I realized that I'd never seen this profoundly emotional man with tears in his eyes.

"The evening your father called for you to go to Cambridge, Tony . . . well, God seemed hard that night. But it was for the best. I knew then that we would not see you after university . . ."

"I should have come back! That's where I went wrong!"

"If you had come back to us, dear, sooner or later, you would have exploded . . ."

A smile creased the old mouth.

". . . causing considerable d-d-damage to b-b-bystanders."

"Father Joe, that person was immature, confused, deluded, unreliable, faithless! I've made a new beginning . . ."

"I know, dear. And it will grow and mature and blossom. But not here."

"You're wrong this time! You were right long ago about being wrong. This has been part of me forever. It's why my marriages didn't work. Why I destroyed the lives of those around me. Even at my least spiritual times, it was still there, a hard little spur of truth. I belong here. Quarr is my home!"

These words seemed to strike deep. He looked totally exhausted. He shook his head imperceptibly.

"That little spur is not a monastic vocation, dear. It's your refusal to accept your true vocation."

"Which is what?"

"You're a husband and a father, Tony. I could see that long ago. The way you thought of Lily and treated her, even as a boy, gently and generously. A husband and father is what God has always wanted you to be. It's a vocation as sacred as ours."

"I've failed utterly at both those things, Father Joe. Not once. *Twice.*"

"Yes, you fought God. One could even say that the first time, you w-w-won. But boundless love, Tony dear, is giving you a second chance."

"Father Joe, dear Father Joe! Please! Don't do this!"

In reply he took my face in his old hands and, as he had in the first moment I ever saw him, gave me the kiss of peace.

Carla was cautious. If she was curious, she kept it well hidden. I fed her curiosity with my reticence about what had happened. That scalpel-sharp intuition must have led her to conclude that it had been big—and that it was best for now to leave well alone.

Had I accepted Father Joe's verdict? Not by any means. I'd rushed away, leaving the old man desolate on his oak stump. It didn't occur to me until much later that it must have been just as hard for him; that he'd probably hoped he would never have to say those words, that I would never put him in the position where he'd have to confess what he really felt. And that for him as for me, this moment had the same aching finality, the same mournful what-might-have-been.

At his venerable age it would have been easy enough—if he really thought he'd get pleasure and comfort from having me around—just to suppress his true feelings and welcome me with open arms. Instead, as ever, he'd taken a deeply unselfish course, rejecting the easy thing, steering me away from a life he felt deeply was wrong for me, would damage me in some way, however much I wanted it. A mistake he would not let me repeat.

That understanding came later when my anger and anguish had gone. My immediate impulse—for the only time in all the years I'd known him—was to go behind his back. He was wrong. I knew it. His judgment was impaired. Perhaps it was the chemo. Quarr was desperate for recruits. Even if they were forty-seven years old. I was needed. I was called.

In any case he wasn't the final authority—not at all. He'd been relieved of his authority, as a matter of fact. The go-to guy, whom I should've approached in the first place, was my old friend Dom Aelred, now and for many years the Abbot, the big dog in the cloister whose word was absolute law.

The Abbot couldn't see me for two days, which meant I had to live in a stew of uncertainty for forty-eight hours, but for a lifetime of peace I could handle that.

Dom Aelred had not a moment's doubt or confusion: Joe was absolutely right. If he said I was not a monk, then I wasn't. I never had been nor would I ever be. If I found that hard to accept, yet still aspired to the monastic way, I should act by St. Benedict's most important principle—the glue of monastic life—obedience. Your Confessor has told you what your vocation is. Obey him. All said in a loving way, of course, or at least his version of a loving way, which had all the warmth of being kissed by a rather cerebral cod. Age and authority had not softened Dom Aelred.

His bluntness exposed another, blunter issue—which Father Joe in his gentleness had perhaps avoided. True, the Church didn't recognize my marriage. But I'd given my word to another human being before a hundred witnesses on a sunny September day that I would love and cherish her till death did us part. Supererogation wasn't required by the State of New Jersey should the parties wish to rescind the arrangement, but perhaps it was required of someone who aspired to the rather higher standards of St. Benedict's Rule. The question of my vocation was moot. I'd already made my choice.

I slunk back to New York, chastened and, as ever after a visit to Quarr, with far more to contemplate than I'd reckoned on. The bedrock of my great idea had been that my whole life had been tending toward Quarr. That Father Joe had been gently leading me back, first to faith, then to my true destination, the cloister. That my monastic vocation had always chafed against the bonds of my marriages, destroying them both.

Alas, something else made just as much sense: it was my delusion of a monastic vocation that had chafed against the bonds of marriage, destroying the first and almost destroying the second. Even at my most apostate, I had kept in the back pocket of my soul the idea that I could leave any situation, opt out of any problem. I had a secret escape route: Quarr. Tony the Monk, my alter ego, had been making excuses for, and rationalizing, my selfishness for thirty years.

Because Tony the Monk had a higher mission, he didn't have to obey the norms by which ordinary, worldly, little people lived. Tony the Monk had savaged people in writing and in person, careless of the damage, regardless of the consequences—even to himself—because he had *contemptus mundi,* detachment from the world. And—less loftly—because he could always flee to his sanctuary to escape retribution. Tony the Monk was so far above the flimsy moral system of other mortals that he was allowed to commit transgressions with impunity—to treat others, his wives or his children or friends or enemies—with utter contempt and lack of humanity. He was entitled to because his heart was pure.

The "something else" that had always lain beside the love Carla and I had together, plotting its murder, that we had never been able to get rid of, our unwanted partner, our Iago, our Unholy spirit, had been, all along . . . me.

Now our marriage could proceed, which it did. As the months crept on, Father Joe's wisdom, like the correct medication for a long misdiagnosed illness, began to have its effect. This isn't to say that our marriage became frictionless, especially given a couple like us, but it no longer had Tony the Monk to contend with. It was free to be a contract between a man and a woman, not between a wife and a guy who thought he was the moral superior of a husband.

Father Joe had been right too about my faith growing and maturing. I could hardly say it was fully Catholic again, though it certainly included a sense of the divine. The spiritual muscles I hadn't used for decades began to acquire some tone, and since they were Catholic muscles too, it was natural to look for a church to work out in.

It was hard. Appalling though the predations exacted on the monastic liturgy were, they were nothing compared to the desecration exacted on the secular. Latin was gone entirely, replaced by dull, oppressive, anchorman English, slavishly translated from its sonorous source to be as plain and "direct" as possible. It didn't seem to have occurred to the well-meaning vandals who'd thrown out baby, bath, and bathwater that all ritual is a reaching out to the unknowable and can be accomplished only by the noncognitive: evocation, allusion, metaphor, incantation—the tools of the poet.

Mass was now said in the language of the region where it was celebrated. Like politics, all Masses were now local—and had about as much dignity. Before "reform," the individual quirks of the priest—whether he was a saint or a thug or merely a potato like old Father Bleary—were submerged beneath the timeless rhythms of a universal script. Now priests had huge discretion in deciding the details of the "modern" Mass, and all those egos were on parade.

At one church I made the mistake of trying, the priest gave a rambling hour-long sermon whose main function, he seemed to feel, was to keep the faithful rolling in the aisles. Several of the utterly irrelevant observations he worked in were lines stolen verbatim from a Letterman monologue earlier in the week. The music was from one of the new Catholic hymnals, which had replaced the august millennial music of the Church with tuneless drivel penned during the seventies and eighties by clerical nonentities whose musical gods were John Denver and Andrew Lloyd Weber. These were accompanied by a sprightly cacophony of guitar, fiddle, and saxophone. The Communion hymn was both better written and more familiar: it was "Raindrops Keep Falling on My Head."

Eventually I found an exquisite little church just north of Columbia University on 121st Street called Corpus Christi, run by a dour, ascetic Monsignor who had no truck with such liturgical atrocities, preached brief, learned sermons, and every Sunday celebrated a full conventual Mass in Latin with the appropriate Gregorian chant. There were other, subtler bonds to Corpus Christi: Thomas Merton had been baptized a Catholic there in 1938 not long before he went off to become a Trappist monk and live by St. Benedict's Rule. And my old pal George Carlin had grown up on the same block in the

1940s, just a couple of buildings from the church doors, no doubt inspiring some of the thoughts that would one day appear on his breakout album, *Class Clown.*

Even if I hadn't found Corpus Christi, I had constructed a means of insulating myself from the hideous practices of the new and improved Church. To some degree in defiance of Father Joe, I'd smuggled out of Quarr a complete copy of the Offices of the day in Latin and said them—most of them—faithfully every day of the week, something I hadn't done since my first year at Cambridge.

It was hard to conceal from Carla that I was sneaking off to Mass several times a week. At first I was rather embarrassed about it, having gleefully derided, for most of our life together, such pious practices. To my surprise, she seemed to respect it. However, I did keep from her that I was still nurturing the inner monk. In the circumstances, it felt almost like infidelity.

The Offices rerooted me in a tradition where, monk or not, I would always be at home. From long ago I knew the power of their repetition, the incantatory force of the Psalms. But they had an added power now. As a kid, the psalmist (or psalmists) had seemed remote to me, the Psalms long prayers which sometimes rose to great poetry but often had simply to be endured. For a middle-aged man, the psalmists' moods and feelings came alive. One of the voices sounded a lot like a modern New Yorker, me or people I knew: a manic-depressive type A personality sometimes up, more often down, sometimes resigned, more often pissed off, railing about his sneaky enemies and feckless friends, always bitching to the Lord about the rotten hand he'd been dealt. That good old changelessness.

Quietly but inexorably, calm and happiness began to descend upon our marriage. There was less tension in the air. Things were going so well we even started fighting a little, just a few tentative jabs, to see how it felt to be swinging at each other again. It felt good.

Father Joe had been right yet again. Looking back, I could also see that he had been quite consistent. Even when I was still at school, so certain about entering the monastery, he had gently been nudging me not toward it but away from it. Those little asides about married couples being just as capable of sanctity as monks or nuns? The observation that Paolo and Francesca were not without hope? The encouragement to go out with a pretty girl, the steady pressure to rescue Judy from her parents and marry her?

Now, twenty-five years, two marriages, and two children later, I was finally accepting that this was my destiny, that I was called to be a husband. And . . . a father.

Another matter. The inchoate sense of responsibility for the death of our tiny sliver of a child still lingered. What if it happened again? What if my seed was toxic?

But what if it wasn't? What if it didn't happen again? How wonderful would that be? Wasn't there a certain egotism in thinking it was all my responsibility? Marriage is a partnership, right? It's about more than love.

Love doesn't hurt. One sunny August day that summer while picnicking at the bottom of our garden, lazy with wine and the hot long grass, we conceived a child. We both knew it instantly. It had the exactitude of an annunciation.

This time there were no mistakes, no black Sunday mornings, no fear of them even. I knew we were in some way under Father Joe's protection. We had never been happier than while waiting for our baby; the world and life seemed complete and satisfactory and sufficient. I kept stopping in odd places and at odd moments, while I was jogging or shopping or shaving or writing, and trying to remember whether it was okay to be so unambiguously happy. Wasn't there something really shitty I'd forgotten? No, there wasn't. Not this time.

Being modern New York parents, we had to know what sex the little sprout was going to be. When the sonogram came in, we were ecstatic. For me the whole process by now had the awe-inspiring force and momentum of a prophecy coming true. Father Joe had said this path had been chosen for me and once I'd accepted it, everything he'd always promised would come with it. The joy, the peace, the love had indeed come with it. On top of all that—a son.

Being modern New York parents, we also had to name him long before he arrived. Of course—Carla agreed by now—he would be named for Father Joe and Quarr. "Joseph" was not an option, since it was Carla's father's name and so open to ambiguity. I set my heart on "Benedict," not just for the obvious reason, but because I truly believed our son to be already blessed. Someone wisely talked me out of this, at least as a first name, pointing out something my British ear was not attuned to: future school chums would quickly convert this moniker into "Bent Dick."

We settled on "Nicholas" and stuck "Bent Dick" in the middle.

And so in the fullness of time, slightly more than a year after I'd run so bitterly from my old friend because he'd insisted I was a husband and a father, a son was born, a little golden boy whose hair was already blond and whose eyes were as blue as the skies over Quarr in spring. Carla had to have a C-section to get him out; they gave him to me in the operating room with the hospital-issue shawl tight around his tiny body, and I took the sweet bundle over to the soft light they supply for fathers to gaze upon their sweet bundles.

And the first thing he did on this earth was to smile at me who was smiling down at him. Back came flooding those ancient words of Meister Eckhart:

> When the Father laughs at the Son and the Son laughs back at the Father, that laughter gives pleasure, that pleasure gives joy, that joy gives love, and that love is the Holy Spirit.

That winter my little sister invited us to celebrate a "Dickensian" Christmas at her farmhouse in Derbyshire with a large number of other family members. Perfect, we thought. His first Christmas in the birthplace of Christmas and on the feast of St. Nicholas.

We flew over in the middle of December to give ourselves time for a trip to the Isle of Wight, where we'd introduce our son to the man but for whom he might not exist.

It was a blustery, squally December day, but Father Joe limped out to meet us on the gravel as soon as he heard we'd arrived. Carla handed him the baby, bundled in his snowsuit, little cheeks red as cherries, huge blue eyes staring at this strange being, and sure enough—who wouldn't at a kisser like that?—he giggled at him.

The joy on the old monk's face as he gazed back at this little boy who was just about exactly eighty years his junior was so simple and intense and pure it lit up the damp gray air around us. He made a tiny cross on Nick's forehead with his big old thumb, kissed him on his cherry cheek, and, as if he was the most precious thing he'd ever held, hugged him for a full minute.

Grandfather Joe.

CHAPTER EIGHTEEN

Sebastian and I hurried up the driveway.

Sebastian—aka Bash—was seven. Unlike Nick, who at nine was off-the-chart tall and strong, an all-round sports guy who held his own at basketball with the black teenagers in Riverside Park, in fact was beginning to think he *was* black despite his ice-blue eyes and Aryan-dream blond hair, Sebastian was of average height, neat and beautiful—just as blond and blue-eyed but definitely from the Italian side of the tree, not like his big bro, who looked as if he belonged in the bows of a Viking warship.

All three of them, including little Lucy, who'd soon be five, were sharp as tacks, but Sebastian was startlingly smart, given to intense quasi-academic crazes. There was usually a pop cultural trigger for these—like a Disney movie—but he'd go way beyond the supporting pseudo-educational promo that showed up on cereal boxes or in *Scholastic* magazine and *Time for Kids.* That wasn't good enough for Bash. He'd plunge into his own research, ransacking the school library and surfing the Web for every piece of information he could lay his hands on—and then master it so that he could hold forth to all and sundry.

Hercules, which had come out the previous summer, had brought on a craze for Greek gods and goddesses, including all the minor nymphs and Muses, many of whom I'd never heard of, and every detail of every legend associated with them. This craze culminated in a terrible heartrending scene when Bash suddenly realized that while Mount Olympus existed, the divinities might not, and so he could never, never *ever* be a Greek god.

In a couple of months, when *Mulan* appeared, his response would be a burning need to learn Mandarin, which he proceeded to do, setting up his own lessons with the Chinese violin teacher of a friend of his. Soon reams of paper covered with Chinese characters would litter the apartment and we'd hear him practicing his singsong vocabulary for hours in his room. This craze would abate only when he got interested in Japanese and Korean as well and time just got stretched too thin. Still, he acquired some proficiency in all three. I was coming home with him one evening in a radio car driven by a stately old Korean gentleman who almost had an accident when Bash asked him something in Korean. They chatted away in Korean for the entire length of West End Avenue, a seraphic smile on the old man's face.

"He have really good accent," he said approvingly as we got out.

I'd been wanting Father Joe to meet his other grandson for a while, but the demands of school and Carla's job made visits to England difficult. She worked at Ogilvy & Mather now, running the North American arm of its interactive division, and the e-craze was nearing its first Alp of incoherent insanity. When we did cross the Atlantic with the kids it was to go to southwest France, where my little sister now lived in a big old run-down château; not much time remained for other family trips. Then a client meeting in London had come up and we'd jumped at the opportunity to get a look at Tony Blair's Cool Britannia (it was February 1998), taking Bash along for the ride.

Quarr was a must-do on this visit. In April it would be Father Joe's seventieth jubilee, and celebrations were planned by the monastery to honor his extraordinary seventy years as a Benedictine. I wouldn't be able to attend these festivities, and I wanted to pay my respects individually.

I had an ulterior motive. With more than a decade of solo writing under my belt, I felt ready to launch a project I'd had in mind for years: a book with or about Father Joe and our forty-odd years of friendship. I hadn't told him about this on previous visits and had no idea whether it would be an appropriate thing for a saintly and self-effacing man to undertake. Was there anything in the Rule forbidding a project like this? I couldn't recall. Clearly St. Benedict had had no qualms about writing books. At least one book.

Since my watershed visit of ten years earlier, I'd been to Quarr fairly regularly. Quarr seemed to reach a certain stasis throughout the nineties. It hadn't shrunk too much further, and the liturgical pendulum had begun to swing back a little—toward the Latin.

Dom Aelred had died of cancer in 1992, to be replaced by a big genial fellow named Leo who also succumbed to cancer a few years later. They were not the only ones; cancer seemed to be becoming an occupational hazard of contemplative monasticism.

Father Joe himself had had another bout in the early nineties, this time a rather unusual form—of the sinus—which can be particularly excruciating because of the pressure it puts on the eyeballs, affecting in turn the vision.

But if the cancer thought that by attacking him in this unexpected quarter it might get the advantage, it had another think coming. For the second time, he'd beaten it, and had been in remission for six years. Other than his asthma, which he affected never to mind anyway since it gave him an excuse to go to Italy, he was hale and hearty and no longer spoke of "not making old bones"—which would have been meaningless by now since he would be ninety next year and looked well set to make his century.

So it was with a certain excitement that I was coming up the driveway. I knew how much Father Joe adored kids—Bash would definitely make his day. And while I'd learned over forty years never to assume that I would leave Quarr with what I came for, I had a good feeling about the book project. It might take a form I could not foresee, would take its own shape acted on by his great soul. But it was going to happen.

A letter from him a couple of weeks before displayed his unchanging, chatty, affectionate self, the writing more spindly but still strong and clear. And I'd spoken to him the night before from London—we communicated mostly by phone now, he having lost all his hesitancy about the newfangled technology. We'd arranged to meet before lunch in his room off the infirmary, overlooking the garden and the sea, where he liked to spend his mornings when it was cold and he couldn't get out.

Bash's big eyes were taking everything in, as they had all the way down from London, the Sussex hills soft and bare in the wintry rain, the ferry pitching in the choppy Solent, cozy inside with the squalls lashing its windows, the apple-green double-deckers that ran on the island, and the always striking neo-Moorish mass of the church and guesthouse, the brooding peace that suffused the place, the sense of home.

"Quarr Abbey," he said, trying out the words.

We went into the church for a quick kneel. Stark and silent, free of the visual turmoil of the New York churches Bash knew, with their melodramatic statuary and flamboyant adornment, stained glass churning with figures, a thousand multicolored stalactites of wax. He said nothing as he gazed into the peaceful gloom, but smiled up at me, as if he got it, understood its appeal.

The monastery was quiet and deserted in the middle of the morning, the monks off about their work. The old Porter greeted us, knowing that we were here to see Father Joseph, and let us into the cloister without a word, leading us back along one side of it. Bash's eyes were wide now, shining with fascination, his lips slightly parted as he absorbed this *very* interesting place. I wondered if a new craze might be a-borning in his hot young brain; if so, for once I might actually be able to keep up with him.

We went up the stairs to the infirmary where we were greeted by a lay brother—one of the very few left—named John Bennett. Brother John was a gentle, laconic, solidly working-class guy from Manchester; over the fifteen years or so he'd been at Quarr, he'd gravitated to the Infirmary, where he was now the Infirmarian or chief medical resource of the monastery and, willy-nilly—given the shrunken size of the community—its only nurse.

He was an unlikely nurse, bulky and muscular with broad shoulders and features. He had a serenity beyond his years, a certain melancholy. Quarr was an aging community and he had seen much sickness, suffering, and death. He'd nursed Father Joe through his two bouts of cancer and most of his other infirmities, and Father Joe loved him dearly.

Brother John was a man of very few words—I doubt that in all the time he'd been at Quarr we'd exchanged as many as a dozen. He nodded quietly at us, cracked the tiniest of smiles for Bash, and led us to Father Joe's room, leaving us silently standing inside.

I'd been here once before, long ago. It was a rather beautiful room, in the old country house that was here before Quarr was built. On the second floor, with a large stone window frame, it overlooked the formal garden behind the monastery, beige and dark gray in the deep of winter. The rain had stopped, but everything was misty and overcast. As ever, off in the distance heaved the wide, restless moat of the Solent.

Father Joe was dozing in a big ornate chair facing the window, a thick blanket tucked around those knobbly knees. As we approached, he woke slowly with a deep sigh.

"Tony, dear, that must be you."

He turned his head to greet us. He had to make quite an effort.

His left eye was sightless, horribly swollen, forced from its socket by internal pressure, the white of the eyeball discolored a gangrenous yellow-green, crisscrossed with broken blood vessels, the pupil staring uselessly off to one side at nothing.

Flashing across my brain came the memory of the terrible epidemic that had ravaged the rabbits when I was a boy, and I would find the poor things in tussocks of grass where they'd crept to die, their staring swollen eyes forced from their skulls just like this.

I knew what it was but didn't want to know, wanted to go back out the door and reenter and discover that all was as it had always been, this terrible new knowledge unknown.

The cancer had returned.

And if he was here, not in the hospital . . .

He pulled his hand from under the blanket and stretched it toward us. His other eye was fine, blinking and twitching out at us as ever. He pushed up his glasses, which had slid down his nose in sleep, and the big mouth bowed upward in a smile of delighted greeting. But the other eye had its own expression, as if it belonged in quite another skull, staring with infinite sadness and resignation into a void.

"Father Joe, why didn't you . . . ?"

"Didn't I tell you, dear? I'm so sorry. I do forget things nowadays."

"Are you going to . . . is there much pain?"

"No. The doctor gave me some lovely drugs to keep the p-p-pain down. I must say I rather like the feeling they give."

"You're going to get better, Joe. You always have before."

Brave sentiments and not at all what I really meant: *you can't go, Joe, you've always been here. I need you to be here always. A world without you is impossible.*

"No, dear, I'm dying. The d-d-doctor's quite certain."

I was dumbfounded. By my own selfishness. By the void into which I was staring.

"This must be Sebastian."

I'd almost forgotten poor Bash. He was rooted to the spot, head down, huge eyes glued on Father Joe from under their finely arched blond brows. His brave look.

He stepped forward, a little hesitant at first, then more certainly, right up to the armchair. Then he leaned forward, trying hard not to look at that awful eye, and kissed Father Joe on the cheek.

The look on the old man's face was like a window into heaven.

He took Bash into the crook of his arm and held him close. His mouth went into its savoring mode, slowly flexing back and forth, as if my little son's presence was the finest wine he'd ever tasted.

"I've had a visit from an angel."

The door opened. In came Brother John with a tray. On it were some crackers and a brimming glass of red wine.

"Oh my goodness, this is the best part of the morning. Won't you have a glass, dear?"

I shot Brother John a questioning eyebrow.

"All right"—his flat Mancunian accent made him sound more severe than he was—"but don't forget it's getting on for lunch. You too, Joe."

He left.

"That's twice as many words as John has spoken to me in all the years he's been at Quarr," I said.

Father Joe chortled.

"It's wonderful that you could come, dear. I was worried that you might not be able to. I know how busy you are."

He took a healthy hit of the wine and smacked his lips.

"Joe, I'd cancel every project I have, if my staying here could somehow . . . stop you . . . going."

"Don't think of it as going, dear. More that God is coming."

" 'He is not far off nor will he be long in coming.' "

"St. Augustine. How nice that you still remember."

He took my hand. Usually his was enveloping and warm. Now it was chilly. And was that a faint, faint trembling?

Bash, perhaps from precocious discretion, more likely from seven-year-old ennui, had moved to the window, engrossed with the shipping on the Solent.

There was one question I had to ask. I thought he might find it worldly and faithless, and spoke so softly he had to lean forward.

"Do you ever worry, Joe, that there might be . . . just nothing?"

"That's a very good question."

His good eye found my face, the dead one staring off at the hopeless horizon.

"No, dear. That doesn't worry me. I'm a little frightened, perhaps. We always are, aren't we? When we have to open a door that's always been there . . . but we've never opened."

"Surely you've nothing to be frightened about, Joe. After the life you've lived . . ."

"I don't mean quite that, dear, though I am a sinner and I've often fallen. I mean frightened by the immensity of what lies beyond the door. A God of love—infinite and eternal. How could I ever be worthy of that?"

Yes, it was trembling. Delicately, but steadily.

His hand tightened its grip a little on mine.

"We're nothing, are we, dear, compared to the perfection of what comes next? Death makes failures of us all."

Brother John returned with my wine—the rest of the bottle, in fact. Father Joe's spirits brightened instantly. He had already polished off his first glass; he wasn't supposed to have more as it would make him sleepy when he had to eat. But no sooner had the Infirmarian retired than he almost bounced in his chair with the excitement of getting an extra glass.

So there we sat with the mist-gray winter light of England slipping discreetly through the leaded window, sipping our wine, for all the world as though we were down the pub having a quick one, and another rather slower. A simple enough pleasure—one of the best—that I'd shared with countless friends, but never with the most precious friend I'd ever had.

The wine wasn't *premier cru,* Quarr not being in the business of keeping a cellar, and I never drink red in the morning; but its perfume and savor were as delicious as any I'd ever tasted. I stopped looking away from Father Joe's poor dead eye and fixed on his good one, where the life still twitched and blinked. As he slurped happily on his truant glass, I flashed back to that Easter weekend getting on for half a century ago, when he had described with gleaming epicurean eye the sumptuous feast the French cooks would be preparing for Easter Sunday . . .

And there'll be wine!

If my belief in the God-force-principle-thing had faltered from time to time, it was completely reaffirmed that morning when I considered how completely brilliant a creation was fermentation. From decay came a pleasure sublime enough to keep decay at bay. Only for a few minutes, perhaps, but some minutes are like no others.

We spoke no more of death. He told me news of Quarr, of the fellow monks we both knew—about whom he was as cheeky as ever—about the new Abbot who had arrived, an energetic man who was already sprucing the place up, planting new trees to replace those destroyed, making the monastery appealing to new postulants, planning for the future. I told him of my work, which was overwhelming that spring but included some of the best projects I'd ever worked on. He chuckled about stuff he couldn't possibly grasp, like the backcourt moves Nick was learning or Lucy's need to get her five-year-old ears pierced, and then Bash joined in, prattling on with a flood of still more urgent New York matters that were way off Father Joe's linguistic radar but which delighted him no end, whatever it was all about.

There we sat, for the first time and the last, grandfather, father, and son, until the wine was gone and the lid of his good eye began to droop.

A bell tolled: the Angelus, end of the midday office and notice to all, guests and community, that they should assemble for lunch. The tolling bell on the other side of the monastery sounded far away. The black figures would be leaving the church now in their double column, the old ones hobbling to keep up, the young ones keeping their pace respectfully slow. Now they had left the church and were moving along the hushed cloister toward the refectory. Every day for more than seventy years Father Joe had made the little trip from prayer to food, two of the very few basics that were the totality of his life. He would never walk even those few yards again. Yet nothing slowed the rhythm of the monastery, quietly, irresistibly flowing on.

I got up. Father Joe drew Bash to him and made a little cross on his forehead with a trembling thumb. I knelt down so he wouldn't have to reach up when he did the same to mine. He was so weak it felt like being stroked with a feather. I took him in my arms and hugged him for a long, long moment.

Brother John came quietly through the door to take us down to the midday meal.

It was time to go.

He looked up at me, his head shaking imperceptibly with the effort. Even his sightless eye seemed full of tears. My own were filling so fast he looked as if he were underwater, slipping away into the depths.

His face creased into one last little smile.

"Good-bye, Tony dear."

"Good-bye, Father Joe."

EPILOGUE

I walk through the drab Victorian streets on a drab Victorian day.

All around me, fussing, limping, waddling, whining, are drab retired men and women in sensible cardigans and driving caps.

I have chosen to walk the shoreline footpath to Father Joe's grave. It's a couple of miles, but it skirts the worst of the Little Haven/Laburnums/Mon Nid cottages, which are still occupied after a century of relentless ridicule—in fact have spawned a whole new generation of newer ones just as hideous. The path then runs along the sea west of Ryde, bringing you to the ruins of old Quarr.

The truth is that while I'm drawn ineluctably to his grave, I'm apprehensive about what my reaction will be. The longer it takes to get there the better.

Six months, but the grief is still raw, open to the bone. In the most unlikely places—the dentist's, restaurants, creative meetings, sitting on the john—I can still be engulfed by sobs. In public I have to excuse myself or pretend something's gone down the wrong pipe. Once, in L.A., a guy actually tried to give me the Heimlich maneuver. I could hardly tell him it was okay, I was only choking on grief.

Curiously, it never happens in church.

Back in the spring, there'd been no question of lingering at Quarr. Bash had to be in school and Carla at work, and our plane left the next morning. Once I might have had the freedom to stay on. But I was a husband and father now.

Before we left, I'd asked everyone I knew—Brother John, the Guestmaster, the Porter—to let me know if Father Joe began to fail. Or when. I could jump on a plane and be at Quarr in hours. I gave them all my telephone numbers.

In New York, work frenzy hit like a hurricane. Ron Shelton and I had a green-lit movie at Warners but the green was rapidly turning to amber as Warners dissolved into chaos. At the same time, I was planning an article about the last voyage of an eighteenth-century pirate which required a three-week cruise from Nassau to Jamaica via Haiti and Cuba on the oldest wooden boat I could find. I was making all the arrangements.

Having heard nothing, I called Quarr in early April and was reassured. Joe was hanging in there. He wasn't going to let a little thing like death cheat him of his seventieth jubilee, which was to be celebrated on Easter Tuesday, April 14, 1998. He would make it. Father Joe had always been a child of Easter, and Easter would bear him up.

Could the miracle be happening? Did he have his old opponent in the corner yet a third time? Why not? He'd beaten so many other diseases so often before.

I sailed away on my pirate voyage, on a boat so authentically ancient that its captain had no phone. I was incommunicado for weeks; in the few desolate places we made landfall, the phones, if you could find them, were always out of order. In Santiago de Cuba you could get through to Spain and Poland but nowhere else.

The night I got back from Montego Bay, I was overjoyed. No

messages, no letters, nothing at all from Quarr. Too late to call there, but what could this be if not good news? A perky voice began to chirp in the back of my mind: *he's done it! Just like all the other times. Good old indestructible Joe.*

I went to bed happier than I had been for months.

But he was already dead.

He'd made it to his jubilee, though too weak to go downstairs for the ceremonies. His brothers stood in for him. A fellow invalid in the infirmary heard him nonetheless burbling away all day on the mobile phone, until one morning there was only silence. He had passed into an unknowing cloud of pain and drugs, and on April 27, 1998, death finally brought him to his knobbly knees.

Six weeks ago. No one had called or even written. Because monks do not live in the world we do, I suppose. Because death is not a disaster, just a door, I suppose.

What did reasons matter that morning?

I wept and wept and wept. And then wept more. I'd never understood the phrase "prostrate with grief," which had always struck me as ridiculously nineteenth-century. Now I got it. I was as weak as you get from a high fever, unable to get up from the floor where I was slumped on my knees, racked by loss.

The tears were not all for Joe. They never are. They were mostly for me—that the safety, certainty, the proximity somewhere of him was gone into the darkness. A spiritual fear far worse than the physical, because flight from the physical is always possible, but there is no flight from the terror of drifting untethered through cold cosmic loneliness. So long as Joe was alive in the world, there was a gossamer-thin thread of connection to the possibility of God, but now . . .

Selfish as ever. I wasn't thinking how it was for him inside that simple holy skull. Was he scared? Was the trembling truer than his words? That the seventy years of mortification and deprivation and dedication might all have been in vain? What terror *that* must be. Suddenly to wonder if faith is rewarded—or whether it's simply its own reward, a pocket watch from management. How I wished I could have been there to hold him as he went. There was no one in the world I would more have wanted to see into the darkness, holding his hand till he slipped from my grasp and his soul walked away into heaven—or oblivion . . .

As if on a leash I was drawn to the church around the corner from my office on Eighty-second and Amsterdam, Santissima Trinita. The tears dried up. I sat. I knelt. I shut my eyes. I opened them. The dumb gilt shed was up in its marble cave in the middle of the altar. If there was anyone inside, he had nothing to say to me.

At least I had seen him and held him before he died. At least my beautiful little boy had kissed him with love like the grandfather he was to him and brought the old dampness to his dear damaged blood-filled eyes. Father Joe meant God to me more than any of these idealized statues, more than the ugly overwrought German stained glass, more than any words or beliefs that have echoed round these walls.

But some, at least, of these saints were once living people, quirky, lumpy, lovable, who had on those who knew them the same effect Joe had on me. The holy are venerated not simply to get favors, but to maintain beyond death that connection they grant you to the divine, to the Better, to whatever that God-thing is out there. The God-thing is inconceivable without a human body as a medium, something we can cling to, that has touched the inconceivable.

My mind wandered over the possibility of praying to Joe, and his personality sprang into my mind, bright and alive, as if he were still present somewhere in the world. This buoyed me, calmed the aftershocks of grief and loss.

My God. Did I, cynic, skeptic, ex-satirist, card-carrying member of the chattering classes, for whom nothing was ever sacred, finally have a saint?

There in the ugly peeling church, so far from Quarr, one last time, I sang the *Salve Regina* for him.

* * *

The spire sprouts from the trees sooner on the footpath route. It gives me chills. In its shadow lies the little square graveyard with its plain stone crosses in neat French rows, like a transported patch of Flanders Field.

I hurry up the driveway. Not because I can't wait to get to Quarr; Quarr feels alien to me. I'm not sure if it's temporary—vestigial pique at their not telling me of his death—or more permanent: without Joe it's of no interest.

I go through the big black door that once opened on my secret Eden. No more Eden. The graveyard is only a few yards away now, off the path, but I can't go in. Not yet. I fear his presence will be so strong I won't be able to stand it—like the Blessed Sacrament when I was kid and it became so present and real I felt like running from the church. "Humankind can only bear so much reality."

I hurry on down the great path through the resplendent sweeping chestnuts whose autumnal leaves still glow warm brown. Everything dear and familiar is changed. What once was a sure haven is now a landscape of loss, devoid of the spirit which animated it for me.

At our favorite spot, the little promontory, still there though each year the sea erodes it farther back into the woods, his image is easier to conjure. The long oval face with its blinking eyes and constant twitching smile, the vast ears, the rabbity triangular nose. Every time I saw Joe, I half expected him to have grown enormous whiskers.

He stands there in the eternal wind: hands under scapular for warmth in the chill, flat feet in black socks and floppy Astérix sandals. This cartoon figure, this still center, this rock of the soul, steady and firm as the huge oak that grows from the crest of the hill.

Father Joe had one last surprise for me.

The first clue came in an obituary a friend sent from England. Apparently some two hundred people had shown up for his Requiem. A good rule of thumb for funerals—especially funerals of those whom people love—is that for everyone who does show up, there are half a dozen others who would have liked to.

That would put this humble, self-effacing, cloistered monk's circle of acquaintance in four figures. Then, in the same obit, I read these astounding words: "He touched the lives of so many people, in England and abroad, in his own Church and not . . . it is hard to give full weight to the extent of his pastoral influence."

Father Joe? *My* Father Joe?

I was never so arrogant and self-centered as to imagine I was his only friend and penitent. I knew he had other people who came to him for help and some "old friends," as he called them, especially as he got older. Other monks at Quarr had penitents or old friends they were permitted to see. Quarr's tolerance of such bonds was greater than that of many other houses or orders.

But—"touched the lives of so many people," which, if you put two and two together, must mean hundreds?

I'd always believed—simply on the evidence of his deep love and abiding concern—that what was the defining friendship of my life was also a prominent fixture of his. All great friendships help both parties discover the uniqueness their self possesses, the "me" they should be. Your true friend joins you on a voyage across the sea of self whose outcome neither can know as they board. And which will change them both.

Common sense suggests it would be hard for one person to maintain in one lifetime more than a few such friendships. It would be taxing physically—the toll it would take on time, energy, patience, concentration—and brutally hard on the emotions, let alone the spirit. Yet as the tributes came in and I dug farther, it became clear that Father Joe had undertaken not just a few, or even a few dozen, but hundreds of such life-altering voyages.

My ignorance arose partly from living on the wrong side of the Atlantic. His European friends must have been more aware of his relative fame. But that I, a journalist, never got a hint of its extent says volumes about his humility. Never in all those years did he once mention that there were hundreds of other Tonys—quite unlike most spiritual mentors, who, though they might be deeply spiritual and operate from the loftiest motives, always revel in their centrality to their followers, are always in growth mode, using their success stories as exemplars for new clients.

Joe had never cited his success with another old friend as holding a lesson for me. Nor, I'm sure, would he ever have held up any aspect of our friendship as useful or inspiring to another. As far as I could tell, he treated every other member of his huge flock the same way. It was immensely disarming and engaging to be treated as if you were the only one in his life; but then, for the time you were with him, you were. He loved the one he was with; spiritually promiscuous, utterly discreet.

One of his fellow monks, when I expressed surprise that I was Not The Only One, said: "Ah yes—everyone thought they were Joe's best friend."

And all of us were right. We all were.

I discovered as I read more tributes and asked more questions that he was best known for saving vocations, especially of priests battered by the storms of experimentation and controversy in the post–Vatican II Church. But most of those who came to him were laymen like me, ordinary people in all walks of life, struggling through the world. Many had known him even longer than I had, some for fifty years, some as long as sixty.

A sizable portion of his ministry was gay, people who'd lost lovers to AIDS or were grappling with it themselves, as well as those tortured by the Church's relentless intolerance of different sexual orientation. (At least among the laity.) Perhaps most unusual, a large percentage of his friends were women. I'd seen for myself long ago his sympathy for Lily and her predicament, so it was no surprise to me, though it seemed to be for certain others. Joe never subscribed to the unspoken clerical conviction that women are for the most part a large and exceptionally annoying species of chicken.

One particular friend was a woman from a city in the North of England whom he called "the mill girl." She had become a single mother in the thirties, in a time and place when that was a terrible row to hoe, and had somehow gotten to know Joe. He remained her friend well into her eighties; she would spend every summer holiday in the Isle of Wight to be near him. At the other end of the spectrum was a discreet telephone and written correspondence in the mid-nineties with Princess Di. Typically, Joe never bothered to share this rather startling intelligence. (The seal of the confessional notwithstanding, one would love to know what he had to say about Camilla.)

Nor was he a chauvinist. He helped many in other churches, notably a man who refers to him as his "main spiritual director"—Rowan Williams, the dynamic new Archbishop of Canterbury. Archbishop Williams recently said in an interview:

> [Father Joe] was a listener of genius—someone who would be well on the way to meet you before you got there. He immediately flung open the doors. He had huge common sense in his advice on prayer.

Joe was a holy chameleon. To me he was irreverent and secular. To others he was an intensely spiritual guide; to yet others a mild but unyielding disciplinarian. To some he was a father, to some a mother. He always did what was appropriate and practical for the person he was with. There weren't two kinds of people in the world for Joe, nor three, nor ten. Just people. He was a prophet of the possible. He soothed the damaged, nurtured the tortured, and reassured the imperfect.

My postmortem discovery of Joe's massive infidelity solved another mystery: where and how had the innocent savant acquired his vast knowledge of people? And the associated ability never to be shocked or thrown or puzzled by any human behavior? To some degree, surely, from how much he saw and heard, how many forms and degrees of imperfection he was exposed to.

But in the end his knowledge came from his bottomless supply of love, a poor, bedraggled, overburdened old word, but in Father Joe's hands, revitalized. For Joe, love was a cure, an emollient, a diagnostic tool, a stimulus, a reward, a nutrient, a guarantor of health and peace. He was the living breathing proof that love will teach you everything you really need to know, even if you choose to live outside the world and its supposedly limitless stocks of knowledge and information.

Father Joe was the human incarnation of Blake's vision: you can find eternity in a grain of sand.

I take as long as possible to walk back up to the abbey, still delaying my visit to the graveyard. The autumn nights are drawing in and the light is fading. The wind is wild in the oaks, whipping the last leaves into a frenzy. They cling to the branches as if they still had some hope. Forget it, leaves. Winter is coming.

I must go in. As I pause at the little iron gate, I see there, among the rows of plain stone crosses in rows, his cross. They haven't made his stone one yet, so it's of wood, two pieces of two-by-four nailed together at right angles. An already discolored plastic panel is screwed to it. It reads "D. [for Dom] Joseph Warrilow." Then his death date in Roman numerals.

Far from an overpowering presence, I feel none at all. I strive to reach him. He seems less alive here than beside the sea where his image was so vivid. Though he is here in front of me, barely six months dead, no farther from me than when we talked for the last time, I can't even visualize him beneath the earth, the dear features fading, the poor cancer-battered eyes rotting, the skull, within which God surely dwelt, whitening into a death's-head.

He is here no more. He is elsewhere. He is everywhere.

TONY HENDRA

FATHER JOE

A READER'S GUIDE

To print out copies of this or
other Random House Reader's Guides,
visit us at www.atrandom.com/rgg

Reading Group Questions and Topics for Discussion

1. One of Father Joe's recurrent themes is to see selfishness as a core modern failing. He "diagnoses" Tony Hendra's sin not as adultery but as selfishness (p. 58), while later he speaks of possessions as being "extensions of the self" and helping to create a "prison of self" (p. 120). In what way is Hendra's sin selfishness, and how is it linked to conspicuous consumption? And what is meant by Hendra's conclusion that "Shop-till-you-drop and true love may well be mutually exclusive" (p. 121)?

2. During their first days together, Hendra says that Father Joe's version of God fits better into his fifties-shaped notion of "she" rather than "he" (p. 67). In the epilogue, Hendra says of Father Joe's ministry, "to some he was a father, to some a mother" (p. 270). Are these two things connected? If you are a believer, do you think of God in a gender-specific way? If not, would you be more comfort-

able with the notion of deity if it were usual to refer not to "God the Father" but to "God the Mother"?

3. Hendra writes that in Europe the Benedictine tradition is "so deep you never heard the stone touch bottom" (p. 77). Later he refers to Father Joe as "thriving after fifteen hundred years of other Father Joes" and expresses excitement at "the discovery of changelessness" (p. 238). A little later he asserts that humanity needs changelessness as well as change. Is changelessness valuable? Is it possible in the modern world? What are the drawbacks, if any, of constant change?

4. Hendra and Father Joe discuss *Macbeth* and depictions of Christ's Passion and Crucifixion, noting that evil acts and people often seem to inspire writers and artists to great art (p. 110). Is this, as Hendra worries, "celebrating" evil? If not, how does art relate to the moral ambiguity it often depicts? Does it transform it? Does it have a redemptive function? Discuss the connection between this and the recurrent attempts in many societies, past and present, to insist that art only depict "good" acts and people.

5. One aspect of Father Joe's Benedictine background that Hendra is attracted to is its ancient historical roots, which can also be expressed as its deeply conservative tradition. Another thing that Hendra admires about Father Joe, however, is that he owns nothing and lives communally. Hendra even says the St. Benedict's Rule concerning possessions and communal living "sounds a lot like communism" (p. 120). Is it possible to reconcile the deeply conservative side of Benedictine tradition with its subversive attitude toward a modern consumer society? Does this in any way mirror our current political notions of right and left? How do you think Father Joe would vote in present-day America?

6. Father Joe says that sex is "almost like a sacrament" (p. 126). He also says we must "take the fear out of sex." What does he mean by

these statements? Do you find Father Joe's attitude towards sex surprising? Inadequate? Dangerous? Illuminating? How could a man who has spent all his life celibate and in a cloister have such definite opinions on the subject?

7. At several points in the book, the supposed dichotomy between sacred matters and humor arises. Hendra says that Father Joe was the only priest who'd ever made him laugh (p. 199). Father Joe responds that we should laugh at priests more often, and that if God is happiness, "God must be laughter too." Discuss what Father Joe means by this insight. Do you see humor and laughter having a place in sacred matters, or should they always be dealt with seriously?

8. Ben explains to Hendra the Benedictine concept of work summed up in the Latin phrase *Laborare est orare:* "To work is to pray" (p. 45). Later Father Joe expands on this, saying that any kind of work done well, with gratitude and enjoyment, for others first and yourself second, "binds us together and therefore to God" (p. 202). Is it possible in the modern world to do work to Father Joe's standards? Does he mean that work is sacred? Could work done to Father Joe's standards have a positive effect on a company? On society in general?

9. Hendra says that Father Joe was, "to me and for the moment, God. God the Other" (p. 100). Later, although he no longer believes in God, Hendra refers to Father Joe as "a body God would from time to time inhabit" (p. 229). In the epilogue, Hendra writes that God is unimaginable without a human body as a medium, something "that has touched the inconceivable" (p. 266). How are these perceptions connected? Does Hendra really mean that Father Joe was God?

10. The word *saint* occurs several times in the book. In the prologue, Hendra defines a saint as someone who practices the "keystone human virtue of humility" (p. 4). Hendra later describes Father Joe

as "a commonsense saint, a saint of what could be done, not what should be done, a practical saint, a saint of imperfection" (p. 203). Does this mean that Father Joe had lower standards than other spiritual guides? Do you find the term *saint* useful in describing Father Joe? Have you known any people you think were saints?

PHOTO: ©JEFFREY SCHIFMAN

TONY HENDRA attended Cambridge University, where he performed frequently with friends and future Monty Pythons John Cleese and Graham Chapman. He is the author of *Going Too Far,* a classic history of modern American satire. He was editor in chief of *Spy* magazine, an original editor of *National Lampoon,* and he played Ian Faith in *This Is Spinal Tap.* He has written frequently for *New York, Harper's, GQ, Vanity Fair, Men's Journal,* and *Esquire,* among other magazines. He is married to Carla Hendra; they have three young children, Lucy, Sebastian, and Nicholas.

ABOUT THE TYPE

This book was set in Requiem, a typeface designed by the Hoefler Type Foundry. It is a modern typeface inspired by inscriptional capitals in Ludovico Vicentino degli Arrighi's 1523 writing manual, *Il modo de temperare le penne.* An original lowercase, a set of figures, and an italic in the "chancery" style that Arrighi helped popularize were created to make this adaptation of a classical design into a complete font family.